LIFELONG LEARNING IN NEOLIBERAL JAPAN

LIFELONG LEARNING IN NEOLIBERAL JAPAN

RISK, COMMUNITY, AND KNOWLEDGE

AKIHIRO OGAWA

Cover image from fotolia.com

Published by State University of New York Press, Albany

© 2015 State University of New York

All rights reserved

Printed in the United States of America

No part of this book may be used or reproduced in any manner whatsoever without written permission. No part of this book may be stored in a retrieval system or transmitted in any form or by any means including electronic, electrostatic, magnetic tape, mechanical, photocopying, recording, or otherwise without the prior permission in writing of the publisher.

For information, contact State University of New York Press, Albany, NY
www.sunypress.edu

Production, Diane Ganeles
Marketing, Fran Keneston

Library of Congress Cataloging-in-Publication Data

Ogawa, Akihiro.
 Lifelong learning in neoliberal Japan : risk, community, and knowledge / Akihiro Ogawa.
     pages cm
 Includes bibliographical references and index.
 ISBN 978-1-4384-5787-1 (hardcover : alk. paper)
 ISBN 978-1-4384-5786-4 (paperback : alk. paper)
 ISBN 978-1-4384-5788-8 (e-book)
 1. Continuing education—Japan. 2. Neoliberalism—Japan. I. Title.
 LC5257.J3O345 2015
 374.52—dc23   2014042147

10 9 8 7 6 5 4 3 2 1

*To my parents, Ogawa Sachio and Masako,
who gave me life and have always nurtured my learning
and intellectual curiosity*

Contents

Illustrations	xi
Preface	xiii

Chapter 1
Introduction	1
Why Lifelong Learning Now?	1
Lifelong Learning as a Global Trend	4
Risk: An Analytical Tool	12
Risk: A Japanese Context	15
Methods	22
Overview of Chapters	25

Chapter 2
Japan's Lifelong Learning: History, Policies, and Practices	29
Three Key Terms	29
Social Education	30
Lifelong Education	34
Lifelong Learning	37
Lifelong Learning Promotion Law	41
Lifelong Learning Council Report in 1992	44
Focus on the Local: Developments in the 1990s	47

Chapter 3
Risk Management by a Neoliberal State	53
Lifelong Learning and Risk	53
Japan's Lifelong Learning in the 2000s	57
"Comprehensive Knowledge"	59
Local Communities: Locations for Realizing the New Public Commons	63
Neoliberal Knowledge	68

Chapter 4
The New Public Commons

The New Public Commons	71
The *Bunka Borantia*	74
Civic Knowledge	78
"Entrepreneurial Self" for Constructing Civic Knowledge	80
Jukugi (Due Deliberation)	83
Real *Jukugi*	88
New Public Commons as a New Growth Strategy	94

Chapter 5
The Japanese "Community School"

Revival of Communication	99
The Japanese "Community School" System	102
Ikiru Chikara (Zest for Living)	106
Integrating School Education and Social Education	110
A Varied Landscape	113

Chapter 6
Becoming a Social Entrepreneur

Why Don't You Initiate a New Style of Working?	117
Vocational Training in Japan	121
After the Lehman Shock	123
The Knowledge and Skills Required to Support the New Public Commons	126
Becoming a Social Entrepreneur: A Challenging Opportunity	131
Taking Risks to Survive in the New Labor Market	136
Postscript	141

Chapter 7
New Knowledge for Youth

Suicide among Young People	145
"Career Education"	149
Changing Trends in Universities	154
Toward Social Inclusion	158
Developing Citizens	163

Afterword
Kizuna

	167

Appendices
    Appendix 1. Japan's Lifelong Learning in the 2000s   175
    Appendix 2. Major Legal and Policy Developments of
        Japan's Lifelong Learning (1947–2011)   177
    Appendix 3. List of Civic Knowledge Sources   181

Notes   185

Japanese Glossary   191

References   197

Index   227

Illustrations

Figure

1.1	Risk—a conceptual map	12

Photographs

4.1	A discussion scene of *bunka borantia* at the Bunka Borantia National Forum in 2007	79
4.2	*Jukugi* demonstration by education officials; proposing problems	90
4.3	*Jukugi* demonstration; categorizing ideas by using sticky notes	91
4.4	*Jukugi* demonstration—a concluding poster	93
6.1	Recruiting poster for the vocational training course to nurture social entrepreneurs who support the New Public Commons	118
6.2	Local people gathering in Toy Square, August 2010	133

Preface

The idea for this book originally came from a conference paper that I presented in Daejeon, South Korea, in 2009. The material for the paper was based on Japan's lifelong learning, and I was looking for some theoretical orientations to support my argument. I owe a lot to Glenn Hook, who was on the same panel as a colleague of the European Japan Advanced Research Network (EJARN) and recommended that I look at the risk scholarship. I am also grateful to Marie Söderberg, organizer of EJARN and colleague in Stockholm, who gave insightful feedback on my work.

This project was based on my research network in the field of lifelong learning over a decade. I was often inspired by my research collaborators—Takemoto Hirokazu, Shimada Yasuko, Ito Misao, Sahara Shigemoto, Takabayashi Mari, Shirai Toru, Okubo Kuniko, Tanaka Hiroko, Yamashita Haruko, Suzuki Shosei, and Sawauchi Takashi. Kondo Shinji, editor of *Shakai kyōiku*, helped me to come into contact with the newest developments on Japan's lifelong learning policies and practices across the country.

I had the good fortune to add further contacts in Aomori to my research network: Kitaoka Seiko, Seino Mayumi, Yatsuyanagi Kakuya, Misawa Akira, Osanai Makoto, Saito Masami, Shikanai Aoi, Narita Harumi and his staff members of Aun, Fushimi Hideto, Kudo Midori, and Ishioka Yuriko. I also benefited from engaging conversations with Sato Sanzo, Lee Young-Jun, Iwata Ittetsu, Kotaya Fumihiko, and Anthony Rausch at Hirosaki University.

Patricia Nelson, Verena Blechinger-Talcott, Sherry Martin, Mitsui Hideko, Roger Goodman, Kariya Takehiko, Ian Neary, Ronald Dore, Joy Hendry, Mitch Sedgwick, Peter Wynn Kirby, Susan Wright, Pia Cort, Katrina Moore, Annamari Konttinen, and Sidsel Hansson offered comments and suggestions on earlier versions of the chapters and research presentations. Special thanks go to Jeff Kingston, who was often the first reader for the chapters and gave me useful and relevant comments. Kuramasu Nobuko helped me access Japanese primary sources.

For the academic year 2009–2010, I was on the postdoctoral fellowship in the German Research Foundation (DFG)–funded research project 1613 Risk and East Asia at the University of Duisburg-Essen Institute of East Asian Studies. During my stay in Duisburg, I had a great chance to become familiar with the theoretical literature on risk. Many thanks go to Karen Shire, speaker of the research project, and Kawai Norifumi, an important colleague of mine. In the following academic year, 2010–2011, my fieldwork was supported by a grant from the Abe Fellowship Program administered by the Social Science Research Council and the American Council of Learned Societies in cooperation with and with funds provided by the Japan Foundation Center for Global Partnership. During my fieldwork, I was affiliated with the National Graduate Institute for Policy Studies (GRIPS) in Tokyo, under the sponsorship of Konno Masahiro and Okamoto Kaoru, and the University of Aarhus Danish School of Education in Copenhagen, under the sponsorship of Susan Wright. I am grateful to all of them.

I am indebted to Theodore Bestor and Davydd Greenwood—two great anthropologists who have inspired me since my graduate days at Cornell.

I thank Nancy Ellegate, senior editor of SUNY Press, for her continuing support.

An earlier version of chapter 3 appeared as "Risk Management by a Neoliberal State: Construction of New Knowledge through Lifelong Learning in Japan," *Discourse: Studies in the Cultural Politics of Education* 34 (2013, 132–144). Part of chapter 1 appeared as "Japan's New Lifelong Learning Policy: Exploring Lessons from the European Knowledge Economy," *International Journal of Lifelong Education* 28 (2009), 601–14. Part of chapter 4 appeared as "The Construction of Citizenship through Volunteering: The Case of Lifelong Learning," in *Japan's Politics and Economy: Perspectives on Change* (London, New York: Routledge, 2009), edited by Patricia A. Nelson and Marie Söderberg. Some of my reflections on the research for this book appeared in "Lifelong Learning in Tokyo: A Satisfying Engagement with Action Research in Japan," *Anthropology in Action: Journal of Applied Anthropology in Policy and Practice* 20 (2013), 46–57.

The photographs in chapter 4 were provided by Yamashita Haruko

(4.1) and Kondo Shinji (4.2, 4.3, and 4.4). Unless otherwise noted, the remaining photographs are mine.

Because of the confidential nature of the material upon which this book draws, no identifying individual names for data sources are provided. Except where otherwise indicated, all quotations are taken from my field notes, and all translations are mine. Furthermore, Japanese individuals' names are written with the surname first. Conversions from Japanese yen to U.S. dollars are made at a constant rate of 102 yen to the dollar.

Many thanks to Deborah and Hannah for their active involvement in numerous brainstorming sessions over breakfast and dinner tables when I struggled to organize my ideas for this book. Their comments were very helpful.

1

Introduction

Why Lifelong Learning Now?

Lifelong learning has become a primary focus in Japan's education policy making. Its heightened importance became evident in December 2006, when the Japanese term *shōgai gakushū* (which directly translates into English as "lifelong learning") was added to Japan's educational charter, the Fundamental Law of Education (*kyōiku kihon hō*). This was the first revision made since the charter's enactment in 1947. Yet, we must ask: Why is the focus now on lifelong learning? This is the primary research question that this book attempts to answer.

In general, lifelong learning encompasses all aspects of learning, which begin in infancy and continue into adulthood (cf. Jarvis 2009a). It includes the learning attained in families, schools, local communities, vocational training institutions, universities, and workplaces.[1] Lifelong learning has become critically important in the promotion of personal development, as well as social cohesion by the improvement of the quality of community life, in the development of active citizenship, and in the sustainment of a global knowledge economy. Policy endorsement of lifelong learning is almost universal (Field 2006), although the practices involved in lifelong learning are varied and contested. Traditionally, researchers have argued that lifelong learning activities in Japan are based on what I would call a cultural model (cf. Schuetze and Casey 2006) that considers lifelong learning intrinsic to individual cultural growth. Japan's lifelong learning is a process that operates in each individual's life. It is designed to promote learning for learning's sake. It is oriented toward the attainment of cultural ends during leisure time (Kawanobe

1994; Okamoto 2001; Wilson 2001; Rausch 2004) and the enjoyment of music (Watanabe 2005) and sports, primarily in the context of an aging society (Ogawa 2005; Ohsako and Sawano 2006). Furthermore, in its promotion of lifelong learning, Japanese society is now shifting from an academic diploma-oriented society (*gakureki shakai*) to a learning society (Fuwa 2001; Sawano 2007). It is also moving toward a knowledge-based economy (Ogawa 2009b; cf. Han 2007).

Japan's lifelong learning policies and practices have been uniquely developed. They flourished at the grassroots level during the post–World War II period. Lifelong learning is an active form of education in Japan. It includes various forms of learning activities that revolve around personal learning and center on hobbies, sports, and liberal arts. Vocational training and recurrent education, which aim to update individuals' knowledge and skills for survival in the labor market, are also parts of personal learning. Meanwhile, social education (*shakai kyōiku*), which includes nonformal learning activities, has been deeply rooted as collective learning in local communities. In 2008, the Japanese Education Ministry[2] announced that the total number of participants in social education courses offered by state-run facilities achieved a record of 34,172,338 people, an increase from 29,377,896 people who participated a decade ago (MEXT 2008a, 15).[3] This means that almost one-third of the Japanese population attended some kind of social education course across the country. What does this really mean?

Nowadays, a variety of learning opportunities related to liberal arts, sports, fine arts, foreign languages, and so on, are provided through government-funded programs at public lifelong learning facilities (see Appendix 1). These include citizens' public halls (*kōminkan*), libraries (*toshokan*), museums (*hakubutsukan*), gymnasiums (*taiikukan*), lifelong learning centers (*shōgai gakushū sentā*), women's education centers, the Open University of Japan (Hōsō daigaku), university extension departments, and private lifelong learning service providers (*karuchā sentā*) (i.e., culture centers, most of which are operated by newspaper publishers and department stores; they primarily target housewives). Further, many NPOs,[4] which were established under the so-called NPO Law enacted in 1998, chose social education as one of their activity areas when they registered. Actually, social education is the second most popular area of activity, after social welfare. The majority of social education NPOs are funded by local governments (Cabinet Office 2011a; cf. Ogawa 2009a). At the same time, some forms of correspondence courses (*tsūshin kyōiku*), including Internet-based courses, are also available.

In this book, my research focuses on state-funded lifelong learning. In fact, the state is one of the key sponsors of lifelong learning activities in Japanese society. For fiscal year 2011 (April 2011–March 2012), the Education Ministry spent a total of 19.8 billion yen ($194 million) for the promotion of lifelong learning (MEXT 2011a). This enormous amount of money may be difficult to imagine. Meanwhile, at the grassroots level, one of my field sites, the city of Hirosaki, which is located in Aomori Prefecture, spent a total of 1.62 billion yen ($16 million) for a population of some 170,000 in fiscal year 2010 (April 2010–March 2011) to support the development of learning activities at twenty-three local public lifelong learning facilities. These facilities included citizens' public halls, libraries, museums, and gymnasiums. This means that the city spent 8,553 yen ($84) per citizen to support their lifelong learning activities. Further, this amount equals 12.7 percent of the total expenses related to education in the municipality (Hirosaki Municipal Board of Education 2010, 88). I believe that Japanese people maintain a variety of learning drives. Those who are eager to learn something new will look for service providers even if they must pay expensive tuition. However, this raises another research question: Why does the state fund these types of learning activities?

A practical or realistic answer may be that offering lifelong learning courses is a government's legal duty to its citizens. Shortly after World War II, in 1949, the Japanese government enacted the Social Education Law (*shakai kyōiku hō*) to support grassroots, nonformal learning activities. This law articulates the concept that lifelong learning is a legal right of the Japanese people. For instance, this law states that both the national and municipal governments are required to make every effort to develop and operate public facilities for lifelong learning so that all citizens can enhance their lives by self-cultivation. Further, it stipulates that state and local public bodies should endeavor to attain educational objectives by establishing institutions such as citizens' public halls, libraries, and museums. In 1990, the government also enacted the Lifelong Learning Promotion Law (*shōgai gakushū shinkō hō*)[5] to prepare the institutional environment for the promotion of lifelong learning. This law prescribes measures including (1) the establishment of lifelong learning councils at national and prefectural levels for the local promotion of lifelong learning; (2) a provision aimed at the development of lifelong learning in designated communities; and (3) surveys for the assessment of residents' learning needs and requirements. However, none of these observations help us understand why lifelong learning is currently garnering special attention.

My argument in this book extends beyond what I have mentioned as a cultural model and attempts to situate Japan's new interest in lifelong learning in international policy making. In fact, current developments in Japan's lifelong learning are generating new patterns of behaviors and outcomes; they are producing new types of disciplinary knowledge for surviving neoliberal Japan.

Lifelong Learning as a Global Trend

The continuing march of globalization has heightened uncertainty in everyday life around the world. Japan is not exempt from this uncertainty. One way to cope with this rapidly evolving environment is to practice lifelong learning: In other words, individuals must engage in continual learning efforts that can help them improve and adapt to society. With the publication of the so-called *Faure Report—Learning to Be* (Faure et al. 1972) by UNESCO (United Nations Educational, Scientific and Cultural Organization), lifelong learning became a worldwide topic of discussion. Since then, as globalization gathered momentum, lifelong learning came into greater focus (Jarvis 2007; cf. Mebrahtu et al. 2000; Stromquist 2002; Suárez-Orozco 2007; Fien et al. 2009; Spring 2009). Sutherland and Crowther (2006) termed the emerging trend of lifelong learning "lifelong learning imagination" in reference to C. Wright Mills' *sociological imagination* (1959). They argued, "The promise of the "lifelong learning imagination" is of a process that enables people to understand their personal circumstances and the habits of mind, knowledge and skills they possess. For this to be useful, it has to be an ongoing process—a lifelong activity that people engage and re-engage in continually in order to improve their understanding and develop new knowledge and skills" (Sutherland and Crowther 2006, 4).

Globally, since the mid-1990s, lifelong learning has been a topic of intensive discussions. International organizations, such as the Organization for Economic Co-operation and Development (OECD) and UNESCO, have actively advocated for "lifelong learning imagination." John Field describes the series of events when "lifelong learning emerged onto the policy scene with the suddenness of a new fashion" (2006, 3). For example, since the 1980s, the OECD has primarily encouraged macroeconomic stabilization, structural adjustment, and the globalization of production and distribution (Schuller 2009), while secondarily paying attention to the preservation of social cohesion (Miller 1997). During the 1990s, new technologies, lifelong learning, and higher education were added to policy priorities. In particular, this addition defined the debates and policies on lifelong learning that occurred in the member states (Moutsios 2009). In this context, in 1996, the OECD held a meeting of education ministers entitled Lifelong Learning for All. These ministers advocated "the continuation of conscious learning throughout the lifespan." They embraced learning undertaken "informally at work, by talking to others, by watching television and playing games, and through virtually every other form of human activity" (OECD 1996, 89). As Moutsios (2009, 474–75) claims, the development of human capital is the main ideology pursued by the OECD; this ideology is promulgated in its formal statements. In 2005, the OECD published a report entitled *Promoting Adult Learning* (OECD 2005) that proclaimed the economistic paradigm—the importance of learning to enhance the human capital of individuals and nations. However, the report states that, despite the benefits, there has been insufficient participation in adult learning. As one policy lever, the OECD recommends the clarification of economic incentives and the introduction of co-financing mechanisms that can increase the efficiency of the provision of adult learning.

UNESCO developed its discourse on lifelong learning in a different manner (Ouane 2009). It avoided the rhetoric of human capital development. UNESCO's approach has been more humanistic since its publication of the *Faure Report* in the early 1970s. It advocated "for the right and necessity of each individual to learn for his/her social, economic, political, and cultural development" (Medel-Añonuevo et al. 2001, 2). The *Faure Report* claims: "Every individual must be in a position to keep learning throughout his life. . . . The lifelong concept covers all aspects of education, embracing everything in it, with the whole being more than the sum of its parts" (Faure et al. 1972, 181–82). In 1996, UNESCO published a report entitled *Learning: The Treasure Within* (Delors 1996). This report was produced by the International Commission on Education for the Twenty-First Century, which was chaired by Jacques Delors, former French minister of economics and finance and former president of the European Commission (1985–95). This report was more balanced than the OECD's report. It recognized the significance of learning for work as well as the human potential for learning. As Jarvis (2007, 69) points out, the report views education as a dimension of all human living: The report began by calling UNESCO's own foundation a hope "for a world that is a better place to live in" (Delors 1996, 14). It also criticized the emphasis placed on "all-out economic growth" (ibid., 15).

The Group of Eight (G8), which is comprised of seven of the world's leading industrialized nations and Russia, adopted the Cologne Charter: Aims and Ambitions for Lifelong Learning in June 1999.

> The challenge every country faces is how to become a learning society and to ensure that its citizens are equipped with the knowledge, skills and qualifications they will need in the next century. Economies and societies are increasingly knowledge-based. Education and skills are indispensable to achieving economic success, civic responsibility, and social cohesion. The next century will be defined by flexibility and change; more than ever, there will be a demand for mobility. Today, a passport and a ticket allow people to travel anywhere in the world. In the future, the passport to mobility will be education and lifelong learning. This passport to mobility must be offered to everyone. (Group of Eight 1999)

The G8 economic summit brought the issue of education and lifelong learning to the forefront for the first time in twenty-five years. The summit argued for greater centrality of education and training in policy making among the member states. The Cologne Charter highlighted the importance of the creation of "lifelong learning," by which people are encouraged to acquire the necessary knowledge and skills for survival in the twenty-first century.

Based on these international developments, this book is a result of my comparative interest in the institutional development of lifelong learning policies and practices between Japan and Europe—two regions where lifelong learning is deeply rooted in the everyday lives of individuals. Yet, lifelong learning has developed in different ways in each culture. Further, my analysis is inspired by several ideas of European origin: risk, social inclusion, and social enterprises. The following questions stimulated my research curiosity: What are the impacts of global policy making on lifelong learning at regional and local levels? How were policy ideas transferred and translated to domestic, grassroots levels? In Europe, lifelong learning activities have been developed based on a philosophy that differs considerably from the Japanese philosophy. In the European policy context, the debate over lifelong learning is treated in a more utilitarian manner; meanwhile, Japanese traditional lifelong learning has been primarily understood as a cultural model. Europeans follow OECD policy and focus greater attention on knowledge production in the globalization of social and economic life. It makes serious efforts to identify the types of knowledge required for economic and social developments. Peters and Besley (2006) described this activity as the creation of a "knowledge culture." This might be considered the foundation for competition in the globally expanding knowledge economy. Lifelong learning is squarely connected to success and to individuals' employment strategies in the knowledge economy because the current labor market demands ever-changing profiles of skills, qualifications, and experiences.

Since the 1990s, in tandem with international economic restructuring, the European Union (EU) has placed a high priority on the need to raise skill levels across Europe (Jarvis 2009b; Milana and Holford 2014). Indeed, the EU is nowadays a key player in making lifelong learning and adult education policies (Milana and Holford 2014). EU policy makers consider lifelong learning to be centered on vocational education and training a significant employment strategy. They wish to create a highly skilled workforce capable of adaptation to both European and global demands in an environment filled with intensified competition. The White Paper on Growth, Competitiveness, and Jobs issued by President Jacques Delors in 1993 was a milestone in the creation of EU policy for lifelong learning. This was crucial for the improvement of the significant unemployment situation in Europe. The follow-up was created during the Luxemburg Summit in 1997, which was held to determine the development of an employment strategy for the EU. Since that time, as Jones (2005, 248) points out, successive European summits have taken active measures on five key structural issues: (1) development of job-intensive growth, (2) reduction of nonwage labor costs, (3) introduction of more active labor market measures, (4) targeting of assistance for long-term unemployed individuals, and (5) investment in human resources. European citizens' increased concerns contributed to the development of the Amsterdam Treaty in 1997, which asked member states to commit to "the development of a skilled, trained, and adaptable workforce and labor markets responsive to economic change."

As mentioned earlier, during the 1990s, lifelong learning was reconsidered for the first time since the early 1970s when UNESCO propounded the idea. At the time, although the OECD emphasized recurrent education as a strategy for the promotion of lifelong education (Tuijnman and Boström 2002, 99), it also actively promoted lifelong learning. Whereas UNESCO provided a broad use of the concept, the OECD narrowed the concept of lifelong learning to include human capital theory, which refers to the supply of productive skills and knowledge in labor (cf. Schultz 1961; Mincer 1962; Becker 1964). In line with the OECD's policy making, the EU translated lifelong learning into the educational policies of the sovereign state and beyond. With respect to this policy move, Borg and Mayo (2005, 207–08) state the following: "Its re-emergence in this context, and in the context of the OECD, has to be seen against the backdrop of a world economic system characterized by the intensification of globalization and the emergence of the neo-liberal ideology."

In more recent policy developments, lifelong learning has been consciously embodied as policy integral to the Lisbon Strategy on the global knowledge economy. When they met in Lisbon, Portugal, in March 2000, the European Council set a new and ambitious goal for the EU: to become, by 2010, "the most competitive and dynamic knowledge-based economy in the world, capable of sustainable growth with more and better jobs and greater social cohesion" (European Council 2000). In particular, the strategy emphasized the need for the EU to adapt to changes in the information society and to boost research and development. Consequently, the European Council published a key policy document, *A Memorandum on Lifelong Learning*, which was based on conclusions reached during the 1996 European Year of Lifelong Learning. This policy document provided a key conceptual framework for current education policy discourse in Europe. On the very first page of the memorandum, the Council adopts the following definition of lifelong learning: "[A]ll purposeful learning activity, undertaken on an ongoing basis with the aim of improving knowledge, skills, and competence." Further, it mentions the following:

> Lifelong learning is no longer just one aspect of education and training; it must become the guiding principle for provision and participation across the full continuum of learning contexts. The coming decade must see the implementation of this vision. All those living in Europe, without exception, should have equal opportunities to adjust to the demands of social and economic change and to participate actively in the shaping of Europe's future. (European Commission 2000, 3)

Lifelong learning is positively and clearly defined as an activity that all citizens should engage in to enrich the quality of their lives. The Commission refers to four broad objectives of learning: personal fulfillment, active citizenship, social inclusion, and employability/adaptability (European Commission 2001, 9; cf. Mulder and Sloane 2009). Nevertheless, in a very practical way, it proposes one crucial aim: the promotion of employability. In fact, a convergence has occurred in economic, industrial, and productive policies aimed at the achievement of the Lisbon objective.

The policy report highlights the enhancement of human capital, which directly leads to employability, by engagement in lifelong learning in the knowledge economy. The memorandum justifies the reason for making the practice of lifelong learning a top priority for Europe: "More than ever before, access to up-to-date information and knowledge, together with the motivation and skills to use these resources intelligently on behalf of oneself and the community as a whole, are becoming the key to strengthening Europe's competitiveness and improving the employability and adaptability of the workforce" (European Commission 2000, 5). The report emphasizes that a comprehensive and coherent lifelong learning strategy for Europe should aim to "guarantee universal and continuing access to learning for gaining and renewing the skills needed for sustained participation in the knowledge society" (European Commission 2000, 10). Economic and social change continues to modify and upgrade the profile of basic skills that everyone should possess as a minimum entitlement. The report mentions five skills as the "new basic skills" (European Commission 2000, 10–11): (1) IT skills, (2) foreign languages, (3) technological culture, (4) entrepreneurship, and (5) social skills. IT skills suggest digital literacy, which is genuinely new. Foreign languages are now becoming important for a larger number of people than they were in the past. Further, social skills—including self-confidence, self-direction, and risk taking—are becoming important because people are expected to behave much more autonomously than they did in the past. The follow-up report entitled *Making a European Area of Lifelong Learning a Reality* (published in November 2001) makes a political commitment to this purpose. It states that the foundations for lifelong learning must be provided by governments through compulsory schooling. Adults who had dropped out of school with ongoing literacy, numeracy, and other basic skills needs should also be encouraged to participate in compensatory learning (European Commission 2001, 22).

Lifelong learning encourages individuals to participate in all spheres of social and economic life. Hence, by extension, it includes opportunities and risks they might face when they attempt to participate. Thus, it affects the extent to which they feel they belong to the society in which they have a fair say. According to a report prepared for the EU spring council in 2007, during the previous decade, most new jobs developed in European countries were generated by the expansion of the knowledge economy (Work Foundation 2007, 9). In fact, between 1995 and 2005, employment across knowledge-based industries rose by 24 percent and significantly erased income inequality in Europe. According to the report, there was no evidence that the considerable growth in knowledge-based industries over the past decade widened income inequality in the EU (as measured by the Gini-coefficient) or in most national economies (Work Foundation 2007, 25). Furthermore, European efforts accelerated after the announcement of the midterm review of the Lisbon Strategy in the so-called Kok Report (European Commission 2004), which calls for more effective investment in human capital. In the report, the following statement is made in the section entitled "Building an inclusive labor market for stronger social cohesion": "If Europe is to compete in the global knowledge society, it must also invest more in its most precious asset—its people. . . . Yet, at present, far from enough is being done in Europe to equip people with the tools they need to adapt to an evolving labor market, and this applies to high- and low-skilled positions and to both manufacturing and services" (European Commission 2004, 33). To produce a "highly educated, creative and mobile workforce," the report asks member states to make lifelong learning schemes available to all—everyone must be encouraged to take part in them (European Commission 2004, 33). A report (European Commission 2005) following the midterm review further states: "The modernization and reform of Europe's education and training systems is mainly the responsibility of Member States. However, there are certain key actions that must be taken at European level to facilitate and contribute to this process. . . . The Community will contribute to the objective of more and better jobs by mobilizing its expenditure policies" (European Commission 2005, 29). In 2005, the Mutual Learning Program was launched for increasing the adaptability of workers and enterprises and investing in an increasingly effective manner in human capital (European Commission Employment and Social Affairs 2008). The program was implemented in 2008 as a priority, given the increasing labor supply, by focusing on the people who are at the periphery of the labor market (Mutual Learning Program 2008). Meanwhile, the European Investment Bank is to mobilize a sum of EUR 50 billion ($74 billion)[6] over the debate (European Investment Bank 2008). The bank focuses on the following three objectives paving the way for technological modernization and the tailoring of human capital to the European economy: (1) improving access to quality education and training; (2) supporting excellence in research, development, and innovation; and (3) promoting the diffusion of information and communications technology networks, including audiovisual activities. Such funding obviously targets masses of unemployed youth, increased migration rates, and an aging population; all theses issues are currently echoed in Japan as well.

Learning is a continuous process spanning a lifetime and is intended to improve and adjust oneself to society. I would like to point out that lifelong learning is a central part of European educational policy discourse. In fact, the flagship "Lifelong Learning Program 2007–2013" was introduced in order to integrate all of the existing programs in the education field into one overall framework program. On March 10, 2008, an EU-wide conference titled "University and Lifelong Learning" was held, with the welcome address given by Mojca Kucler Dolinar, the Slovenian Minister for Higher Education, Science, and Technology. It confirmed the above point:

> When we speak about lifelong learning as a twenty-first century educational approach, we often forget that lifelong learning is not a separate process conducted in parallel to formal education; lifelong learning must be acknowledged and incorporated into formal education. In this present-day age of rapidly changing technologies and organizations, the individual's capacity to learn and to adapt to the needs of the environment in terms of new skills and knowledge is increasingly appreciated. The simple ability to learn is no longer enough. (European Union 2008)

Learning can occur across the full range of our lives and at any stage. Europeans believe that this comprehensive education strategy allows for social equity and ultimately helps in attaining the goal of a knowledge economy. In March 2010, the Lisbon Strategy was succeeded by the new Europe 2020 strategy which aimed to make the EU "a smart, sustainable, and inclusive economy" (European Commission 2010).

Meanwhile, what about Japan? Obviously, the European lifelong learning policy, which focuses on human capital development, can provide a lesson for Japan, where the economy and society have remained persistently sluggish over the past two decades. Almost simultaneously with European development, lifelong learning has risen to become a top priority in Japan's education policy agenda based on apparent stimulation provided by international policy making on lifelong learning. However, Japan's lifelong learning in the 2000s is emerging quite uniquely. It is actually producing a specific kind of knowledge and skills. In the remainder of this book, I present a detailed analysis of the development of Japan's new lifelong learning, which employs the concept of *risk*. I argue that one's choice of engagement in lifelong learning is intimately associated with the perception of risk.

Risk: An Analytical Tool

Risk is an important analytical tool in this book. Risk is defined as the probability of harm and injury (Garland 2003, 50). This probability cannot be determined with absolute confidence. Thus, I discuss risk in the context of uncertainty. Risk, which is recognized as an emergent modality of governance, has captured the sociological imagination in recent years. Over the past few decades, scholars across disciplines have documented a modality of risk governance that is emerging globally. This modality of risk governance entails the production of new forms of knowledge, new subjectivity, and new regulatory space. Three major approaches to defining risk in sociocultural research that have been developed are the following: (1) the cultural-symbolic approach, primarily advocated by Mary Douglas;[7] (2) risk society by Ulrich Beck;[8] and (3) governmentality by Michel Foucault.[9]

	Constructionist	
		Governmentality (Foucault) / Poststructuralism - How do the discourses around risks operate in the construction of subjectivity and social life?
	Risk Society (Beck) Critical structuralism - What is the relationship of risks to the structure?	
	Cultural /Symbolic (Douglas) Functional structuralism - Why are some dangers selected as risks and others not selected?	
Individual		**Social**
Subjective		**Collective**
Technico-scientific - What risks exist? - How should we manage them?	**Realist**	

1.1. Risk—a conceptual map. Created based on Lupton (1999a, 35) and Taylor-Gooby and Zinn (2006, 47).

In the first approach, risk is viewed largely as a matter of perception related to specific or cultural issues. Works of symbolic anthropology by Mary Douglas (1992) highlight the ways that risk cannot be isolated from culture. In other words, individuals' risk perceptions are culturally biased. They are never fully objective or knowable outside of belief systems. As Douglas and Wildavsky (1982, 6–7) explain, individuals' responses to, and perceptions of, risk can only be understood against the background of their embeddedness in sociocultural backgrounds, rather than by individual cognition. Furthermore, the meaning of risk is not static. It is constantly constructed and negotiated. Mary Douglas, a functional structuralist, primarily analyzes risk by attempting to identify the ways that underlying cultural structures, hierarchies, and categories serve to define risk knowledge and practices (Lupton 1999a).

Proponents of the second approach define risk as a strategy related to instrumental rationality. This approach essentially adheres to the realist view of risk. It is viewed as a product of reflexive modernization or second (late) modernity, to distinguish it from industrial modernity or first modernity. This approach is inspired by Ulrich Beck's groundbreaking work in *Risk Society* (1992). Beck defines risk as a "systematic way of dealing with hazards and insecurities induced and introduced by modernization itself" (21). This view assumes that a fundamental social transition is occurring. Society is changing from an industrialized society to a risk society. Simultaneously, uncertainty is simply replacing conventional trust and belief in progress by science and technology. In late modernity, risk refers to that which cannot be known—it refers to unquantifiable uncertainties. Beck employed the notion of reflexivity to describe a modern society that "is confronted with problems that are (unintentionally) self-inflicted" (Arnoldi 2009, 50). "All around the world, contemporary society is undergoing radical change that poses a challenge to Enlightenment-based modernity and opens a field where people *choose* new and unexpected forms of the social and the political" (Beck 1999b, 1, emphasis in original). Reflexivity is a response to conditions that arouse fear or anxiety. It is active, rather than passive. Reflexive modernity is termed "reflective" because it represents an era in which society begins to confront itself rather than external others. The term "reflexivity" is also used by Anthony Giddens, who pays greater attention to the operation of reflexive modernization at the individual level. He claims it is a defining characteristic of all human action; it involves the continual monitoring of action and its contexts (Giddens 1990, 36–37; cf. Giddens 1991, 1998b, 1999). The macrosocial process is characterized by uncertainty related primarily to constant changes and cultural fragmentation—the breakdown of norms and traditions. The concept of predictability or certainty, which was a major characteristic during the first modernity, has currently collapsed. Entry into the second modernity has left our everyday lives more susceptible and fragile to unpredictable risks. This forces us to survive the new logic of the organizing society.

Another important part of Beck's theory on risk society concerns individualization. This can be defined as "the disintegration of the certainties of industrial society as well as the compulsion to find and invent new certainties for oneself and others without them" (Beck 1994, 14; cf. Beck and Beck-Gernsheim 2002). Individuals must produce their own biographies in the absence of fixed and obligatory traditions. They remain conscious of their social context and their own roles as actors within it. Mass education, improvements in living standards, new social movements, and changes in the labor markets contribute to the process of individualization. One reality of the contemporary life we face is expressed as follows: "We live with an increasingly large quota of uncertainty and we are often overwhelmed. What are we to do in a *different* context? How can we tackle a *new* problem? Or, more simply and generally, *what* are we to do, which choice should we make? Many of our tasks become exercises in problem solving, compelling us to acquire information, study the instructions, and, in the end, make a choice" (Melucci 1996, 45, emphases in original). Reflexive individuals retain a level of "liquidity" similar to the sense defined in Bauman's *Liquid Modernity* (2000). This flexibility allows them to manage and respond to risk and uncertainty. Although uncertainties continue to expand, the best preparation is to remain flexible. Flexibility allows individuals to make adjustments as they acquire and interpret new knowledge and skills (cf. Ekberg 2007, 354). Both Beck and Giddens, so-called critical structuralists, develop their theories based on Marxist critical legacy with a focus on social conflict, as well as inequalities, dissent, and the need for social change in relation to risk (Lupton 1999a). They critique the ways that social institutions—including families, states, work, science, economic systems, and legal systems—wield power over individuals and reduce their capacity for agency and autonomy.

The third approach relies on the concept of governmentality, which was developed by Michel Foucault. This approach primarily refers to questions of how institutions organize power and govern populations and how risk is used in various technologies of government. The governmentality approach is characterized by "the ensemble formed by the institutions, procedures, analyses and reflections, the calculations and tactics that allow the exercises of this very specific albeit complex form of power" (Foucault 1991, 102). The domain of government covers a variety of human dramas:

> The things with which in this sense government is to be concerned are in fact men [sic], but men in their relations, their links, their imbrication with those other things which are wealth, resources, means of subsistence, the territory with its specific qualities, climate, irrigation, fertility, etc: men in their relation to that other kind of things, customs, habits, ways of acting and thinking, etc; lastly, men in their relation to that other kind of things, accidents and misfortunes such as famine, epidemics, death, etc. (Foucault 1991, 93)

Risk is understood—under the Foucauldian perspective, which is generally framed as poststructuralism—as one of the heterogeneous governmental strategies of disciplinary power by which populations and individuals are monitored and managed, so the goals of democratic humanism can be met (Lupton 1999b, 4). One of its central preoccupations concerns the relationship between power and knowledge. Power relations are always implied, along with knowledge. Individuals are believed not to possess social identities. Rather, their identities are constantly shifting. They are products of dynamic interactions that occur between power and knowledge. Thus, this governmentality perspective offers the most relativist or socially constructionist position on risk (Lupton 1999b, 6). In fact, what we understand to be risk is a product of historically, socially, and politically contingent ways of seeing. As Ewald (1991, 199, emphasis in original) stated, "Nothing is a risk in itself; there is no risk in reality. But on the other hand, anything *can* be a risk; it all depends on how one analyzes the danger, considers the event."

Risk: A Japanese Context

On November 20, 2009, Ulrich Beck gave a keynote speech at the annual conference of the German Association for Social Scientific Research on Japan held in Berlin. To describe the speech, which was entitled "World Risk Society: The 'Cosmopolitan Turn,'" Beck contributed a brief paragraph to the conference abstract book:

> Basic concepts of the theory of reflexive modernization cannot be simply applied in different contexts of the world. . . . This "cosmopolitan turn" criticized the universalistic assumptions and expectations of the early theory of risk society. The point is that the theory itself has to be cosmopolitanized. . . . This means that basic concepts like "risk" and "individualization" have to be adapted and transformed to a multi-path outlook of modernity. These concepts have to be re-interpreted in order to be "usable" in different societies and contexts. More than that: In order to understand the "post-universalistic" European path we have to relate it to and compare it with different South-East-Asian paths (for example). This is a basic challenge to social theory to develop an epistemology/methodology for path dependencies and their comparison. (Beck 2009b)

Indeed, most scholarship on risk is based on experiences that occurred in Germany and the United Kingdom (UK) at the end of the twentieth century. These have been described as "post-traditional" (Giddens 1994, 56) because old traditions were called into question.

Currently, risk is a major research topic for Japanese social science scholars (e.g., Tachibanaki 2004; Hook and Takeda 2007; Okuma-Nyström 2007; Hook 2010; Kingston 2010; Chan et al. 2010; Suzuki et al. 2010; Bradley 2012; Ito and Suzuki 2013; Ogawa 2013; Azuma et al. 2014; Williamson 2014) who are contributing an East Asian perspective to the global discourse on risk (cf. Calhoun 2010). For example, among the most current accounts, Glenn Hook edited a special issue of *Japan Forum* devoted to risk and security in Japan (Hook 2010). Highlighting the lacunae in the literature on risk in Japan, the articles examined Japan's security policy in relation to China and North Korea and discussed the intersection of risk at international and societal levels by focusing on U.S. bases in Okinawa and on terrorism/counterterrorism. Further, Chan and colleagues (2010) provide an account of risk from the perspective of social policies related to families and the labor market. Meanwhile, Kingston (2010) points out increases in risks since the early 1990s as one of the key concepts required to understand contemporary Japan. These risks are analyzed based on vivid descriptions of negative net equity in housing, an expanding precariat, child abuse, suicide, and growing socioeconomic divides. All of these Japanese accounts relate to the "logic of risk distribution" that is growing in importance as a political issue (Beck 1992, 19–22).

In the emergence of active policy development on lifelong learning in Japan over the past decade, I have observed that the promotion of lifelong learning as a state policy reduces risks for both the state and the individual. Risk management poses a new challenge to the state and to international organizations. It also poses a challenge to ordinary citizens at grassroots levels. It has generated demands for new sets of laws, regulations, and instruments to manage various kinds of risks. It has also introduced new modes of interaction between the state and the individual. Meanwhile, little research has been conducted to examine these types of interactions between institutions and to observe the impact of individual participation. Further, there has been some criticism of the existing risk scholarship. In his book, Jakob Arnoldi, a Danish scholar who studies risk, points out that many social theorists, including risk scholars, have difficulty understanding the major changes occurring on an institutional scale that highlight the transition from one epoch to another (Arnoldi 2009, 5). With respect to the contemporary situation, this applies to the transition that is occurring from welfare statehood to neoliberal politics. Further, as Mythen (2007, 802) notes, the risk society thesis is a macrotheoretical endeavor that is not sufficiently attentive to empirical evidence.

I address these issues in my qualitative ethnography, which showcases Japan's lifelong learning through the lens of two types of risks: (1) governmental risk, as inspired by Foucault's notion of governmentality, and (2) socioeconomic risk, hinted at by Beck's notion of individualization that occurs in risk society. What kinds of knowledge does the Japanese state deploy in its lifelong learning policies to counteract these risks? How do ordinary people create, circulate, mediate, react, and absorb these risks in their everyday lives? I explore how the "large processes" (Tilly 1984) of institutional change—from the welfare state to neoliberal politics—shift the responsibility of risk management in economic, social, and political institutions from states to markets; from public to private, as well as third-sector/civil society bodies; and from collectives to individuals. Neoliberalism is commonly viewed as an economic doctrine that endorses individual freedoms and rights. It seeks to limit excessive state intervention by the actions of decentralized authority. Human action has become characterized by economic rationality. This ideology has gained dominance in advanced industrial countries such as the United Kingdom, the United States, and Japan, since the 1980s.

My first topic of investigation will focus on governmental risk. Specifically, I will focus on how risk is employed in various technologies by the government and on the power that risk may hold over people. In particular, I will explore forms of neoliberal government and its innovative distribution of responsibility between the state and the individual. I believe that the strength of the governmentality approach lies in (1) its capacity to analyze specific forms of risk rationality and technology; (2) the different types of agency and identity involved in practices of risk; and (3) the political and social imaginations linked to these practices (cf. Dean 1999a). Furthermore, Ong (2006, 12) stresses the importance of the study of neoliberalism as a specific type of governmentality. For example, current neoliberal regimes rely increasingly on self-governance that allows individuals to accept additional responsibility for themselves. In fact, Dean (1999b) regards governmentality as a study of the conduct of conduct: modern power conducts the subjects into conducting themselves in certain ways. I would argue that this activity appears to develop because of education. Rose (1999, 234) claims, "One is always in continuous training, lifelong learning, perpetual assessment, continual incitement to buy, to improve oneself, constant monitoring of health and never-ending risk management." Under the learning initiative, individuals are expected to be autonomous, self-responsible, prudent subjects who rationally weigh the pros and cons of choices.

I locate the current discussion on *atarashii kōkyō*, or the New Public Commons, within Japanese education policy making and in relation to discussions on governmental risk. The concept of the New Public Commons was first presented in the early 2000s during discussions on possible revisions to be made to the Fundamental Law of Education. Since the term *shōgai gakushū*, (lifelong learning), was added to the Fundamental Law of Education in December 2006, discussions in both policy and academic circles have centered on the kinds of lifelong learning policy that Japan should specifically formulate. In my fieldwork, I have observed that the major theme of these discussions revolves around how lifelong learning might support the New Public Commons. The New Public Commons may serve as a foundation for solidarity, which can, in turn, enable good citizens to improve society. It can also function as a sphere in which citizens in general, or those interested in a particular cause, can voluntarily participate (New Public Commons Roundtable 2010a). I argue that Japan's new lifelong learning, primarily developed in the 2000s, contributes to the actual formation of this public sphere. It is expected to produce a new type of disciplinary knowledge referred to as "comprehensive knowledge" (a literal translation of *sōgōteki na chi* in Japanese) that, in turn, is expected to support the creation of the New

Public Commons. A reframing process is also involved with respect to the relationship between the state and the individual.

This very governmental risk should be interpreted as a new metanarrative that is strongly linked to the government's neoliberal projects. Japan's new lifelong learning policies in the 2000s were introduced specifically as a method of risk management in contemporary Japanese society, which was once described as general middle-class society. However, at present, its population is socioeconomically polarized. It is popularly referred to as *kakusa*. In other words, it is a negative revelation of neoliberal economic measures implemented in the early 2000s. In fact, the current political discourse on neoliberalism represents more than a policy shift aimed at deregulation and liberalization. It reasserts the interests of economic elites and restores a more direct expression of class power. Against the backdrop of the deepening socioeconomic nationwide divide, in imagining the realization of the New Public Commons, the Japanese neoliberal state has attempted to manage the risk of governing society by the introduction of a strong lifelong learning initiative. "Comprehensive knowledge" generated by state-sponsored lifelong learning activities is disciplinary in nature. This knowledge aims to undertake problem-solving activities exclusively in local communities or *chiiki*—the daily centers of people's lives, thoughts, and behaviors. In fact, local communities, which serve as key actors in Japanese civil society, were reinstitutionalized as places for the practice of lifelong learning activities so that people might enhance social solidarity and collective consciousness by engaging in problem-solving activities as members of the community. In this context, local community can be understood as an entity in which people cooperate to govern aspects of their own lives (cf. Bowles and Gintis 2002).

My second topic of investigation will focus on socioeconomic risk. I will primarily employ Beck's notion of individualization to demonstrate how the process of individualization involves shifts from public to private social security and includes the privatization of economic risk in ways that affect individuals. This process is also associated with the creation and actualization of new boundaries for individual responsibilities. Individualization means that one must choose among risks, conform to one's internalized standards, and be responsible for one's self while simultaneously remaining dependent on conditions outside one's control (Lupton 1999a, 70). Individuals must turn inward to cope with anxiety and insecurity. These self-choices require intense and continuous negotiation with others that involve risk-taking. Thus, individualization itself carries and creates new socioeconomic risks.

We are facing a qualitative shift in the experience of contemporary capitalism expressed through labor market change and the new relations of employment it generates. The traditional lifetime employment practice in Japan has not functioned well because many of the businesses with the practice can no longer maintain it due to their increasing exposure to global competition. This deterioration of the practice has naturally led to the increase in risk in the livelihoods of workers. As Boltanski and Chiapello (2007) argue, these new risks appear in the form of growing wage discrepancies, benefit (or social insurance coverage) inequalities, and family instability. They generate a novel set of contingencies associated with the neoliberal labor market. In other words, Japan's labor market is becoming fluid: workers who used to enjoy high job security under the lifetime employment system now face lower salaries or even risk losing their jobs. The labor market indeed serves as "a signifier" (Doogan 2009, 143), par excellence, of societal transformation. It embodies the outcomes of technological change, industrial and occupational restructuring, deregulation, flexibilization, and individualization. This scenario was definitely echoed in contemporary Japanese society (cf. Genda 2001; Kaneko 2007; Iwata and Nishizawa 2008; Shibuya 2010).

In the early 2010s, Japan experienced a sharp rise in labor market dualism. The share of nonregular workers represented more than one-third of the total number of employed people (MHLW 2011). Nonregular workers included part-time workers, short-term contract employees, and dispatch workers employed by temporary work agencies. Socioeconomic risks were disproportionately experienced by social groups, including the less educated, those with limited or outdated skills, and young people. Because ordinary people face socioeconomic risks, the Japanese state aims to develop competency-based skills and experiences in the form of new knowledge to be transmitted by vocational training, an important component of lifelong learning. This type of training includes competencies (1) in building relations with others, (2) in self-understanding and self-management, and (3) in problem solving and career planning. These competencies form the foundation of *ikiru chikara* (zest for living), an educational mission Japanese schools currently attempt to instill in their students.

At a later point in this book, based on a theory that Stephen Lyng termed "voluntary risk taking" (Lyng 2004), I describe a type of vocational training course developed by the Japanese government in the late 2000s. This vocational training course was primarily intended to nurture people who would support the New Public Commons. These participants were expected to serve as social entrepreneurs who would establish NPOs in their local communities. I discovered that socially vulnerable unemployed men or men with limited skills or education were encouraged by the state to participate in these courses. They were asked to voluntarily take risks by becoming social entrepreneurs. The theoretical conception of voluntary risk-taking is based on the notion of edgework (Lyng 1990; 2004). The term *edgework* was originally coined by Hunter S. Thompson (1971). He used this term to describe activities that put "one's physical or mental well-being or one's sense of an ordered experience" at risk (Lyng 1990, 857). In his research on edgework, Lyng initially focused on risk taking in the leisure realm of high-risk sports, including skydiving and Alpine mountain climbing. However, his research program quickly expanded. Its focus was "dictated by the decision to make *voluntary* risk-taking the primary conceptual issue" (Lyng 2008, 107–108; emphasis in original). Lyng further noted that certain high-risk occupations, such as firefighting, police work, combat, and bond trading, hold attractions for some individuals that are similar to high-risk leisure activities (ibid.). I believe the work of social entrepreneurs fits the criteria of voluntary risk-taking behaviors found in edgework. Edgework "means overcoming the group and the routines of social life, overcoming fear and other weaknesses and evolving as person" (Arnoldi 2009, 141). During my fieldwork, I documented the series of narratives produced by participants in the abovementioned vocational training course. This series of narratives emphasized self-descriptions of how participants developed new skills and knowledge by participation in edgework. We can link these narratives to ideas related to the construction of the reflexive self (Giddens 1991, 5).

As an extension of elements in my previous work, *The Failure of Civil Society?* (Ogawa 2009a), this book argues that Japan's neoliberal state has attempted to reorganize the public sphere by the generation of new disciplined knowledge based on a strong lifelong learning initiative. I demonstrate challenges encountered at the grassroots level in the pursuit of lifelong learning as individuals survive neoliberal life in contemporary Japan. Ultimately, my analysis of Japan's lifelong learning in this book aims to contribute a new corpus of knowledge about global developments in lifelong learning in three main respects. First, this book is one of only a few comprehensive accounts that exclusively document Japanese policies and practices related to lifelong learning, which is a significant form of education in the Japanese education system. Second, this book will provide an ethnographic account of Japanese neoliberal politics during the 2000s by employing the concept of risk. Anthropologists have compiled an extensive ethnographic catalogue of the ways that neoliberalism re-engineered and refashioned social and political spaces and populations, including local communities, citizenship, family, and gender roles, in addition to transforming learning (e.g., Hilgers 2002; Ong and Collier 2005; Ogawa 2009a; Greenhouse 2010; Ogawa 2013). Only a limited number of nuanced accounts are currently available that describe the state-society interactions, processes, and practices by which neoliberalism has become entrenched in institutions credited with its dissemination (e.g., in particular, Asian experiences). By employing the idea of "globalization from below" in the sense of Arjun Appadurai (2001), this book documents the challenges encountered at the grassroots level in pursuing lifelong learning and in surviving the risks of contemporary times. Third, I explore how institutional arrangements in different countries have succeeded in filtering or mitigating the disruptive effects of neoliberal globalization. My analysis provides some lessons for Japan's new lifelong learning; it brings to light the policies and practices that Japan can adopt and adapt for sustainable human development.

Methods

I conducted multisited ethnography (Marcus 1995) in both Japan and Europe to investigate how people create, circulate, mediate, react to, and absorb the risks in their everyday lives and the kinds of strategies they deploy to do so. Over the past decade, I did fieldwork in Tokyo (in Sumida and in my neighborhood, Suginami) and Aomori, as well as in Stockholm and Copenhagen. As a trained anthropologist, since 2001, I have been documenting the efforts of a civic group that promotes lifelong learning in Sumida, eastern Tokyo (Ogawa 2009a). The civic group, known as SLG (a pseudonym), is a third-sector organization that is considered an NPO created under the 1998 NPO Law. It offers a lifelong learning program at a local public lifelong learning center. This group stands out among other lifelong learning providers in Japanese society because the organization's operations are performed primarily by ordinary local-resident volunteers. Volunteer participants plan and implement courses, distribute information, and promote the virtues of lifelong learning in the community. During my observations of SLG's activities, I witnessed volunteers' independent approaches and sensibilities as they molded community-oriented learning. Their learning was considerably enhanced by their participation in volunteer activities aimed at activation of the local community. The volunteers provided support and guidance for independent and individual learning activities.

From 2001 through 2003, I worked as an unpaid staff member at the SLG secretariat. I continue to serve as a volunteer. Meanwhile, I developed my own research "networks" (Bestor 2002) with volunteers located throughout Japan who work at public lifelong learning facilities, including local lifelong learning centers, libraries, and museums. Further, I formed relationships with researchers who shared similar research interests. These volunteers actually identified themselves as *bunka borantia* (culture volunteers). I became *engaged,* in Thomas Eriksen's sense (2005), in the national network of *bunka borantia* (2005–present). With the assistance of these networks, I discovered another interesting field site, in Hirosaki, where active social education activities were being conducted at the grassroots level. This site is located in Aomori Prefecture, at the northern tip of the Japanese mainland. This location sounds marginal, but during my first visit in the summer of 2007, I realized it was culturally rich. Although the city's current population is approximately 170,000, the city originated as a castle town (*jōka machi*) under the leadership of the Tsugaru family during the Edo period. Hirosaki High School, one of several elite public high schools that operated during the pre-World War II period, was established in 1920. That school is now a part of Hirosaki University. Dazai Osamu, a popular author, graduated from the school. I was introduced to a café where Dazai often spent time as a student. This café became my favorite place to conduct interviews. Then the network in Hirosaki introduced me to an interesting vocational training course focused on the nurturance of social entrepreneurs in the city of Aomori. I had the opportunity to conduct participant-observation-based research during this course. I conducted intensive fieldwork in Aomori Prefecture between 2010 and 2011. In tandem with the research conducted in Aomori, I also conducted fieldwork in my neighborhood, Suginami, Tokyo. I regularly observed a series of board meetings held at a public junior high school. I conducted extensive follow-up interviews with board members and parents. Further, many meetings (however, I assume, not all) held at the Education Ministry were opened to the public by the new Democratic Party of Japan (DPJ) government, which ended more than half a century of almost uninterrupted rule by the Liberal Democratic Party (LDP). Discussions concerning the New Public Commons were also available on its website (http://www5.cao.go.jp/npc/index.html), for example. Hence, I took advantage of these opportunities to observe their policy-making discussions. This series of direct observations was followed by intensive interviews with meeting participants and bureaucrats. To gain background knowledge, I also conducted interviews with former bureaucrats who were involved in the education policy discussions.

At the same time, the perspectives I gained in my comparisons of Japan and Europe were significantly enhanced by my daily interactions in Stockholm, Sweden, where lifelong learning activities, such as various kinds of study circles and vocational training, are deeply rooted in the lifestyle. I am currently participating in a Swedish-language course for immigrants as part of my own lifelong learning activities. My comparative perspective was further enhanced by participation in an open seminar series held at the Danish School of Education, University of Aarhus, in Copenhagen, Denmark (2009–2011). This school has become a core research center for European lifelong learning policy. It is one of several base institutions that host the European master's degree course on lifelong learning. This course is sponsored by the EU's Erasmus Mundus Program. In addition to my participation in these long-term fieldwork experiences, I scheduled several short trips to Japan to collect documents and conduct interviews in Saitama, Shizuoka, and Toyama. These opportunities allowed me to observe significant patterns in Japan's lifelong learning.

In due course, I wanted to test the power of anthropology with respect to policy analysis (Shore and Wright 1997; Shore et al. 2011; Goodman 2002 in the context of Japan). The arguments I present in this book were primarily inspired by Shore and Wright (2011, 1): "From our perspective, policies are not simply external, generalized, or constraining forces, nor are they confined to texts. Rather, they are productive, performative, and continually contested. A policy finds expression through sequences of events; it creates new social and semantic spaces, new sets of relations, new political subjects, and new webs of meaning." Policy can be studied as contested narratives that define the problems of the present in ways that either condemn or condone the past and that may project only one viable pathway to their resolution (Shore and Wright 2011, 13). We anthropologists are primarily interested in the native point of view that embodies how people make sense of things. Thus, during conventional participant-observation-based fieldwork, I analyzed official policy reports and legal documents, as well as discussion records. I considered them "significant cultural texts that shed light on the way policy problems are framed and contested" (ibid., 15). I attempted to document what people would say and think about policy narratives and how policies affect their everyday lives. Ultimately, I aimed to offer policy initiatives and practices that Japan should consider when it attempts to (re)build its own novel lifelong learning policies.

In addition, this project examines policymaking in an era of globalization. Traditionally, education policies are assumed to constitute core national policies. However, major changes have occurred in this trend in recent years. Currently, an increasing number of education policy concepts do not actually originate in any country. Rather, they originate from international organizations such as the OECD, UNESCO, and the EU, as shown earlier in this chapter. The Japanese phenomenon can be considered a good example of what Dolowitz and Marsh (2000, 5) refer to as "policy transfer." This is a situation in which policy making in one political setting (or in my case, international organizations) plays influential roles in another political setting (or domestic policy-making activities) (see also McCann and Ward 2013). I believe that the growing overlap between national policies and international perspectives is an effect of globalization. Furthermore, education policies are not solely the subject of global debates on policy making. They also relate to global dynamics because they can be influenced by changing trends in the labor market. This is exactly what is occurring in the case of lifelong learning, my research topic. I explored the manner in which countries employed lifelong education policies in the context of their national growth strategies as a means to compete on the international stage in an era of globalization. Education policy reforms constitute efforts to build a global community so countries can move together toward the creation of a knowledge-based society and a flexible workforce. In this book, I investigate the impact of lifelong learning policy discussions on Japan.

Overview of Chapters

Chapter 2 provides an overview of the institutional development of Japan's traditional lifelong learning activities during the post–World War II era (chronologically beginning in 1947 and ending in the early 2000s), which has been described as a cultural model. I examine three key words: *shakai kyōiku* (social education), *shōgai kyōiku* (lifelong education), and *shōgai gakushū* (lifelong learning). Each of these terms has appeared in Japanese education policy documents. They look similar. However, they are significantly different. With respect to policy documents related to education policy making, I argue that the consistent focus on the local and, in particular, local communities, has become the solid foundation of Japan's lifelong learning.

The rest of the book examines new developments in Japan's lifelong learning policy and practices in the 2000s and beyond, based on my application of the concept of risk. Chapters 3, 4, and 5 primarily examine governmental risk. In chapter 3, my key argument is that the promotion of lifelong learning assists the neoliberal state to manage the risks of governance or governmental risk. Implementation of a new lifelong learning policy in the 2000s involves the employment of a political technique that aims to integrate the currently divided and polarized Japanese population—popularly known as *kakusa*—into the newly imagined collective: the *atarashii kōkyō*, or New Public Commons. In its examination of the macropolicy discourse on Japan's education policy, this chapter demonstrates Japan's inflections of neoliberal governmentality that include innovative distribution of responsibility between the state and the individual by the construction of new knowledge known as "comprehensive knowledge." In fact, this new knowledge lies at the epicenter of the national education policy discourse aimed at the generation of social solidarity in local communities.

Chapter 4 argues that a dynamic grassroots interaction has developed between the New Public Commons and the *bunka borantia*. Because they produce knowledge, referred to as *shimin chi* or "civic knowledge," in their daily volunteer activities, the *bunka borantia* play a key role in the ongoing societal restructuring that continues to occur under the New Public Commons. The Japanese neoliberal state is strongly expected to mobilize these disciplinary "knowledge-constructing" subjects for the public in the hopes of managing governmental risk. The *bunka borantia* are pointing Japanese society in the direction of the entrepreneurial self. In addition, I document a policy development in which the Education Ministry attempted the systematic production and reproduction of certain disciplinary subjects by the introduction of *jukugi*, a discussion technique. Finally, this chapter demonstrates that the New Public Commons, supported by citizens such as the *bunka borantia*, is part of a new growth strategy in Japan, where the economy and society have remained persistently sluggish over the past two decades.

Chapter 5 provides an account of local communities in contemporary Japan, extending my argument on governmental risk. It sheds light on Japanese society's current efforts to institutionalize the "community school" in its public education system. Beginning in the early 2000s, an increasing number of community schools have been developed at the grassroots level across the country. These schools function as centers for community solutions or problem-solving activities within local communities. Furthermore, this chapter argues that the establishment of public schools as local community centers is a move towards the integration of formal school education and nonformal, community-oriented social education—the cornerstone of Japan's new lifelong learning in the 2000s. The formal school system is actually being rebuilt on the foundation of Japan's rich tradition of social education.

Chapters 6 and 7 provide narratives related to socioeconomic risk: chapter 6 focuses on vocational training, a key component in conventional lifelong learning activities that can help improve individuals' knowledge and skills and help them adapt to the demands of the labor market. Traditionally, the Japanese government has been the principal organizer of public vocational training programs. Recently, the government funded a new type of vocational training program, which trains individuals to become social entrepreneurs. These courses were primarily developed as a response to conventional firms not hiring as many people due to the persistently sluggish economy. However, this chapter questions the usefulness of this new program. It demonstrates how ordinary people, and, in particular, the socially vulnerable unemployed, were, practically speaking, heavily influenced by the state to enroll in these types of training courses. Because they were asked to become social entrepreneurs, they were expected to undertake unreasonable socioeconomic risks, even though they were deeply overwhelmed by the reality of their lack of immediate financial support.

Chapter 7 highlights "career education," a newly introduced course in Japanese schools. This course primarily attempts to generate new knowledge for Japanese students by the provision of education on the four "basic and versatile competencies" defined by the Central Council for Education. I argue that, because employment styles are changing, the knowledge imparted to students by the Japanese education system should also change. The new knowledge involves competency-based skills and experiences and encourages youth to commit themselves to their own society. Further, I argue that career education has been developed in the context of the management of new risks that young people face because of socioeconomic changes that occurred and continue to occur during the transition to the neoliberal economy. Finally, I claim that career education is an effective tool for the promotion of the social inclusion of youth. It could act as a foundation for the development of citizenry of contemporary neoliberal Japan.

The afterword contains my reflective account based on the results of fieldwork I conducted on lifelong learning policies and practices over the past decade. In particular, with respect to the disastrous earthquake that hit eastern Japan on March 11, 2011, I argue that the new emphasis on lifelong learning contains increased meaning in postcrisis Japan.

2

Japan's Lifelong Learning

History, Policies, and Practices

Three Key Terms

This chapter provides a chronological overview of the institutional development of Japan's lifelong learning activities that began in the post–World War II era. The period examined ranges between the late 1940s and the early 2000s. I examine three key terms: *shakai kyōiku* (social education), *shōgai kyōiku* (lifelong education), and *shōgai gakushū* (lifelong learning). Each of these terms has appeared in Japanese education policy documents. Although these terms appear similar, in reality, they differ significantly. To explain the differences, I primarily examined policy documents produced by the Social Education Council (*shakai kyōiku shingikai*), the Central Council for Education (*chuō kyōiku shingikai*), the Lifelong Learning Council (*shōgai gakushū shingikai*) (all of which are advisory bodies to the education minister), and the Ad Hoc Council on Education (*Rinji kyōiku shingikai* or *Rinkyōshin*) (a private advisory body to the prime minister organized in the 1980s). Members of these councils included academic scholars, businesspersons, public officials (prefectural governors and mayors), and journalists. All members were directly appointed by the designated ministers of each council. During the post–World War II period, policy reports produced by these councils played very influential roles in the direction of all education policy making performed in Japan (see appendix 2 for a list of major education policy developments). A consistent focus on the local, and, in particular, local communities, or *chiiki*, became the solid foundation for Japan's lifelong learning. Local communities were firmly institutionalized as key locations in which lifelong learning policies would be actively practiced. Later, during the 2000s, the significance of local communities was reaffirmed in the development of Japan's new lifelong learning policies. This will be discussed in chapter 3.

Social Education

The history of Japanese contemporary lifelong learning can be traced to learning activities referred to as *shakai kyōiku,* (social education) that developed during the early post–World War II period. The literal meaning of the term *shakai kyōiku* is "social education." This term alludes to general educational activities conducted in society. Simply put, social education can be defined as all types of education other than school education. Social education was developed with the goal of providing learning opportunities to members of the younger generation who were unable to attend high school due to poverty (Sasai 1998). During the early postwar era, only a limited number of students could attend high school. In September 1945, just one month after the war ended, the Education Ministry announced the guidelines for education that were aimed at the development of a new Japan (*shin nihon kensetsu no kyōiku hōshin*). The guidelines included the concept of social education. In October 1945, the Ministry established the Social Education Bureau (*shakai kyōiku kyoku*). The promotion of social education has become a key pillar in Japanese education policy since that time (Sato 2009, 8–9).

When the term *social education* is used in the context of international scholarship related to lifelong learning, the term *nonformal education* for adults and youth appears to be a better translation of the Japanese phrase. The term *shakai kyōiku* refers to informal but organized programs conducted in local facilities other than schools. These include organized sporting and cultural activities. *Adult education* might be considered an equivalent to *shakai kyōiku* (cf. Jarvis 1983). However, Japanese *shakai kyōiku* also includes youth activities. Thus, the English equivalent does not fully encompass the actual meaning of the Japanese term. Similarly, the Japanese academic research association devoted to *shakai kyōiku* translates the term to mean "adult and community-oriented education." However, in this book, I use the literal translation, *social education*, to maintain the original Japanese conception of learning activities.

These learning activities are supported by the Social Education Law that was enacted in 1949, shortly after the end of World War II. As Fuwa (2001, 129) points out, the law hoped to offer a wealth of learning opportunities aimed at the development of knowledge, skills, sentiments, and physical capacity essential to individuals' personal growth and maturity throughout the lifespan. The law also made significant contributions to the reconstruction and revitalization of communities by its efforts to build a democratic Japanese society after the war by encouraging citizens' learning. Japan's social education is officially defined in the Social Education Law as follows: "Article 2: In this law, "social education" implies systematic educational activities (including physical education and recreation) primarily provided for out-of-school adults and youth. It excludes educational activities conducted in schools as part of the curriculum, in accordance with school education." The Social Education Law further stipulates the framework of social education or non-formal education policies in Japan and notes the responsibilities of national educational authorities and local public bodies at various levels to educate the public: "Article 3: The State and local public bodies shall assist in the maintenance of a congenial environment in which individual citizens can engage in cultural and educational activities . . . it will assist them in daily living by providing various kinds of facilities, sponsoring meetings, and making informative materials available for social education in accordance with the prescriptions of this law and [its] regulations."

As mentioned earlier in this chapter, social education began to supplement school education for citizens who were unable to attend high school during the early postwar era. The role of social education as an alternative form of education continued primarily until the share of junior high school students who continued on to senior high school exceeded 90 percent in the mid-1970s. The Law for the Promotion of Youth Class (*seinen gakkyū shinkō hō*), enacted in 1953 (and abolished in 1999), also contributed to youth education. However, despite the dramatic increase in students' attendance in senior high school, this tradition of social education remains vigorous in contemporary Japan.

The most distinctive phenomenon related to Japanese social education activities is the fact that they are community oriented. They have been conducted mainly at citizens' public halls known as *kōminkan* that began to be established during the post–World War II period. One survey suggested that 16,566 citizens' public halls were located across the country in fiscal year 2007 (April 2007–March 2008). This figure shows a decline from 19,063 public halls that operated one decade ago (MEXT 2008a, 10). This decline is primarily related to mergers of halls to cut costs. Despite this decline, 13 million people attended social education courses offered at local citizens' public halls. Of these 13 million people, 8.57 million were women (ibid., 15–16). Further, 236 million people visited citizens' public halls. This total implies that each Japanese citizen used the public facility in some manner at least twice per year (ibid., 21). The establishment and management of these halls are required of local public bodies, primarily at the municipal level, by the Social Education Law, Article 5. Interestingly enough, Sasai (1998, 181) points out that, although Japan has a centralized legal structure, social education is significant because it establishes a basis for "decentralization."

Social education activities are diverse. They respond to individuals' voluntary and spontaneous drive for learning. Indeed, citizens' public halls play active roles in the stimulation of educational and cultural activities at grassroots levels. Services offered by the citizens' public halls include the provision of a variety of programs: lectures, art exhibitions, film shows, and athletic meetings. In addition, citizens' public halls offer regularly scheduled courses, such as youth study classes, women's classes, and parent education courses. Programs address social issues that affect contemporary society. They also provide programs focused on the liberal and fine arts, including literature, art, music, dance, and sports. For example, in fiscal year 2007 (April 2007–March 2008), 469,546 courses were offered at citizens' public halls throughout the country. Among these courses, 245,367 were focused on liberal arts and hobbies (52 percent), 98,279 were focused on home economics (21 percent), 77,556 were focused on sports and recreation (17 percent), and 34,405 were focused on citizenship and community solidarity (7 percent) (MEXT 2008a, 17). Suzuki (1994, 32–33) explains that learning themes in social education can be classified into two categories: socially "necessary/relevant topics" (*hitsuyō kadai*) and individually "desired topics" (*yōkyū kadai*) (see also Yamamoto 1996). Socially necessary topics include current social issues. I understand the essence of social education involves an examination of whether individual learners are committed to socially relevant topics.

Usually, each citizen's public hall provides conference rooms, small rooms for learning (or classrooms), a small library, a kitchen, and a gymnasium. Learning activities provided at citizens' public halls are coordinated by social education officers (*shakai kyōiku shuji*). According to statistics available (MEXT 2008a, 15), 3,004 social education officers were active. This total decreased by half from the total number available one decade earlier (6,035 officers in 1999). Of the number of officers, 2,505 officers (83.4 percent) worked full time and 332 (11.1 percent) were women. The prefectural and municipal boards of education employ social education officers in their administrative offices under the provisions of the Social Education Law. These social education officers provide professional and technical advice and guidance to all those engaged in social education. The qualification for social education officers can be obtained at undergraduate programs in social education at universities, to be followed by practical involvement in social education development for more than one year. University graduates who work in the field of social education for more than three years and complete a series of social-education courses designated by the Education Ministry can also obtain the qualification. Meanwhile, ordinary citizens can also become involved in social education policymaking by becoming volunteer members of their local boards of social education (*shakai kyōiku iinkai*). Board members are regularly recruited by municipalities (see Chapter 5 with regards to the local board of social education).

Libraries (*toshokan*), museums (*hakubutsukan*), and gymnasiums (*taiikukan*) are conventionally important institutions that facilitate social education. Libraries are crucial to the success of grassroots learning activities because they collect, arrange, and store books and written records and make them available for general public use. Therefore, libraries respond to public needs and to the demand for educational, cultural, and recreational knowledge. The Library Law (*toshokan hō*) enacted in 1950 is based on the Social Education Law. It strongly emphasizes that libraries should "contribute to the enhancement of education, science, and culture in the nation" (Library Law Article 1: Purpose of this Law). According to the Japan Library Association (2010), 3,196 libraries were located throughout the country in 2010. The number of libraries is increasing. Of the number of libraries, 62 were run by prefectural governments, 3,114 were run by municipal governments, and the remaining 20 were run by private entities. During fiscal year 2009, 290 million people used the libraries (April 2009–March 2010). Museums are also important facilities that collect, store, and display artifacts from history, arts, folklore, industry, and so on. Several types of museums are available, including general museums, fine art museums, history museums, science museums, planetariums, zoological gardens, and botanical gardens. The establishment of museums is included in the Museum Law (*hakubutsukan hō*) enacted in 1951. Museums "are offered for people under educational care, and for the conduct of necessary business to serve people's cultural attainment, research, recreation, etc., and to conduct research and surveys related to these materials" (Museum Law Article 2: Definition). As of October 1, 2008 (MEXT 2008a, 11), 1,248 public museums were in operation in Japan. Of these museums, 449 (36.0 percent) were fine arts museums and 436 were history museums (34.9 percent). At the same time, 47,925 public gymnasiums and 17,323 private gymnasiums were in operation throughout the country (ibid., 10). These facilities promoted sports among local citizens.

In addition, youth education is offered at Youth Outdoor Learning Centers (*seishōnen shizen no ie*) and Youth Friendship Centers (*seishōnen kōryū no ie*). These organizations are currently under the direct control of the National Institution for Youth Education (*kokuritsu seishōnen kyōiku shinkō kikō*). As of 2008, the number of these youth facilities, that are not, however, limited to the abovementioned facilities, amounted to 1,229 located throughout the country (ibid., 10). These facilities promote youth independence as well as sound development by facilitating their participation in experiential activities. Finally, 380 women's education facilities (ibid., 10), were located throughout the country. These facilities include the National Women's Education Center (*kokuritsu josei kyōiku kaikan*) and local women's education centers.

Lifelong Education

In 1971, the Social Education Council produced a report with a title translated as: *On the Arrangement of Social Education to Cope with Rapid Changes in the Social Structure* (originally, *Kyūgekina shakai kōzō no henka ni taisho suru shakai kyōiku no arikata ni tsuite*). Indeed, the time was right for this type of report because Japan, as the second largest economy in the world, was experiencing a period of prosperity. People were experiencing changes to everyday life, such as population increase, nuclearization of family life, industrialization, urbanization, and internationalization. The report claims:

> [B]ecause of exceedingly rapid, large-scale social changes, education has failed to play a pioneering role in society, in some respects, and it cannot even keep pace with society in others. A tendency exists to place an excessive burden or expectation on school education alone. This loses sight of the educational trinity of home education, school education, and social edu-

cation. . . . A pressing need now exists to re-examine every phase of education from the viewpoint of lifelong education. (Social Education Council 1971, 10)

The concept of lifelong education does not simply imply continuous learning throughout the lifespan. Rather, it also effectively combines three functions: family, school, and social education (ibid., 80–81). In other words, the report states that the functions of family education, school education, and social education should be complementary. Each of these forms of education must demonstrate the usefulness of its own educational functions. Each should cooperate with and supplement the others. Further, in the abovementioned report released by the Social Education Council in 1971, special cooperation between school education and social education was mentioned. The policy rationale states: "Owing to the need to address diverse educational problems that occur throughout the course of life, school education alone, because it is limited to a prescribed period, is inadequate. Therefore, it is important to provide people with a flexible type of education that can meet the ever-changing multifarious demands of individuals and communities. Accordingly, the role of social education in lifelong education must be considered" (Social Education Council 1971, 10). The Council report directly reflected the use of the term *lifelong education* (or *shōgai kyōiku* in Japanese), which was initially presented by Paul Lengrand, a theorist and practitioner in adult education and a member of the UNESCO Secretariat, at the Third International Committee for the Facilitation of Adult Education in 1965. The context of the UNESCO conference focused on the concept that learning throughout life is required if an individual hopes to respond actively to changes that occur in the world. Lengrand claims that lifelong education plays a significant role in helping individuals address ongoing social issues from the perspective of individual learning (see Lengrand 1970). In 1966, just one year after the UNESCO conference, the Central Council for Education specifically mentioned the concept of wide-ranging education throughout the lifespan, although the Council did not use the actual term *lifelong education* (Central Council for Education 1966).[1]

Interestingly enough, the introduction of *lifelong education* to Japanese society occurred almost in parallel to the advocacy of a learning society, or *gakushū shakai*. This Japanese term first appeared in Japanese policy documents at the end of the late 1970s (cf. Sawano 2007). Meanwhile, in Japanese academic circles, Arai Ikuo (1982), an education scholar, introduced the concept of the learning society. This concept was originally an American idea expressed in Robert Hutchins' book *The Learning Society*. Hutchins (1968) claimed that, in addition to offering part-time adult education to every man and woman at every stage of his or her adult life, the learning society had succeeded in transforming values in such ways that learning, fulfillment, and becoming human had become its aims. He claimed that all institutions were directed towards these aims. Further, in 1975, UNESCO's *Learning to Be* (Faure et al. 1972) was translated into Japanese. The so-called *Faure Report* also cited the idea of the *learning society* (ibid., 160), which became the foundation for lifelong education promotion at that time.

In 1981, the Central Council for Education produced a policy report entitled *Shōgai kyōiku ni tsuite* (*On Lifelong Education*). Publication of the report marks the beginning of Japan's efforts to transform the nation's educational structure so that its key foundation would become lifelong education. Japan officially presented the Japanese term *shōgai kyōiku* (lifelong education) in its education policy documents. In the beginning of the report, the Council defines the meaning of lifelong education:

> In response to rapid changes in society, individuals today, based on their spontaneous intentions, are seeking appropriate, modern learning opportunities for self-improvement and self-development. Because individuals learn throughout their lives and choose appropriate learning measures and methods in response to their needs, it is evident that the concept of lifelong learning exists. Therefore, the idea behind the promotion of lifelong education is that a wide variety of educational functions in society shall be prepared and improved, and their correlations shall be considered. In other words, the concept behind lifelong education states that the entire educational system should be structured to assist individuals' cumulative learning throughout their lives so they might live increasingly meaningful lives. (Central Council for Education 1981, part 1, chapter 1)

In other words, the Central Council for Education proposed that lifelong education should encompass learning that occurs during all stages of life. It should include both formal and nonformal learning. Thus, learning programs should contain all types of educational activities. These activities should be conducted in formal schools, companies, local citizens' public halls, libraries, museums, gymnasiums, and so on.

The major rationale of these policy developments stems from the fact that Japan as a society greatly values school credentials. Japan is popularly referred to as *gakureki shakai* (the "credentialed society"). Since the Education Order (*gakusei*) was promulgated in 1872, Japan has emphasized the role of formal school education in an effort to catch up with advances achieved by Western countries. The development of school education has significantly contributed to the nation's prosperity over the past century (cf. Rohlen 1983; White 1987; Kawanobe 1994; Okano and Tsuchiya 1999; Fuwa 2001). Fuwa (2001, 131) points out that Japanese society has traditionally considered school education to be the most important standard of social estimation throughout a person's lifespan. Given this background, Okamoto Kaoru, a former career bureaucrat at the Education Ministry and currently a professor of education policy at the National Graduate Institute for Policy Studies in Tokyo, claims that the promotion of lifelong learning primarily began to mitigate this overenthusiasm towards and overestimation of the value acquired at an early age of diplomas achieved through formal education (Okamoto 2006; cf. Okamoto 1994). In other words, lifelong learning began to mitigate the overemphasis on "names" of universities. He further maintains, "To cope with this serious problem, the promotion of continuing education following completion of initial education and, more importantly, the appreciation and proper evaluation of the outcomes of such learning, have been emphasized" (Okamoto 2006, 75) in Japanese society.

Lifelong Learning

In the mid-1980s, the term *shōgai gakushū* (lifelong learning) often appeared in the Japanese policy domain due to the promotional efforts of the Ad Hoc Council on Education, an advisory body to Prime Minister Nakasone Yasuhiro (1982–1987) of the LDP.[2] Lifelong learning includes all types of educational efforts that can be from formal schools, homes, workplaces, and local communities. The major difference between lifelong education and lifelong learning is, as Okamoto (2004, 16) notes, positioning. The term *education* refers to something that we learn from someone else. However, the term still sounds passive. The term *lifelong learning* places an emphasis on individuals as agents of their own learning. Meanwhile, Japanese community-oriented social education lost momentum in the 1980s. It was replaced by a more individual-based, leisure-oriented learning offered at private culture centers. This point is discussed later in this chapter.

In 1984, the Ad Hoc Council on Education was founded. An inauguration statement was released by Prime Minister Nakasone:

> Rapid social changes that occurred in recent years have greatly affected the situation vis-à-vis education. These changes have exposed a variety of problems and difficulties, including a social climate in which excessive value is placed on the educational backgrounds of individuals, excessive competition occurs during entrance examinations, young people are experiencing behavioral problems, and other problems are caused by the inflexible, uniform structure and methods used in formal education. . . . At the same time, an increasingly strong demand has been expressed for the adaptation of the educational system in response to these social and cultural changes, including the revision of industrial and employment structures to support the progress of an information-intensive society . . . and the growing internationalization in a variety of areas. (Ad Hoc Council on Education 1988, 323)

As a result, the Ad Hoc Council was charged with the administration of educational reforms based on a long-term perspective. It would receive the support of all relevant government authorities so that it could transmit the idea of lifelong learning as a key concept in Japanese education as Japan moved into the imminent twenty-first century.

Between 1984 and 1987, the Ad Hoc Council on Education produced four policy reports. Its main discussion theme was whether the transition to a lifelong learning system should become the basic direction for national educational reform. The Council claimed that Japanese education should make a dynamic shift and focus on lifelong learning rather than on the maintenance of a credentialed society in which academic backgrounds were excessively emphasized. The Council aimed to restructure the overall Japanese societal model (see Uchida 1987; Schoppa 1991; Ichikawa 1995; Hood 2001; Kawachi 2008; Shimizutani 2011). However, what the Council foresaw was a more ambitious concept—"a lifelong learning society" (*shōgai gakushū shakai*)—in which wide-ranging learning opportunities would be provided at all stages in the lifespan. It foresaw a society in which people would learn while working and where due regard would be given to individual lifestyles (Ad Hoc Council on Education 1988, 15). Further, to achieve these learning activities, the Council recommended roles and responsibilities for the respective sectors of the educational system to expand and improve integrated opportunities available throughout a person's approximately eighty-year lifespan, and to enhance full cooperation among families, schools, and local communities. Thus, society would reap the benefits of a horizontal learning system (as opposed to vertical or hierarchical systems in which students must climb the educational ladder) (Ad Hoc Council on Education 1988, 71–78).

Furthermore, it is interesting to note that the Ad Hoc Council on Education clearly defined local communities as the sites where such lifelong learning policies and practices would be implemented. The third report envisioned the way these local infrastructures for lifelong learning would develop:

> It is necessary to shape the foundations to support learning activities suited to a lifelong learning society and to develop attractive and energetic communities that encompass the distinctive characteristics of each locality. To this end, and based on the fundamental principle that, by their own initiatives, learners should choose the ways and means of learning suited to their needs, and community structures should be developed in which all members of the community cooperate in the promotion of lifelong learning activities. These local initiatives should expand and spread throughout the country. (Ad Hoc Council on Education 1988, 176)

This important point—the local initiative—would become a key policy element in Japan's new focus on lifelong learning in upcoming decades. This is the basis of this book. In August 1987, the Council concluded its discussion. It declared three basic viewpoints for educational reform: (1) an emphasis on individuality, (2) a focus on the transition to a lifelong learning system, and (3) development of methods to cope with ongoing social changes (Ad Hoc Council on Education 1988, 278–82).

Upon receipt of this 1988 report, the government adopted a wide range of measures to address the policy recommendations. The ultimate goal was to develop a lifelong learning society. The measures included the development of promotional mechanisms for lifelong learning and the organization of departments and councils that would be responsible for lifelong learning in government. For example, the Education Ministry modified its organizational structure in 1988, and the Social Education Bureau became, or, more accurately, was upgraded to become, the Lifelong Learning Bureau (*shōgai gakushū kyoku*). The new bureau was expected to play a significant role in the coordination of ministry-wide policy making by managing other bureaus, including the formal school education bureau. In 2001, the bureau changed its name to the Lifelong Learning Policy Bureau (*shōgai gakushū seisaku kyoku*) to mirror the administrative reforms implemented.

The infrastructure development for lifelong learning, which was discussed by the Ad Hoc Council on Education, was continuously elaborated. A policy report entitled *Development of a Lifelong Learning Infrastructure* was submitted in 1990 by the Central Council for Education. It identified formal school education as the foundation for lifelong learning, and it noted that the foundation for lifelong learning should arise from the voluntary will of the people. It also highlighted the importance of building infrastructure. The report highlighted three points as urgent issues:

1. Lifelong learning should be based on individuals' spontaneous and voluntary willingness to pursue quality in their lives and vocational abilities, as well as to enrich their individual selves.

2. Lifelong learning should continue. It should include measures and contents considered appropriate by each individual.

3. Lifelong learning encompasses organized intentional learning opportunities provided by school and society. It also includes activities such as participation in sports, cultural events, recreational programs, volunteer activities, and so on. (Central Council for Education 1990, part 1, chapter 3)

Consequently, national and local governments were asked to develop lifelong learning infrastructures to allow and assist individuals to conduct their learning activities. Three specific tasks were mentioned:

1. The first task is to provide educational information and consultation so that individuals may select appropriate

learning opportunities and, consequently, engage in learning.

2. The second task is to promote lifelong learning to encourage individuals who possess latent learning demands to establish information programs, and to perform appropriate assessments of the learning results to further increase individuals' desire to learn.

3. The third task is to develop cooperation among all types of lifelong learning facilities so they may respond to learning demands by developing learning opportunities. (Ibid.)

In the 1990s, the Japanese government at various levels, particularly prefectural levels, actively began to build public facilities to promote lifelong learning. These facilities were referred to as lifelong learning centers (*shōgai gakushū sentā*). Their development was encouraged by the positive sentiments created by the asset-inflated "bubble" economy that flourished after the late 1980s when the government experienced an increase in tax revenue. According to statistics available (MEXT 2008a, 10), 384 lifelong learning centers were developed at prefectural and municipal levels. These centers were considered central institutions responsible for the promotion of each community's lifelong learning activities.[3] Meanwhile, the role of universities and junior colleges was addressed with respect to lifelong learning. The Central Council for Education encouraged universities and junior colleges to establish lifelong learning centers. These centers spearheaded the promotion of adult education by the initiation of organized systematic and continuous extension courses, as well as by the provision of educational information and consultation related to learning opportunities (Central Council for Education 1990, part 2, chapter 2, section 2). The role of higher educational institutions was further explored in the upcoming proposals presented later in the 1990s, and it will be discussed in the next section.

Lifelong Learning Promotion Law

In Japan 1990 was significant because that was the year the Lifelong Learning Promotion Law was enacted. The law announces its objectives in its initial paragraph:

Article 1: As learning opportunities are currently required for every person throughout his/her lifespan, the objective of this law is: to define measures for lifelong learning facilitation that should be planned by local public bodies to define measures required; to improve a wide range of learning opportunities in specific districts; and to promote policies for the facilitation of learning activities in local communities. These objectives will be achieved by the establishment of councils to conduct surveys and discuss matters important to lifelong learning.

To achieve these objectives, first, the law defines the roles of prefectural governments. In article 3, the prefectural boards of education are required to fulfill the six conditions listed below:

1. To collect, arrange, and provide information related to learning opportunities in school-centered education, social education (including sports activities referred to as learning), and cultural activities.

2. To conduct research and surveys to explore citizens' learning needs and to assess learning results.

3. To develop learning methods appropriate for each community.

4. To conduct trainings for leaders and advisors involved with citizens' learning.

5. To provide consultation and reference services and, especially, to encourage cooperation among institutes and organizations with respect to school education, social education, and cultural activities.

6. To conduct a variety of programs to provide learning opportunities to citizens.

Further, article 5 notes that both the national and prefectural governments should outline basic plans for the provision of various opportunities for lifelong learning. The plans should include content related to different types of lifelong learning opportunities, as well as content related to persons who would conduct programs required for the comprehensive provision of lifelong learning opportunities. Meanwhile, article 10 calls for the establishment of a Lifelong Learning Council within the Education Ministry to support lifelong learning policies related to school education, social education, and cultural activities. Article 11 also aims to improve the lifelong learning structure at local levels and to establish Prefectural Lifelong Learning Councils wherever possible. In 1991, an additional report published by the Central Council for Education focused on the reform of educational systems (Central Council for Education 1991). The policy proposal attempted to present the development of lifelong learning as the role of formal school education. A statement in chapter 3 of part 1, which addresses the background of the educational reform, as well as some of its perspectives, states:

> [A]ll aspects of education should be reconsidered from the viewpoint of lifelong learning. This would make the fixed educational system (school education) more flexible and blur the distinction that exists between school education and society.
> . . . [S]chool education should not be considered complete once an individual's work in society begins. After compulsory education, free choice allows some individuals to continue advanced education or to enter working society. Likewise, an individual should choose whether to work in society while engaged in study at a senior high school or university, or to return to school after a period of work in society. Furthermore, it is not necessary to complete one's education within the school system. Today, diverse learning opportunities are available outside of school education. Many of these opportunities are in no way inferior to school education.
> If individuals were to view school education as a part of lifelong learning and if they allowed for the expansion of people's choices, their attitudes toward school education would change and the mental pressure caused by school education during early life stages and their effect on later life would ease. (Central Council for Education 1991, part 1, chapter 3)

In this context, the role of universities and junior colleges was given serious consideration. The Council report recommended that universities and junior colleges provide (1) part-time education to adults, (2) a quota for the special admission of working people, (3) a credit transfer system, (4) open lectures in response to highly advanced learning demands, and (5) extension programs. The Open University of Japan was established in

1983 by the University of the Air Foundation. It has played a significant role as a lifelong learning institution.[4] Over the past three decades that have passed since its establishment, some one million people have studied at this distance-learning university. More than fifty thousand of these individuals have graduated with bachelors' or masters' degrees (Open University of Japan 2011). In fact, during the early 1990s, a significant amount of discussion occurred in relation to university education in the University Council (*daigaku shingikai*), an advisory body to the education minister established in 1987. The University Council mentioned that the role of the university system in the training of human resources would become increasingly important. It would signal the direction in which Japan would move, maintain vitality in various fields, and contribute to society (University Council 1991). The Council expected to diversify Japanese university education, reflect people's ideas and lives, and exert positive effects on the subsequently expanding numbers of people who would work and continue to study. It recommended the introduction of evening/weekend courses, as well as the acknowledgment of learning acquired in educational institutions other than universities.

Lifelong Learning Council Report in 1992

Following passage of the Lifelong Learning Promotion Law, the Lifelong Learning Council (LLC) was established in 1990 to serve as an advisory body to the education minister. The Council submitted its first policy report in 1992. It stated that its final goal would be the construction of a lifelong learning society. To achieve this goal, it proposed four key agenda items:

1. High-level continuing learning activities for adults: The promotion of systematic and continuing recurrent education for adults who would require new advanced professional knowledge and skills due to progress in technological innovation and due to changing economic structures.

2. Volunteer activities as learning: The encouragement of voluntary activities that would utilize a wide range of knowledge and skills acquired through learning in the community against the background of an increase in holidays and the growth of economic affluence.

3. Outside-school activities for children and youth: The development of education for children within their families and the encouragement of social and educational activities for youth in the community outside of school. The aim would be to cultivate, by experience, basic ways of thinking, behaviors, communications, and human relations required for everyday social life.

4. Learning activities related to contemporary issues: The extension of opportunities to learn about contemporary issues. For example, new constructions of values related to human rights, citizenship, gender, the environment, the aging society, nuclear power, and gene splicing and their impacts on the globalizing society. (LLC 1992, part 1, chapter 4, section 2)

With respect to the last agenda, the LLC highlighted nineteen examples of contemporary issues that could be addressed through lifelong learning activities.[5] Yet, Japan's traditional lifelong learning institution, citizens' public halls, had already provided these kinds of programs as socially "necessary topics" (or *hitsuyō kadai*), mentioned earlier, since the early post–World War II era (also see Ogawa 2005, 352). However, Fuwa (2001) argues that this first report produced by the LLC demonstrated, from multidimensional perspectives, the principal targets for the development of lifelong learning and highlighted concrete measures required to realize them. The report provided many suggestions for directions to be taken in the upcoming decades (see also Sasaki 1992). Further, volunteer activities were introduced by the state into the field of lifelong learning in a highly strategic manner (see chapter 4 for a more detailed account). Ultimately, in 1999, the LLC clearly stated that all types of learning that resulted from lifelong learning activities would be useful for (1) individual career development; (2) volunteer activities; and (3) revitalization of local communities (LLC 1999a, part 1)

During the 1990s, under the Lifelong Learning Promotion Law, lifelong learning was formally institutionalized in Japanese society. The policy included the organization of administrative systems to provide strong support for the promotion of learning at local levels and to develop a wide variety of learning centers. Lifelong learning was supported primarily by the Education Ministry. However, efforts were extended even further as lifelong learning policies became part of national comprehensive efforts (cf. Kagawa and Miyasaka 1994). Sixteen ministries, with the exception of law, foreign affairs, and defense, became involved with lifelong learning policymaking under the Lifelong Learning Promotion Law. Diverse learning opportunities were provided by other administrative bodies. Because individuals could choose to learn or begin new activities to enrich their lives, these programs addressed all stages of life (Miura et al. 1992, 86–87). During that time, at the national level, the Ministry of International Trade and Industry (MITI, changed to the Ministry of Economy, Trade, and Industry, METI, in 2001) was transformed into a different agency that aimed to promote lifelong learning activities in Japanese society.[6] In fact, in cooperation with the Education Ministry, MITI played a significant role in the development of the Lifelong Learning Promotion Law enacted in 1990. MITI's active participation in the promotion of lifelong learning expanded its scope. It was no longer limited to the concept of traditional social education. MITI established the Lifelong Learning Development Office (*shōgai gakushū shinkō shitsu*) within the Industrial Policy Bureau of the Ministry and created a budget for the implementation of lifelong learning programs. The major assignment of this office was the facilitation of private industry programs related to citizens' learning. In particular, MITI pursued the promotion of lifelong learning from the perspective of leisure (*yoka*) activities. The policy rationale was that the leisure industry during the late 1980s/early 1990s was buoyed by positive economic sentiment because of the bubble economy. Ordinary people began to enjoy affluent lives. Lifelong learning was considered an activity that would enrich their lives (cf. Amano 1989; Wilson 2001; Okamoto 2001). The Economic Planning Agency also directed the focus of lifelong learning towards leisure activities within the overall sphere of national life. The Ministry of Transportation combined lifelong learning with the travel boom and the popularity of recreational sightseeing. Furthermore, MITI pursued traditional vocational training (see Chapter 6 for a more detailed account), a key part of lifelong learning, through the medium of the Chambers of Commerce and Industry (*shōko kaigi sho*). Vocational training and human resources development were also supported by the Ministry of Labor. The Ministry of Health and Welfare (currently known as the Ministry of Health, Labor, and Welfare) provided learning programs for the elderly in an aging society (cf. Ohsako and Sawano 2006). The Ministry of Home Affairs explored the possibilities of lifelong learning promotion from the perspective of local community revitalization. The National Police Agency provided traffic safety education classes.

With respect to lifelong learning opportunities offered by private industry, the development of "culture centers" (*karuchā sentā*) should be mentioned. These consisted of a new type of educational institution operated by private businesses. These *karuchā sentā* occupy distinctive places in Japan's lifelong learning (Hatano 1995; cf. Yamamoto 2001). Newspapers and broadcasting companies, as well as department stores, banks, and electric power companies, offer extension services, such as lectures and courses focused primarily on hobbies and liberal arts. Statistics available reveal that, as of November 1, 2005, 698 culture centers operated throughout the country; 190,998 courses were offered at these centers. A total of 7,097,867 people attended these courses; 80.8 percent of attendees were women and most of these women were housewives (METI 2005). Originally, the provision of learning activities at culture centers began in the 1950s. These centers became one of the most popular learning outlets during the 1980s. Their major difference from traditional social education was that, while social education was practiced mainly at the community level, these newer institutions allowed people who shared the same interests to become acquainted with one another and broaden their circle of associations beyond the communities in which they lived (Miura et al. 1992, 195). Further, these centers operate for profit. Thus, course participants must pay on average 1,374 yen ($13) per hour (METI 2005). In contrast, social education courses offered at citizens' public halls are often provided free of charge or a discounted cost (say, a couple of hundred yen) per session. Alternatively, they might cost only several thousand yen for an entire course because these courses are subsidized by local governments.

Focus on the Local: Developments in the 1990s

Japan's lifelong learning experienced dynamism at the local level during the 1990s. Japan saw the establishment of an administrative framework, as well as the expansion of lifelong learning opportunities. The creation of a lifelong learning council at the prefectural level was recommended by the Lifelong Learning Promotion Law. Statistics (MEXT 2010a) reveal that 35 of the 47 prefectures in Japan have organized these types of councils based on this recommendation. In the remaining 12 prefectures, the committees for social education perform the same kinds of functions. Further, the traditional social education sections (*shakai kyōiku ka*) in the Japanese public administration gradually changed the names of the lifelong learning sections (*shōgai gakushū ka*).

During the late 1990s, the LLC produced a series of annual policy reports that explored a new type of lifelong learning in Japan. Each of these reports focused exclusively on the role of local communities in the provision of lifelong learning activities. As mentioned earlier, in its 1988 report, the Ad Hoc Council on Education pinpointed local communities as the primary locations for the practice and implementation of lifelong learning policies. In a report published in 1996, the LLC recommended that lifelong learning opportunities be expanded further in local communities (LLC 1996). One measure made higher educational institutions accessible to local communities (ibid., part 1, chapter 1, section 2). To respond to learning demands from local residents, the LLC also recommended that the government actively build public facilities to support learning activities in local communities. These learning activities would encompass traditional social education. At the same time, the LLC noted that primary and secondary schools should be deeply rooted in local communities (ibid., part 2). In the following year, the LLC proposed several measures to help people make the best use of the results of lifelong learning (LLC 1997). Most importantly, it pointed out that learning results should be used for the development of local communities (ibid., part 2). Furthermore, the knowledge and skills acquired in lifelong learning should also be used for volunteer activities in local communities (ibid., part 4). This second point was clearly mentioned in the 1992 report presented by the LLC. The report identified volunteering as an integral part of lifelong learning activities. In 1998 the LLC produced a concluding report that noted that Japan's new lifelong learning should be supported by the traditional community-oriented social education that Japanese society had enjoyed to the fullest over the past half-century (LLC 1998). Social education in the future should consider the characteristics of each local community. Local residents will be expected to participate actively in social education administration (ibid., part 2). To promote lifelong learning, the report also mentioned the importance of networking with private sectors. These include for-profit businesses, as well as NPOs, which Japan institutionalized as a new third-sector organization in 1998 (ibid., part 3). In 1999, the LLC produced a report focused on children. It emphasized the importance of children having real experiences in actual daily life and in nature (LLC 1999b). Children's education had formerly been limited to formal school education. However, the LLC clearly presented its intention to include children in the lifelong learning policy framework. It recommended that children accumulate a variety of experiences in local communities, and it also recommended that adults should support the development of community infrastructure that would offer these types of experiences. The LLC also mentioned *ikiru chikara* (ibid., part 3, chapter 6, section 2), which translates literally as "zest for living." The term implies the ability to survive in the contemporary world and was originally introduced in 1996 in a policy proposal created by the Central Council for Education (Central Council for Education 1996). *Ikiru chikara* was specifically defined as abilities individuals can employ to solve problems independently. It also means to learn and think by oneself. The Central Council for Education emphasized the nurturing of these types of abilities in children. This *ikiru chikara* development was focused on the institutionalization of the "community school" aspect of Japanese schools (see chapter 5 for a more detailed argument related to community schools). These points related to the education of children were newly added when the Social Education Law was revised in 2001. In reality, this active introduction of local communities became a solid foundation for lifelong learning policy making and for its implementation later in the 2000s (see the path of development discussed in chapter 3).

During my examination of the 1990s, I discovered three interesting developments related to the promotion of lifelong learning in Japanese society. First, the number of prefectures and municipalities that openly declared they would promote lifelong learning activities increased over time. In Japanese, these declarations were called *shōgai gakushū toshi sengen* (a declaration of a lifelong learning city). In 1979, only two municipalities had agreed to participate. Ten years later, their number had increased to thirty-seven (Miura et al. 1992). As of May 1, 2010, eighty-six municipalities throughout the country had declared the creation of public entities that favor the promotion of lifelong learning (MEXT 2010a). However, this number represented only 5 percent of all Japanese municipalities. These declarations were made during the local diet sessions. In many cases, the managing agencies charged with the promotion of lifelong learning are maintained under the aegis of the lifelong learning sections or under mayors' offices. Following the enactment of the Lifelong Learning Promotion Law, lifelong learning policy making was also implemented as a direct initiative by mayors. The city of Kakegawa, which is located in Shizuoka Prefecture, is well known as the first lifelong learning city (*shōgai gakushū toshi*), established in 1979. A quotation taken from the City of Kakegawa's Declaration of Lifelong Learning appears below:

> To feel just a little more happiness,
> To gain a healthier sense of life,
> Always ask one another what we should do, and
> How we should continue to learn during our lives.
> April 1, 1979, City of Kakegawa

Shinmura Junichi, the mayor in 1979, published a book, claiming that lifelong learning policies developed by municipalities are a matter of "local pride" (Shinmura 2007). He argues that the promotion of lifelong learning by local municipalities can serve as an indicator of community development. He notes that each municipality should pursue its own style of learning. Under the declaration, each public entity creates its own program for the promotion of lifelong learning. Efforts can include building lifelong learning centers, holding conferences, advocating the virtue of lifelong learning activities, conducting surveys on lifelong learning activities, and hiring consultants to provide guidance to local residents and to advise on learning subjects.

Second, local bodies that promote lifelong learning as public entities have hosted *manabipia* on a yearly basis since 1989. These consist of annual national festivals sponsored by the Education Ministry. The Japanese word *manabipia* is a combination of *manabi* (learning) and *utopia*. Each festival site is designated by the Ministry. The purpose of the festival is to enhance citizens' motivation for lifelong learning, to facilitate their participation in learning activities, and to contribute to the promotion of lifelong learning by the provision of sites for citizens to practice their lifelong learning activities. These festivals are conducted on a nationwide scale (MEXT 2001). In 2009, the national festival was held in Saitama Prefecture. It was held over five days (October 30–November 3) at the Saitama Super Arena. The festival began with an opening ceremony that was followed by the main event entitled Talking about Lifelong Learning in the Twenty-first Century, sponsored by Saitama Prefecture. The keynote speaker was a university professor who taught in the local prefecture. The professor described the importance of human networks: Human beings are nurtured by connections made with other people and by conversations with other people. Humans are influenced by other people. By developing relations with other people, we learn about one another. This, in itself, is a type of lifelong learning. The program included symposia, panel discussions, lectures, research meetings, and exhibitions (sponsored by the host prefecture, as well as by related organizations and private businesses). In addition, the festival offered a classical concert, a chorus contest, dance and theater performances, a short marathon, and an arts and crafts gallery. All programs were designed to serve as presentations of the results of lifelong learning activities. They propagated the significance of lifelong learning. Their perspectives included community development, gender equality, the aging society, ways to raise healthy youth, sustainable human development, and so on. The festival headquarters reported that more than 2 million people attended the festival (Saitama Prefecture Education Department 2010).

The third and final point is that NPOs established under the 1998 NPO Law have begun to play significant roles in the provision of community-oriented lifelong learning programs. In fact, the so-called "third sector method" (Miura et al. 1992, 100; cf. Shiraishi et al. 2001; Sasaki 2006) gained prominence when local municipalities began to face financial restrictions that affected their ability to offer diverse programs for lifelong learning. By applying this method, administrative bodies, in cooperation with private entities, can establish new organizations to utilize private-sector vitality. One example of an institution managed by the third-sector method is what I refer to as "SLG (pseudonym)," an NPO that operates in eastern Tokyo (Ogawa 2009a). SLG was founded as an NPO under the 1998 NPO Law. It was established with funds provided by the local ward government. Residents are actively involved in its operation. They engage in course planning and serve as volunteers (cf. Sato 1998, 2004). Another method that can be employed to promote lifelong learning is the creation of a foundation (*zaidan*). In Toyama Prefecture, *toyama kenmin shōgai gakushū karreji* (or Toyama Citizens' Lifelong Learning College) was established in 1988. It is managed by a foundation devoted to culture promotion (*bunka shinkō zaidan*) that is funded by the prefectural government. The college functions as a core non formal learning institution in the prefecture. It absorbs former lifelong learning programs and administrations previously offered by the prefectural government. This college is one of the most successful examples of organizations that offer lifelong learning programs via the third-sector method.

Since the early post–World War II period, the Japanese state has supported the unique, active development of grassroots learning activities that began with social education. Legal and policy developments that occurred over the past half-century, as argued in this chapter, have solidly institutionalized individuals' learning practices. Japanese lifelong learning is very rich (see Kagawa et al. 2007, for comprehensive accounts of Japan's lifelong learning policies and practices). Indeed, several reasons encouraged the Japanese government to promote lifelong learning. One of the major reasons was the need to overcome the diploma-oriented society. It was also necessary to provide learning opportunities in response to the growing society's demand for leisure-oriented learning activities. More importantly, individuals were required to learn, so they could better cope with social, economic, and technological changes towards a knowledge economy. The active development of lifelong learning in grassroots Japan during the late 1990s was also stimulated by international policy developments aimed at the promotion of lifelong learning by OECD and UNESCO, as introduced in chapter 1. However, one question remains unanswered: Why has lifelong learning become popular now? The development of Japan's lifelong learning during the 2000s is a crucial case we must observe, so we can adequately address this question.

In the remainder of this book, I will directly explore the abovementioned research question by combining a policy document analysis with my ethnographic findings. Indeed, Japan has been actively developing new interesting practices under the name of lifelong learning in the 2000s. In this chapter, I have argued the old or traditional style of lifelong learning, which has been popularly described as a cultural model in the lifelong learning scholarship. In the following chapters, meanwhile, I will develop a new account about Japan's lifelong learning in the 2000s. The Japanese state has nowadays stepped into establishing new policies in the field of lifelong learning in a very strategic manner. I observe that the policy development is an important attempt by the Japanese state, as well as individuals, trying to survive in the contemporary neoliberal era. For a detailed analysis on the contemporary lifelong learning phenomenon, I employ the concept of *risk,* which I particularly identify as "governmental risk" and "socioeconomic risk" in chapter 1. In the next chapter, I discuss the fact that the Japanese neoliberal state is building up a new kind of knowledge through an active lifelong learning initiative. The knowledge is called *sōgōteki na chi* or "comprehensive knowledge" for surviving amid new modes of governmentality, informed by neoliberal principles, which have risen to prominence in the twenty-first century.

3

Risk Management by a Neoliberal State

Lifelong Learning and Risk

> The nurturing of an independent-minded individual is an important agenda in contemporary education. It is also becoming crucial to generate a sense of "public" to foster the active participation of such an individual in society. . . . Lifelong learning should play a key role in developing this sense among Japanese citizens.
>
> —Central Council for Education 2008a, 6

Lifelong learning can be defined as continual learning efforts at any stage of life that help people improve their lives and adapt to society. Japan has a rich tradition of learning activities at the grassroots level, and researchers have argued that lifelong learning in Japan primarily follows a cultural construct revolving around personal learning centered on liberal arts, painting, sculpting, and sports (cf. Schuetze and Casey 2006). The latest available survey on Japanese lifelong learning (Cabinet Office 2008a) revealed that nearly half of the respondents (47 percent, to be precise) had taken up at least one lifelong learning activity. Meanwhile, lifelong learning is gaining attention in Japan's contemporary education policy making. Its heightened importance became evident in December 2006, when the term *shōgai gakushū* (lifelong learning) was added to the Fundamental Law of Education—Japan's educational charter. This was the first amendment to the law since its enactment in 1947. Furthermore, the current discussion on the topic goes beyond the scope of cultural construct, through the introduction of a new term: *atarashii kōkyō* (the New Public Commons). Since the early 2000s, this term has been widely discussed in the Japanese policy-making circle, in relation to the revision of the Fundamental Law of Education. The concept of the New Public Commons can serve as a foundation for solidarity, which, in turn, can enable conscientious citizens to improve society. It can also function as a sphere wherein people in general, or those interested in a specific cause, voluntarily participate. In the ongoing policy discussion, Japan's new lifelong learning initiative is primarily expected to contribute to the formation of this public sphere. It is expected to produce a new type of disciplinary state-sponsored knowledge that, in turn, is expected to support the creation of the New Public Commons. Armed with this new knowledge, citizens can contribute spontaneously to activities like agenda setting and problem solving at the grassroots level and respond suitably to a constantly changing social and political life. Through a new lifelong learning initiative, this social imagery—the New Public Commons—involves an attempt to redefine the boundaries of moral responsibility between the state and the individual, emphasizing more the virtues of self-regulation.

Over the past decade, I conducted extensive ethnographic fieldwork on Japan's lifelong learning (Ogawa 2009a), drawing on Foucauldian poststructuralist theoretical insights. In this chapter, I argue that promoting such lifelong learning is an action that manages the risks of governance for the state. Clearly, engaging in lifelong learning activities toward updating knowledge and skills is more of a risk-managing activity for individuals trying to enhance their flexibility in the knowledge economy–based labor market (Ogawa 2009b). However, my focus in this chapter is on the state. In fact, one of the most recent comprehensive policy papers on Japan's education (MEXT 2009a) used the Japanese term *risuku* (or risk) six times in the 403-page document. Twice, it was used to discuss the significance of lifelong learning—unprecedented in policy discourse—and four times, it was used to imply a natural threat in the context of science/technology promotion policy. Here is an excerpt from the policy paper in the section on lifelong learning: "It is necessary for the state to support an individual's learning which makes it possible to acquire knowledge and skills and for economic independence, as *risks* of the expansion of non-regular type of jobs and the bankruptcy of corporations are prominent, and socioeconomic divide and poverty issues are major social problems" (MEXT 2009a, 80, emphasis added by the author). Implementing the new lifelong learning policy indeed involves the employment of a political technique toward integrating the currently divided and polarized Japanese population—popularly called *kakusa*—into the newly imagined collective, namely, the New Public Common. After World War II, Japan generated a relatively equal society in terms of chances and outcomes. In a welfarist society, the state tended to act as the general risk manger—insuring its citizens, indemnifying them against losses, protecting them from social harm and economic disaster, and regulating economic risks and environmental dangers. Behind these functions were conceptions of responsibility, relations between social groups, and techniques of insurance, all of which converged to produce a distinctively social mode of managing risk and promoting solidarity (Garland 2003, 61). However, since the 1990s, Japan's societal model of a divided society has gradually replaced the general middle-class or "90 percent middle-class" society prevalent since the 1960s (Economic Planning Agency 1967; cf. Tachibanaki 2005; Chiavacci 2008; Hashimoto 2009a, 2009b). In its economic survey of Japan, the OECD identified the country's increasing inequality and poverty levels as its major economic problems (OECD 2006). While this socioeconomic dividedness stems from disparities of income, the matter is not confined to this aspect. It could potentially lead to social exclusion—"the loss of social cohesion resulting from growing inequalities and the return of mass social and economic vulnerability for an increasing part of the population" (Bhalla and Lapeyre 2004, 1).

Sociocultural research on risk provides a rich source of ideas on the theme of social change and selfhood (e.g., Douglas 1966; Giddens 1990; Foucault 1991; Beck 1992; Beck et al. 1994). The nature of risks has indeed changed in the present scenario. A risk connotes few opportunities for gain and a greater possibility of loss. It is broadly considered as involving a threat, hazard, danger, or some form of harm. Further, risks today refer to unquestionable uncertainties. They have become more global, less readily identifiable, more problematic, less easily managed, and more anxiety-provoking, leading Ulrich Beck to describe contemporary society as a "risk society" or "second modernity" that Anthony Giddens terms "reflexive modernization." Meanwhile, the existing risk scholarship has been argued in the Western context, mostly in Germany and Britain, as mentioned in chapter 1. However, in fact, risks tend to arise in new and challenging ways in contemporary Japan as well.

In Japan, the rolling back of the welfare state and rise of neoliberal politics, conspicuous factors since the tenure of Prime Minister Koizumi Junichiro (2001–06) of the LDP, has rendered the social safety net inadequate for many sections of society (cf. Arnoldi 2009). Globally, neoliberal governments have indeed sought to depart from the classic postwar model of the risk-managing state (cf. Yergin and Stanislaw 1998). The current political rationale tends to consider that the risks previously governed through techniques such as social insurance are now better governed by individuals. This change has made the life of ordinary individuals much more precarious in terms of life planning and career building as well as in relation to issues of identity and sense of self (e.g., Sennett 1998; Bauman 2000). These trends, propagated by a series of neoliberal political measures, have intensified and accelerated the socioeconomic dividedness of contemporary Japanese society. I argue that a strong lifelong learning initiative is currently functioning as a lever for social integration. Imagining the realization of the New Public Commons manages the concerns of what I call "governmental risk" (see chapter 1) of such dividedness through producing new disciplinary knowledge; it shifts responsibility onto the individual, deploying the discourse of "self-responsibility" (Hook and Takeda 2007). Risk is indeed understood as one of the heterogeneous governmental strategies of disciplinary power by which populations and individuals are monitored and managed so as to best meet the goals of democratic humanism (Lupton 1999a, 4; cf. Foucault 1991). In its contemporary form, governmentality is a neoliberal approach to the political rationale dominating since the 1980s, which endorses individual freedom and rights and seeks to limit excessive intervention by the state through decentralized authority (cf. Harvey 2005). Further, neoliberalism constitutes a particular set of social relations between the government and the governed (e.g., Ferguson and Gupta 2002; for accounts in the context of Japan, see Miyazaki 2010, for example).

Through the lens of risks, this chapter explores Japan's inflections of neoliberal governmentality with the new distribution of responsibility between the state and the individual through the construction of new knowledge supporting the concept of the New Public Commons. It is examined primarily through the analysis of macropolicy discourses on Japan's education policy, combined with the findings from my ethnographic fieldwork. As the national policy makers specify the local as the arena wherein lifelong learning should be defined and implemented, local individuals participate in the new forms of state-sponsored knowledge production and circulation through lifelong learning activities. The construction of new knowledge through the lifelong learning initiative is a reflection of the "risk society" that Japan faces, and it is a risk-managing strategy for neoliberal Japan.

Japan's Lifelong Learning in the 2000s

As mentioned in chapter 2, since the early post–World War II period, lifelong learning activities have been solidly supported by the Social Education Law of 1949. Under this law, the local governments at the prefectural and municipal levels are required to provide lifelong learning opportunities to residents. These activities have been primarily organized in local citizens' public halls. One recent survey suggested that there were 16,566 citizens' public halls nationwide (MEXT 2008a, 10). Further, the law requires that each prefectural and municipal government have at least one social education officer. In 1981, the Central Council for Education proposed that lifelong education encompass learning that takes place at all life stages and includes both formal school education and nonformal social education (Central Council for Education 1981). Thus, contemporary lifelong learning programs contain all types of educational activities. These activities may be carried out at schools, companies, citizens' public halls, libraries, museums, or various other facilities. Further, the Lifelong Learning Promotion Law was enacted in 1990, improving the institutional arrangements of lifelong learning opportunities.

The 2000s have seen the rapid establishment of lifelong learning as one of the top priorities on the national policy agenda, as Japan seeks to create a dynamic, sustainable, and knowledge-based society in today's constantly changing world—an outcome of the era of globalization. The 2003 report published by the Central Council for Education emphasized the importance of realizing a lifelong learning society, where every citizen would be able to freely use numerous learning opportunities at any stage of life and where the attainment of such learning would be evaluated properly in order to meet the enormous changes taking place in society (Central Council for Education 2003). This policy philosophy was manifested when the Japanese government led by Prime Minister Abe Shinzo (2006–2007) revised the Fundamental Law of Education in December 2006. The revised law, chiefly known in the media for promoting patriotic education, also stressed the significance of lifelong learning: "Article 3: Mission of Lifelong Learning: Each nation can learn to improve itself and its citizens can strive to enhance their lives throughout their lifetimes, wherever and whenever; we aim to take advantage of our learning outcomes for the betterment of our own society." After this amendment, the task force on lifelong learning at the Central Council for Education submitted a policy report to Japan's education minister, Tokai Kisaburo, on February 19, 2008, which stated that Japanese society should promote lifelong learning in order to survive in the new era. Moreover, the report confirmed the incorporation of lifelong learning as an integral part of the national education policy (Central Council for Education 2008a).

New perspectives on the development of the concept of lifelong learning in Japan were articulated in the abovementioned 131-page policy report. The initial portion of the report explained the key conceptual framework of lifelong learning in Japan, linking traditional personal learning to the knowledge construction that contributes only positively to society:

> Learning is an individual activity based on a person's own interests and motivations. Promoting such learning activities makes it possible for people to have healthy, sound lives. Also, acquiring and updating knowledge and skills for a working life makes it possible to have an economically stable life. At the same time, this kind of learning activity should contribute to the development of an individual's abilities. Such individuals will ultimately contribute to the overall galvanization of society and the sustainable development of this country. (Central Council for Education 2008a, 3)

The present policy discussion on lifelong learning is actually beyond the scope of the old cultural model that focuses on learning liberal arts, hobbies, and sports. This is because the newly advocated knowledge base is disciplinary in nature: lifelong learning is primarily argued to contribute to the quality of the public sphere that is termed the New Public Commons. In fact, during my fieldwork on Japanese lifelong learning over the past decade, I observed an obvious shift in lifelong learning activities from the cultural model to a model exploring something different under the name of lifelong learning. There is a stronger emphasis on the responsibility of each Japanese citizen in learning and active problem solving. As mentioned in chapter 2, 34,405 courses on citizenship and community solidarity were offered in the framework of social education during the fiscal year of 2007 across the country (MEXT 2008a, 17). The courses discussed what the role of citizens and the role of the local community should be at citizens' public halls in their local communities. Further, women's education centers and lifelong learning centers were becoming the major providers of such courses in their local communities, and the number of such courses has been solid since the late 2000s (cf. MEXT

2011b).¹ Nowadays, lifelong learning is centrally located as part of an individual's contribution to this new public sphere.

"Comprehensive Knowledge"

The grand challenges posed by contemporary times have necessitated the acquisition of new knowledge. The lifelong learning initiatives currently in operation can be expected to produce a certain type of disciplinary knowledge that exclusively supports the creation of the New Public Commons. One of the major new points in the ongoing discussion on lifelong learning in Japan is symbolized by the term *sōgōteki na chi*, or "comprehensive knowledge" (Central Council for Education 2008a). The Central Council for Education described this knowledge as an indispensable asset in the contemporary world. The Council did not narrowly interpret "comprehensive knowledge" to mean simple knowledge and skills nor a certain kind of specialized knowledge. Rather, it referred to it as the "ability to identify problems as well as to evaluate them flexibly" (Central Council for Education 2008a, 4). The policy rationale is presented below:

> Japanese society is currently experiencing dramatic changes, as administrative reforms and the economic deregulation process are being implemented across the country. . . . As a result, social services formerly furnished by the government are now being transferred to the private sector. Under the circumstances, as part of her or his self-responsibility, each individual is expected to independently decide what she or he needs to know. Thus, learning opportunities should be guaranteed and supported by the state so that the Japanese people are afforded flexibility in deciding upon what they need to know. (Ibid.)

Actually, this argument reminds me of Robert Reich's *The Work of Nations*, which claims that there is contemporary demand for symbolic analysts who "solve, identify, and broker problems by manipulating symbols" (Reich 1991, 178). Reich continues, "They simplify reality into abstract images that can be rearranged, juggled, experimented with, communicated to other specialists, and then eventually, transformed back into reality" (ibid.).

One component of "comprehensive knowledge" is *ikiru chikara* (zest for living, or the ability to survive in the contemporary world) (Central Council for Education 2008a, 6), which was briefly mentioned in chapter 2. It is described as the most relevant knowledge and skills for children. It advocates that no matter how much our society has changed, it is important to acquire abilities to independently solve problems, learn and think, judge the significance of situations, and act accordingly. For adults, it is called *ningen ryoku* (the ability as a human being) whereby one needs all the knowledge and skills necessary as an independent human being to survive by participating in and contributing to society (ibid.).

More specifically, concerning "comprehensive knowledge," an education bureaucrat who was involved in this lifelong learning policy making told me that Japan's Education Ministry was looking at "key competencies" that the OECD wants to promote as essential skills for the personal and social development of people in modern, complex societies. The OECD defines three categories of key competencies: (1) interacting in socially heterogeneous groups, (2) acting autonomously, and (3) using tools interactively (see Rychen 2003, 85–104; cf. Tatsuta 2006). These three are indeed complementary. However, the second category, acting autonomously, seems particularly relevant to my argument as it induces the competencies that empower individuals to manage their lives responsibly. Acting autonomously means "participating effectively in the development of society, in its social, political, and economic institutions (e.g., to take part in decision processes), and functioning well in different spheres of life—in the workplace, in one's personal and family life, and in civil and political life" (Rychen 2003, 91). The bureaucrat mentioned that Japan intends to enhance individual competencies as a collective (or the state) in order to cope with the demands and challenges of the contemporary world.

Domestically, this policy trend was reflected in the new Fundamental Law of Education, which was revised in December 2006. While the original law enacted in 1947 deemed the nurturing of the "independent spirit" and "spontaneous spirit" of the individual one of the main aims of education, the subsequent revisions deleted these phrases. The aim of education became, among others, the cultivation in the minds of children of "a sense of morality," "autonomous self-control," "a sense of public spirit and duty," and "a respectful attitude toward tradition and culture"—all of which reflected the conservative neoliberal values and philosophy advocated by the ruling LDP at that time. In fact, the recent development of lifelong learning policy and practices should be understood in line with the educational reform led by neoconservative politicians. The last action undertaken by the Koizumi administration in this regard was the submission of the revision proposal for the Fundamental Law of Education to the National Diet in April 2006. The revised law was passed and enacted under Abe Shinzo in the same year as he claimed in his policy speech that the purpose of education was to nurture nations that have the will to mold the state and society with dignity (Cabinet Office 2007). Following the revision, the 2008 policy report produced by the Central Council for Education concluded its proposed initiative on lifelong learning as a national campaign aimed at "*Nihon wo tsukuri naosō*" or reinventing Japan (Central Council for Education 2008a, 18). The reform had indeed reflected some conservative values and philosophy; it is embodied as the process of reorganization of the Japanese public sphere through the lifelong learning initiative (cf. Ichikawa 2009, 109).

The background of this development lies in the introduction of the concept of the New Public Commons. In Japanese society, the term "public" or *ōyake* has traditionally meant the state or something for which the bureaucracy assumes responsibility (see Ogawa 2009a, in particular, chapter 4). However, the concept of "public" has been strategically expanded through the education policy, involving a subtle shifting of responsibility to the people and a concomitant diminution of state responsibility. This policy rationale of the New Public Commons can be attributed to a statement made in 2000 by the prime minister's Commission on Japan's Goals in the Twenty-first Century (*"21 seiki nihon no kōsō" kondankai*), established by Prime Minister Obuchi Keizo (1998–2000). As the central elements of reform that Japan would need to focus on, the commission emphasized the importance of empowering individuals and creating a new public sphere.

> By "public space" we do not mean the traditional top-down public sphere. . . . We are referring to a new kind of public sphere created through the combined power of individuals, who regardless of their personal affiliations, consciously engage with one another and with society of their own free will. It is a public space that permits diverse "others," is considerate of others, and support others. At the same time, once a consensus has been formed, everyone should obey it. (Prime Minister's Commission on Japan's Goals in the 21st Century 2000, chapter 3, 8)[2]

The discussion record for the revision of the Fundamental Law of Education was developed following this statement:

We [the Japanese people] are stepping into a new era in which we are supporting a sense of values that we call the New Public Commons. That is, we try to independently solve the social problems we face, including the life improvement issues connected with the daily lives of the local community as well as matters related to the global environment and human rights. It is expected of people to try to use their abilities and time for others, for the local community, and for society, of their own volition. To support the New Public Commons, what one needs is a conscious awareness of oneself as an active participant in the formation of state and society, the courage to practice social justice, and an attitude of respect for traditional Japanese social norms. (Central Council for Education 2003, 5)

In all the quotations cited above, personal learning as a cultural construct, in which nearly half of the Japanese population is currently engaged in some form or another, is now directly linked to the new lifelong learning initiative as a tool for active participation in the Japanese social and political spheres. The policy tries to promote their learning activities among the population. Their learning is a medium of social construction: personal learning is translated into collective learning. Through lifelong learning activities, the Japanese people are encouraged to become involved in something that positively impacts society. These activities will allow them to use their knowledge, skills, and experience exclusively for improving society. In fact, as an ultimate goal, the policy proposal prepared in 2008 by the Central Council for Education proclaims that instead of simply being accumulated, knowledge should be "circulated" (*junkan suru*) in society (Central Council for Education 2008a, 8). The circulation of knowledge is expected to create a new flow of energy in society and generate another learning motivation. Thus, knowledge is expected to circulate among different organizations, generations, and local communities. Through the discussion of new disciplinary "comprehensive knowledge," the Japanese state embodies a problematization of the neoliberal ideology and formulas of rule that the state tries to generate. In fact, knowledge construction directs attention to the principles of reason as inscriptions in which the current divided population "come together to govern, shape, and fashion the conduct of conduct" (Olsson and Petersson 2008, 63).

Local Communities: Locations for Realizing the New Public Commons

Gaining knowledge of governing practices plays a significant role in helping the common man negotiate the complexities of everyday life and establish networks with his fellow citizens. Interestingly, the discussion on new "comprehensive knowledge" brings *chiiki* (local communities) to the policy discourse. They are considered ideal locations for realizing the New Public Commons through the practice of newly gained knowledge. The key policy document on lifelong learning written in 2008 claims, "In order to facilitate such knowledge construction, local communities will be expected to set up their agendas and achieve them through their own efforts. Instead of the government, local people will be expected to play the role of service providers on the basis of their own knowledge. Not only individuals but also the local community needs to enhance learning capabilities in order to respond adequately to the changes we are now facing" (Central Council for Education 2008a, 4). The interim report submitted to the Education Minister by the Central Council for Education in January 2007 provides a relevant insight regarding this point. The report discusses a distinctive view on lifelong learning:

> People who have knowledge, skills, and experience are now expected to spontaneously and actively participate in the agenda-setting and problem-solving activities of their local communities; in order to facilitate these activities, the government needs to support learning related to history and culture in the communities. Also, in collaboration with schools, public lifelong-learning facilities, businesses, and NPOs, local residents are expected to jointly develop their own learning toward problem-solving activities in their communities. The government needs to support these learning efforts. (Central Council for Education 2007, 6)

The Tokyo Metropolitan Government is a frontrunner in implementing these national policy proposals. In December 2008, the Lifelong Learning Council of the Tokyo Metropolitan Government published a report that provided two meanings of the term "local communities" (Tokyo Metropolitan Government 2008). The first was an interpretation of the term in the conventional sense in the Japanese language to mean just a geographical area. The second referred to it as the relationality among human beings, as a term representing the various networks established among local people. The report stated that it was vital to create a safe, trust-based support network when considering the reconstruction of Japanese society (ibid., 6). Such networks would be generated when people were positively involved in various types of problem-solving activities in their communities (ibid., 7). Local communities would thus be considered as a social resource for generating the new "comprehensive knowledge." Practically speaking, this new knowledge would be an essential foundation for building grassroots skills to embody devolution—a distinctive administrative technique of rationalization in a neoliberal government, and devolution has been devised to manage "governmental risk."

The logic underlying the above concept is that people living in the same community unite and try to devise ways of improving their daily lives jointly under the sense of value advocated in the concept of the New Public Commons. In doing so, they can establish some kind of social solidarity and develop a collective consciousness through undertaking problem-solving activities as members of one community. This policy discourse would also work to strengthen trust and voluntary associational relations in civic life, which are popularly described as "social capital" (Putnam, 2000). As Japanese society is veering toward a socioeconomic divide, I consider this policy development as a risk-managing activity by the state in its governance of society. Risk is profoundly social. It is constructed as a factor that hinders the generation of cohesion and solidarity in the nation. The new form of knowledge construction that is achievable through lifelong learning works to instill or aid in a sense a collective belongingness as Japanese. In fact, Japan's new lifelong learning policy is considered as a means to alleviate the negative impact of such a divide by imagining the realization of the New Public Commons.

Stratification of the Japanese populace in contemporary Japan is economically and socially bifurcated, and bipolarization—particularly among the youth—is a reality today. Japanese society is in fact becoming two-tiered, divided into the rich and the poor. The *Asahi Shimbun*, a major national daily, presented a story in the editorial section, on November 4, 2009:

> First, let me introduce a resident of Tokyo in his 30s. He is a university graduate but makes a living as a dispatched day laborer. He delivers packages or sorts warehouse inventory,

and earns 6,000–7,000 yen at the end of each grueling day. He wants to get married and start a family some day but is aware that it would be difficult to achieve this given his current income level. "When I don't even know if I'll have work tomorrow, how can I make plans for my future?" he laments.

This editorial appeared following an announcement by a welfare minister that Japan's relative poverty rate had touched 15.7 percent in 2007, one of the highest rates among the OECD member countries. The OECD average for the mid-2000s was 10.6 percent. The data for 2007 was much higher than that found in the 2004 survey conducted by the OECD; Japan's relative poverty rate was placed at 14.9 percent, the fourth highest among the 30 OECD member nations. Meanwhile, this rate was between 7 percent and 8 percent in the 1980s. Previous LDP administrations never released the country's poverty rates. The relative poverty rate was disclosed for the first time by the new government, led by former prime minister Hatoyama Yukio's DPJ.

Poverty is indeed difficult to measure. The relative poverty rate represents the proportion of the population whose disposable income is less than half of the nation's per capita median disposable income (which was 2.28 million yen in 2007 or about $22,000). The relative poverty rate is the most accurate indicator, as it is pegged to income and living standards in the society in which a person lives. The article in *Asahi* went on to state, "Today, there are people who cannot even meet their basic needs, no matter how hard they work. This is what the relative poverty rate of 15.7% implies." This rate indicates that almost one in six people are struggling to make a living. The welfare ministry's announcement of the relative poverty rate for 2007 underlines the fact that Japan is no longer a prosperous nation where most households can consider themselves to be middle class. Further, when I was finishing this book in the summer of 2014, I read a new report that Japan's poverty rate in 2012 was 16.1 percent, and 16.3 percent for children under eighteen years, both of which were the worst figures since 1958 when the survey started (*Mainichi Shimbun*, July 16, 2014).

On September 1, 2010, the Ministry of Health, Labor, and Welfare (MHLW) announced that the Gini coefficient, a measure of income distribution inequality, had registered a record 0.5318 in 2009 (MHLW 2010a; the closer the Gini coefficient is to 1, the worse the inequality).[3] This trend can be attributed to the drastic changes in the labor market liberalization started by former prime minister Obuchi following the burst in the 1990s of the bubble economy. It was further promoted by the Koizumi administration in the early 2000s under the name of neoliberal deregulation and structural reform (*kōzō kaikaku*).[4] Many Japanese firms have accelerated restructuring and laying off of workers, mostly youth; the rate of unemployment reached 5.1 percent in 2009, a record high level in Japan's history, according to the Ministry of Internal Affairs and Communications (MIAC 2010), as well as replacement of their full-time employees with young nonregular workers in order to save labor costs and survive in the fiercely competitive global market (Tarohmaru 2009). While the Japanese traditional working style—lifetime employment—is on the verge of a breakdown, such precarious employment is fast becoming the dominant mode of working (Ishiguro 2008). Furthermore, the number of so-called working poor, whose income falls beneath the poverty line of around 2 million yen ($19,000) per annum—many youth fall in this category—has also risen. According to current news reports, the number of people who receive *seikatsu hogo* (livelihood protection), a core poverty policy in post–World War II Japan, exceeded 2 million as of March 2011, the same level as in 1952 shortly after World War II (*Asahi Shimbun*, June 14, 2011).[5] Meanwhile, there are 1,739 millionaires in Japan, the second highest number in the world, following the United States (*Financial Times*, June 23, 2011).

This divided society has the omnipresent character of a risk society: it possesses the collective consciousness of anxiety, insecurity, uncertainty, and ambivalence. With the collapse of social solidarity and coherence, however, local communities have not disappeared, as Scott Lash (1994) argues; rather, they are being rediscovered and re-institutionalized around risk. According to Lash, risk is now the collective bond holding communities together as imaginary risk communities (ibid., 157–68, in particular). Local communities are in fact being imagined and rebuilt as locations where people would embody the social and political values of the New Public Commons. In a 2005 report, the Council on National Life (*kokumin seikatsu shingikai*), a subcommittee of the Cabinet Office, actually identified local communities as a new form of associational entity constructed by citizens through a synthesis of traditional area-based and theme-based communities. According to the report, local communities would be based on people "with a shared consciousness of what the problem is and how it should be solved"; the term was defined as "the aggregate of connected people dealing with the issue" (Council on National Life 2005, 3). On this policy development, as Dean and Henman point out, "[g]overning is fundamentally spatial because it is about 'acting at a distance,' creating particular sites as 'containers' of power and authority, coordinating diverse locale, linking center with periphery, metropole with colony" (Dean and Henman 2004, 490). Local communities provide a location to practice lifelong learning and are recognized as what Dean and Henman call "containers" for directly linking the government and the governed. Following the revision of the Fundamental Law of Education in 2006, local learning movements are now increasingly examining ways of including agenda-setting and problem-solving activities involving local people in the lifelong learning programs at local citizens' public halls, libraries, museums, and so on. Also, the community policy unit (*chiiki seisaku shitsu*) as well as the community development support unit (*chiiki zukuri shien shitsu*), both of which were created in 2001 and 2004 respectively in the Lifelong Learning Policy Bureau of the Education Ministry, support the governmental strategy to emphasize community building through learning activities. In fact, the units aim to play key roles in linking education policy making at the local level with community development and the need to create the units stemmed from the increasing number of people who wished to be involved in community-based learning and from the demand for empowering local communities. It had become crucial to galvanize the local communities by catering to their own strengths, and lifelong learning thus became a core element of the local revitalization program (cf. Suzuki 2004; Senuma 2006).

The abovementioned argument can be considered to be in line with the global efforts made by the states stepping in to implement education policies to actively involve the at-risk for being socially excluded, including the youth (cf. Kelly 2001; Te Riele 2006; Wishart et al. 2006). In Japan, in recent times, local communities are being re-institutionalized as important places that afford the youth proper access to learning opportunities connected to lifelong learning. For example, since 2004, the Japanese government has been establishing "community schools" in its public education system at the primary and secondary levels.[6] As part of this initiative, children are encouraged to get actively involved in their communities just as adults are involved in their local school activities. In other words, people from the community volunteer to carry out teaching and learning activities in the school. By mobilizing volunteers among the locals, the community school policy contributes toward enhancing educational skills in the community (see chapter 5). Further, communities play a significant role in offering various types of work-experience programs to students in the recently introduced "career education" course in Japanese schools (see chapter 7). Through active interaction with the local adults, the community school system primarily aims at reducing any risks of local children being socially displaced in their adolescence. Specifically, this system ensures that not just parents and teachers but also the local adults provide proper guidance to the students. Meanwhile, volunteers working at local public lifelong learning facilities, such as libraries and museums, play a significant role to include the youth in their social activities (see chapter 4). Furthermore, one of the new vocational courses recently funded by the state is offered by community-based local NPOs—civil society organizations established under the 1998 NPO Law in Japan (see chapter 6). The course aims at training people to become social entrepreneurs, but more practically, workers for NPOs, mainly because conventional businesses are unlikely to hire people in the current persistently sluggish economy. The courses are not limited to the youth, however. Recruiting the unemployed from the entire community, the local NPOs retrain them, that is, offer new knowledge and develop skills necessary for the operation of voluntary NPO activities. In the summer of 2010, these courses were started across the country, first in Aomori Prefecture, the northernmost tip of the Japanese mainland, followed by the Niigata, Chiba, and Aichi Prefectures and others. All of the abovementioned activities, that is, giving access to lifelong learning, should be part of the major efforts to bring the at-risk for being socially excluded into the mainstream Japanese society, and local communities are the focal points of such efforts.

Neoliberal Knowledge

In this chapter, I frame the strategies adopted by the Japanese state under neoliberal governmentality from a risk perspective in the context of lifelong learning. The risk society is a reconstruction of modernity, which is oriented around the production of new "comprehensive knowledge." The state promotes lifelong learning as one of the foremost priorities on the agenda of the national education policy; in particular, it intends to support the concept of the New Public Commons. The state discourse on lifelong learning is expected to produce disciplinary knowledge, presented as "comprehensive knowledge," in order to primarily contribute to the quality of the public sphere. Further, I would argue that the Japanese state is replacing the Keynesian techniques of social intervention used in the implementation of welfare statehood by mobilizing lifelong learning among the population. Against the backdrop of the deepening socioeconomic divide nationwide, in imagining the realization of the New Public Commons, the Japanese neoliberal state is ultimately trying to manage the risk of governing society or "governmental risk" through the introduction of a strong lifelong learning initiative: the idea that knowledge is the epicenter of the movement aiming at generating social solidarity in local communities. As Mok (2007, 18) points out, the development of such new knowledge through lifelong learning can be considered as part of the capacity-building efforts being made by the neoliberal state, by revitalizing nonstate sectors in education provision, in the midst of the challenges posed by neoliberal globalization. Cynically, however, this new neoliberal paradigm does not care so much about the content of disciplinary "comprehensive knowledge," as long as citizens are able to independently solve their problems by themselves. Even though "discipline" is a specified knowledge, the neoliberal knowledge does not mean such knowledge. The "comprehensive knowledge" produced under the new lifelong learning initiative is considered a tool for reorganizing and changing the conditions governing people's lives at the grassroots level, and it is at the center of the transformation in contemporary society. In the rest of this book, I have further documented various representations of knowledge and skills embodying "comprehensive knowledge" for surviving neoliberal Japan.

4

The New Public Commons

The New Public Commons

The New Public Commons (*atarashii kōkyō*) has been a policy buzzword in Japanese society since the late 2000s. Prime Minister Hatoyama Yukio (2009–2010) of the DPJ, who ardently promoted the concept of the New Public Commons, declared during his tenure that he "would like to establish a society in which public affairs are shouldered by not only the public sector but also local communities, NPOs, and others" (Prime Minister Hatoyama's Cabinet E-mail Magazine 2010). In other words, the New Public Commons is a sociopolitical imagery attempting to redefine the boundaries of moral responsibility between the state and the individual, with greater emphasis on the virtues of self-regulation. The policy was further advocated under the administration of Hatoyama's successor, Prime Minister Kan Naoto (2010–2011). In October 2010, Prime Minister Kan newly established the Council on the Promotion of New Public Commons (*atarashii kōkyō suishin kaigi*) under a direct initiative called "The Prime Minister in Action." He introduced the following thoughts in the first meeting: "I believe that the area of the New Public Commons, together with the work undertaken by public or private entities, of which the latter includes profit-making businesses, should, in a sense, be the foundation of society and the core basis for *societal restructuring*. I hope the Council will play a leading role and present a model in this regard" (emphasis added by the author). I watched a live broadcast of this speech on the Cabinet Office website.[1] There was live streaming of all discussions on the New Public Commons, and all meeting documents (both handouts and detailed discussion records) were also available.[2] Thus, watching the discussions over the Internet became an important part of my fieldwork in Japan (when I could not be physically present in the discussion room). Indeed, one of the major changes I experienced during my ethnographic fieldwork, which I primarily conducted from 2010 to 2011, was that many government meetings, particularly at the state level, were made public (including over the Internet) in comparison to my previous fieldwork experience in Japan (2001–2003). The major reason for this change could be attributed to the 2009 DPJ government, in particular, under Prime Ministers Hatoyama and Kan, which created a strong antibureaucratic discourse after the old-fashioned LDP adherence to bureaucratic rule in Japan for most of the post–World War II period. Such government information was not so easily accessible under the former LDP government, and information disclosure was considered a paramount factor in generating the New Public Commons in Japanese society. The disclosure of the poverty rate, which I mentioned in chapter 3, is a good example. "In this society everyone has a place to go and a role to play. People value the pleasure of helping others, and by generating new markets and services they allow economic activity to thrive. When the fruits of such activities are properly returned to society, people can live better lives. Thus, such a society develops in a virtuous cycle."[3]

The seed idea for the New Public Commons was presented a decade ago by the Prime Minister's Commission on Japan's Goals in the Twenty-first Century, which was established by Prime Minister Keizo Obuchi, whom I briefly mentioned in chapter 3. As the central focus of structural reform for Japan, the commission emphasized the importance of developing "a new kind of public sphere created through the combined power of individuals, who regardless of their personal affiliations, consciously engage with one another and with society of their own free will" (Prime Minister's Commission on Japan's Goals in the Twenty-first Century 2000, 17). Further, the policy discourse on New Public Commons can be identified as a direct outcome of the emergence of volunteerism in Japanese society after the Hanshin-Awaji earthquake on January 17, 1995. At that time, approximately 1.3 million volunteers acted to aid victims of the disaster, leading the Japanese government to institutionalize a new third-sector initiative in Japanese society. Consequently, the so-called NPO Law was enacted in 1998. Since then, the number of NPOs has increased continually across the country. As of July 31, 2011, when I was conducting fieldwork, nearly forty-five thousand NPOs had been incorporated (Cabinet Office 2011b). They are primarily collaborative partners with local governments, mostly at the municipal level, in providing social services, including elderly care and nonformal social education, at the same time replacing the role of government. Originally started during the conservative LDP regime, the New Public Commons policy discourse has been carried over to the DPJ's Third Way politics.[4] The third sector, which includes the NPOs, has been placed more strategically than before throughout Japanese society.

Earlier, I had pondered the question of who was to lead this "societal restructuring" process at the grassroots level or in local communities in Japanese society. Prime Minister Kan mentioned that the Council on the Promotion of New Public Commons itself would play a key role in this issue. Considering Prime Minister Kan's background as a social activist and after examining the discussion records of the Council members, I assumed that the restructuring process was not likely to be implemented as a top-down initiative. The state's primary role would be to prepare the social environment to support the new public sphere. Meanwhile, the New Public Commons Declaration mentions that "in Japan, communities and individuals once played important roles in providing public services, and it is still possible for the Japanese public to recover this role" (New Public Commons Roundtable 2010b, 3). These words made me recall *bunka borantia* (culture volunteers—volunteers in local public facilities for lifelong learning, such as citizens' public halls, libraries, and museums). They would lead the ongoing societal restructuring process. They would be the key actors to generate the New Public Commons in their local communities.

The *bunka borantia* voluntarily take up the governmental imperatives advocated under the New Public Commons. In this chapter, I label them as "knowledge-constructing" subjects. My argument concerning these "knowledge-constructing" subjects resonates with the concept of cultural citizenship (see Dudley et al. 1999).[5] Nowadays, citizenship is considered to have a major impact on the cultural processes of society. It is argued to be a dynamic, contextual, contested, and multidimensional notion. This concept is very different from the older liberal notion, or what the British sociologist T. H. Marshall ([1950]1992), in his *Citizenship and Social Class*, describes as rights or formal membership in a polity. In postwelfare, neoliberal, advanced industrial societies, including Japan, the idea of citizenship is best conveyed through responsible consumers of social services, and the role of the state is only to facilitate this consumption, preferably through private providers. In keeping with this view, greater emphasis has been placed on the responsibilities of citizens to maintain order in society. The widespread privatization of formerly public areas can be conceived as a new form of responsibility for citizens. Meanwhile, the neoliberal practices of government offer ordinary individuals new opportunities to participate in various arenas of action "to resolve the kind of issues hitherto held to be the responsibility of authorized governmental agencies" (Burchell 1996, 29; cf. Foucault 1991). Such a profound shift from the Keynesian welfare state to that of neoliberal politics represents a deliberate cultural restructuring and engineering based upon the neoliberal model of the "entrepreneurial self" (Peters 2001). I see this very characteristic in the emergence of *bunka borantia* in contemporary Japan. As Rose (1998, 151) argues, this kind of subject is conceived as an active, self-creating individual seeking to enterprise him- or herself.

I argue that, while interacting with the neoliberal state, the *bunka borantia* are active in learning, producing, accumulating, and applying a certain kind of knowledge in their daily lives, which they use to deal with constant changes. This knowledge, which the *bunka borantia* call *shimin chi* (civic knowledge), exclusively supports the New Public Commons. Japan's new policy on the New Public Commons strongly encourages the building up of such disciplinary subjects as the *bunka borantia*, who can generate civic knowledge. The new policy equips, enables, or shapes the subjects to survive the pervasive changes currently sweeping through society. In tandem with the *bunka borantia* development, I document a recent policy development: the Education Ministry tried to systematically produce and reproduce, in a more direct manner, such disciplinary "knowledge-constructing" subjects through the introduction of *jukugi*, a discussion technique. This chapter further suggests that the Japanese state steps in to generate the New Public Commons, a social infrastructure for managing the risk of governing society or what I call "governmental risk" in chapter 1. The realization of the New Public Commons is an effort to reinvigorate the persistently sluggish economy and society of the past two decades by enhancing social solidarity and collective consciousness at the grassroots level.

The *Bunka Borantia*

During my ethnographic fieldwork in Japan in the early 2000s, I met with some of the *bunka borantia*; they were key players in local public facilities for lifelong learning, such as citizens' public halls, libraries, and museums. *Bunka borantia* was a relatively new term in the Japanese lexicon. It initially referred exclusively to volunteers working in local public facilities for lifelong learning. The term was originally advocated by the former chief of the Agency for Cultural Affairs (*bunka chō*), the late Kawai Hayao, a well-known Jungian psychologist, when he assumed this position in January 2002. Kawai, who was actually the head of the Prime Minister's Commission on Japan's Goals in the Twenty-first Century, which claimed the original idea of New Public Commons, described *bunka borantia* as follows:

> I am often asked what *bunka borantia* means. Recently, in this country, volunteering has begun to gather much attention. Many people might associate volunteering with social welfare activities. There is no formal definition of the term in policy documents. I believe it is unnecessary to define the term strictly, as this would limit the scope of activities associated with the term. *Bunka borantia* broadly implies volunteering that helps others enjoy cultural activities while the volunteers themselves enjoy the activities. (Agency for Cultural Affairs 2002, 1)

With respect to volunteering in Japanese society, social welfare and disaster relief are traditionally popular fields. Volunteering opportunities in public lifelong learning facilities are currently gaining attention among people at the grassroots level. A member of the *bunka borantia* explained the difference between two types of volunteering, *bunka borantia* and social welfare volunteers, to me. While volunteers at citizens' public halls, libraries, and museums mainly attempt to create something new, social welfare volunteers are primarily expected to help others. The former tries to organize creative activities that contribute to the public good. They serve as guides at museums by sharing their knowledge, skill, and experience. Further, the current expanded meaning of the term encompasses local community development through dramatic and musical performances and cultural resource management.[6] This initiative of the *bunka borantia*, which focuses on the local community, is directly in line with the policy discussion that aimed to create the New Public Commons.

Kokubo Keiko is a key member of the *bunka borantia*. She was in her early forties when she began her long career as a volunteer in the late 1970s. Her first volunteer experience involved archiving news clippings at the library of the women's education center that was newly established in her neighborhood. She had fulfilled her duties with regard to the raising of her children and wished to undertake a new responsibility. She considered enrolling in college, but she ultimately chose volunteering over her other interests, as it provided her with the opportunity to peruse vast amounts of new information, thereby satisfying her intellectual curiosity.[7] In simple terms, Ms. Kokubo and her peers (all women) clipped articles from newspapers and magazines. Together, they read, organized, and classified news articles. She stated that during the course of their work, she and her colleagues tried to better understand the nature of the activities for which they had volunteered. As a research agenda, they were interested in exploring the qualities that volunteers should ideally possess; in other words, they wished to understand how they could locate volunteers like themselves in society and glean reasons for participating in volunteer activities. What Ms. Kokubo and her peers actually intended to do was to find and solve problems existing inside public lifelong learning facilities by bringing citizens' perspectives to such facilities. For the benefit of the user, Ms. Kokubo and her peers could even play an important role in connecting public officials and ordinary people for improving the quality of public life.

Ms. Kokubo was born in Taiwan during World War II, and her family moved to a prefecture in Kyushu, southern Japan, after the war. Her father taught ethics at a high school. She stated that she had been used to discussing social and political affairs with her father ever since her childhood. Although Ms. Kokubo's mother attended a college in Tokyo, she withdrew owing to illness. At that time (that is, before the war), it was extremely rare for women from the countryside to attend college in Tokyo. Further, her mother's marriage had been arranged by her parents without her consent. Ms. Kokubo, who dreamt of becoming a designer, attended a fine arts college in Tokyo. She was a junior during Anpo (the anti U.S.-Japan Security Treaty movement) in 1960. She told me that this event was one of the most influential experiences in her life. "At that time, I only knew that something important had happened in this country," she said. "But I didn't know what I should do. So I wrote to my father, and he wrote back with only one line on a postcard: 'Think and decide for yourself.'" After Ms. Kokubo received the postcard, she willingly started participating in demonstrations. The day the security treaty was ratified at the National Diet, she spent the night at Shinagawa station. She was tired and downhearted over the hopeless situation, and she thought of becoming a journalist instead of a designer. She wished to have a job whereby she could convey her opinions to society.

After graduating from college, Ms. Kokubo joined a publishing company that specialized in women's fashion. A couple of years later, she married a co-worker and resigned from the job. During the 1960s, it was the social norm for Japanese women to resign from their jobs when they married. Hence, although Ms. Kokubo believed that women should continue working after marriage, she merely followed the custom. She also confessed that she was a little frustrated with her job. Instead of pursuing trendy fashions, she felt the need to do something different; she would prefer writing stories that could bring about social change. After marriage and the birth of her son, she became a very active member of the Parent-Teacher Association (PTA) of her son's school. In addition, as a freelance writer, she continued to achieve career growth.

In her writing, she highlighted the issues in daily life; she selected common problems and visualized them. Gaining a variety of information through volunteer activities, as mentioned earlier, personally motivated her and satisfied her intellectual curiosity. During her conversation with me, she often used two Japanese words—*manabi* and *kizuki*—when describing her volunteer work. For Ms. Kokubo, volunteering was a great opportunity for *manabi* (learning), which is available to all of us—volunteers, officials of public lifelong learning facilities, and users, and ultimately, such *manabi* could cause a change in ourselves. In her view, all the stakeholders would do well to adopt the same standpoint. Working with volunteers would even provide new perspectives to public officials. Further, the process would serve as a lifelong learning opportunity for them. Ms. Kokubo also used the Japanese term *kizuki* (becoming aware of) when referring to the act of learning something new. She believed that her repeated exposure to *kizuki* during her volunteer work had aided her personal development. Ms. Kokubo subsequently tried to convert what she had learned through her volunteer work into a new volunteer opportunity.

After twenty years of working with other volunteers on archiving news clippings, Ms. Kokubo stopped her activities at the women's education center and created an independent network with other volunteers working in public facilities for lifelong learning across the country. The major motivation was to build a collaborative relationship with the government at various levels. Ms. Kokubo's network has been transformed into a network-based group called *bunka borantia*, in which I myself am a participant. Since 2005, the people connected to her network have been organizing an annual series of national gatherings of the *bunka borantia* in association with the Agency for Cultural Affairs. In the four occasions during the late 2000s, some one thousand people attended the gatherings. The participants reveal an interesting trend in demographic diversity. I identified three categories: women, local civil servants, and youth. Women form the major category of participants supporting this network, in keeping with their long-standing status as the backbone of social movements in Japan (cf. LeBlanc 1999; Chan-Tiberghien 2004; Chan 2008). The female participants are primarily housewives in their fifties and sixties. These female participants are part of a concrete example of political action by women and for women that is inextricable from the cognitive processes that are mobilized in political conversation, study and lifelong learning, and local political action, as Sherry Martin claims in her study on Japan's lifelong learning and democracy (Martin 2011). The second category of participants comprises civil servants, who are mostly from the prefectural and municipal levels and are in charge of affairs related to lifelong learning; they participate in these gatherings in their official capacity. Some of the retired civil servants, who were previously engaged in lifelong learning policy making, remain active participants. Moreover, the people in this network are making serious efforts to attract the youth. Thus, there has been a gradual but steady increase in the number of young volunteers joining this network, who make up the third and last category. For example, at the 2006 meeting, more than half (53 percent) of the participants were in their twenties (18 percent) and thirties (35 percent)—a major change in the demographic data of Japanese volunteerism, which is usually dominated by retired seniors (Bunka Borantia National Forum 2007, 2; cf. Ogawa 2009a, 57–58, for demographic data of the volunteers).

Civic Knowledge

The *bunka borantia* might realize that they are simply complementing the work originally initiated by the government as part of cost-cutting policies in public administration, a political preference advocated by neoliberalism, which is indeed true. I confirmed several cases in my previous studies (Ogawa 2009a) where introducing volunteers halved administrative costs, including personal expenses; these volunteers simultaneously replaced bureaucrats in implementing the publicly financed lifelong learning program. Meanwhile, I observed that the *bunka borantia* were effecting a change in contemporary Japanese society through collaborative engagement in the formulation of the state discourse on the New Public Commons.

By networking at the national gatherings of the *bunka borantia*, the participants aim to accumulate and circulate the grassroots knowledge generated through their daily activities at public lifelong learning facilities. Their construction of new knowledge includes learning to coordinate volunteer activities, collaborating with the government at various levels, involving themselves in community development as volunteers, and acquiring decision-making tools for diversified stakeholders—all of which can be categorized as practical knowledge, which the participants would call "civic knowledge" (*shimin chi*). I locate the construction of civic knowledge as a vibrant, grassroots response to the state-sponsored "comprehensive knowledge" argued in chapter 3. If I were to select some keywords from the records of the national gatherings, they would be *management, coordination, partnership*, and *quality of volunteerism* (Bunka Borantia National Forum 2007, 19; see Appendix 3 for a list of civic knowledge sources). I have found these words to be representative of the volunteers' newly acquired knowledge. For the *bunka borantia* armed with civic knowledge, volunteering at citizens' public halls, libraries, and museums is a means to support and enrich the New Public Commons from below. It is an opportunity to better society through civic engagement.

Another key member of this *bunka borantia* network, Ms. Sato, a

4.1. A discussion scene of *bunka borantia* at the Bunka Borantia National Forum in 2007.

woman in her sixties, offered me the following description: "What we are trying to do is simple: recognize one another, achieve unity amid diversity, and build and implement our own agenda; such knowledge (or civic knowledge) could not be accumulated in public administration, which prefers uniformity or dealing with its population in a uniform manner. Our networking focuses on each individual and extending support to him or her. It enables empowerment through new knowledge production." Ms. Sato is a former deputy mayor in her municipality and is currently organizing an NPO that promotes grassroots empowerment through gender equality. She added, "Collaborating with citizens armed with such knowledge is probably the only way that the government can survive. Collaboration might take a lot of time, but it is worth the wait." Mr. Iwata, an engineer in his thirties and an active course-planning volunteer at a local lifelong learning center in Tokyo, had the following to say: "Within our network, for example, I love that everybody is different. Although it might be difficult to reach an agreement, I appreciate that we enjoy the process. We are changing, and the government is trying to change too."

The *bunka borantia* realize that civic knowledge can be a powerful and essential tool in inducing or encouraging ordinary people to participate in the New Public Commons. Civic knowledge can also provide a framework for self-creation that buffers both the state and the individual. Their knowledge is indeed framed as relational learning. Through the *bunka borantia* network, the participants are trying to institutionalize the civic knowledge generated through their collective learning as a social institution. In fact, the construction as well as consumption of civic knowledge, through volunteer activities at public lifelong learning facilities, is a solid foundation for supporting the concept of the New Public Commons.

"Entrepreneurial Self" for Constructing Civic Knowledge

Thus far, I have analyzed the interaction of macropolitical discourse, or the New Public Commons, with the *bunka borantia*, a group of what I call "knowledge-constructing" subjects who are active in public lifelong learning facilities at the grassroots level across the country. Over the past two decades, the Japanese state has been assuming the strategic role of facilitator and providing the conditions for self-governing citizenship. Below, I provide an example of volunteering in the context of lifelong learning, a political technique that was introduced into Japanese politics in 1992, with the aim of generating "knowledge-constructing" subjects. The implementation of the lifelong learning policy is linked to different micropractices in which such subject making is fostered in local communities.

As I briefly mentioned in chapter 2, the Lifelong Learning Council (LLC), an advisory body to the education minister, proposed this policy. The LLC sought to redefine the limited public understanding of volunteering as a charity by describing it as a lifelong activity in which all strata of society can actively engage (LLC 1992). More importantly, it clearly stated that volunteering could be identified as an integral part of lifelong learning activities. In other words, the LLC encouraged voluntary activities in the community through the use of the citizens' wide range of knowledge and skills. The logic employed was that the personally gathered knowledge and skills could become essential resources for society. On the one hand, an individual equipped with such knowledge and skills could achieve the crucial objective of lifelong learning activities in the form of self-actualization by supporting public lifelong learning facilities in local communities—mainly at citizens' public halls, libraries, and museums—as a volunteer. On the other hand, these volunteer activities could be expected to contribute to the enhancement of local cultures through individual participation in these facilities. This was one of the key policy developments since the LLC tried to change or redefine the conventional style of Japanese lifelong learning, which consisted mostly of pursuing liberal arts, hobbies, and sports. The policy report even claimed the conceptual equalization of lifelong learning with volunteering activities in such facilities. Since the LLC's statement, people at the grassroots level have increasingly begun to avail themselves of volunteering opportunities. They serve as guides at museums, assistants at libraries, and course planners for community-oriented lifelong learning programs. According to the statistics available, of the 4,000 museums (which include both public and private) across the country, 759 invited volunteers in 2004—a significant increase from the 139 that did the same in 1993—with some 250 additional museums considering the introduction of volunteers (Kinoshita 2005,12). The ongoing *bunka borantia* development should be placed within this lifelong learning policy development.

One way of examining this subjectivity development is a facilitation technique by the state to mobilize its population. Simon Avenell's work highlights how the Japanese state has been facilitating volunteerism since 1945 (Avenell 2010a, 2010b; see also Cruikshank 1999). However, the "knowledge-constructing" subjects are not just representative of how individuals are constrained against their will *by* discipline but of how individuals create their own selves *through* discipline (cf. Starkey and McKinlay 1998). In fact, the governing technique employing the concept of knowledge construction aims to increase people's capacities rather than making them into docile individuals. Rather than determining people's subjectivities, the facilitation technique, through the state's policy, "elicits, fosters, promotes, and attributes" them (Edwards 2008, 6). In her or his local community, the "knowledge-constructing" subject (like the members of the *bunka borantia*) produces knowledge that proves indispensable for the governing of the local community. The knowledge produced becomes a means for the person's participation as a responsible subject in the governance of society, and the process through which she or he constructs this knowledge becomes a technology for the governing of the self. During my fieldwork, what I observed was that a subject armed with the new knowledge became the "entrepreneurial self" (Peters 2001)—the form of self-government currently promoted and stimulated. Generally speaking, entrepreneurship is about using resources to produce a commodity that meets needs and offers an income. It also includes an "element of alertness"—that is, a speculative, creative, or innovative attitude that entails seeking opportunities in a competitive environment.[8] Entrepreneurship is a risky business. However, as Giddens (1998a) argues, as in the social regime, risk is not to be prevented but is the condition for profit—a kind of stimulating principle. The entrepreneurial self-attempts to perceive itself as operating within a certain environment and having certain needs that the self can satisfy through creatively produced goods (Simons and Masschelein 2008, 53).

Becoming an entrepreneurial self through the construction of new knowledge is a risk-hedging activity for the *bunka borantia*, which needs to survive in a contemporary society dominated by a neoliberal governmentality rooted in self-responsibility, competitiveness, and decentralization. People are largely motivated to participate in the activities undertaken by the *bunka borantia* because they try to be collaborative partners when the neoliberal state promotes the devolution of state power to smaller localized units. Ms. Kokubo, a member of the *bunka borantia*, pointed out with regard to volunteering, however, that she did not believe in working according to the instructions of higher authorities (or the government). She explained her philosophy of volunteering as follows: "When we volunteer, we should not blindly accept or follow the requests of the government. We need to understand what we are expected to do and then reflect on the meaning of what we are doing. Otherwise, we will end up becoming mere subcontractors of the government. It is 'risky' for us." She continued, "Just supporting the government's work is not enough; it means nothing to us. We can be creative, and propose something novel to the government from our perspectives as citizens." For her, it was important to reflect on how she was involved with society through her volunteer work, and how she transformed herself as well as society in the process.

The neoliberal policy, characterized by "a 'folding back' of the objectives of the government upon its means" (Dean 1999a, 174), entails breaching the conventional divisions between the state and society. Japanese devolution has so far been conducted through policy collaboration between the state and its citizens, who are mostly organized under NPOs, and this collaborative relationship today is popularly known as *kyōdō* (collaboration). It has become fashionable for the neoliberal state to introduce techniques aimed at reducing the cost of public administration while mobilizing concerned citizens in local communities. Volunteer mobilization in citizens' public halls, libraries, and museums, referred to earlier in this chapter, should be included in this devolution process. As the neoliberal modes of governance encourage the transformation of public realms, the *bunka borantia* consciously avoid becoming subcontractors of the government, which is a crucial risk they face. They try to become entrepreneurial selves, viewing the process of devolution as an opportunity to create a reflective space for innovation and creativity in Japanese policymaking and its implementation. Jointly working with public officials and constructing new or civic knowledge makes it possible for the *bunka borantia* to participate in Japanese social and political life while cultivating an entrepreneurial spirit. Their networking initiatives have also made it possible for them to mobilize their knowledge effectively. Civic knowledge production is a crucial part of being an entrepreneurial self for enhancing the quality of the New Public Commons, changing the conventional relationship between the state and the individual.

Jukugi (Due Deliberation)

In tandem with this grassroots development of the *bunka borantia*, I observed an interesting policy making that the Education Ministry tried to systematically produce and reproduce, in a more direct manner, such disciplinary "knowledge-constructing" subjects through *jukugi*. *Jukugi* is an education policy implemented at the state level that fosters painstaking discussion and contemplation on issues and seeks a solution at the grassroots level. It was becoming a nationwide phenomenon when I was doing fieldwork in Japan in 2010.

The concept of *jukugi* was debated intensively in Japan's National Diet in fall 2010. The phrase was indeed often used by lawmakers of both the ruling DPJ and the opposition LDP. Prime Minister Kan himself, who used the term a great deal, had a "divided Diet" (*nejire kokkai*)—in which the two houses were dominated by ruling and opposition parties, respectively—as the background of his speech, and the only way to move politics forward was for Mr. Kan to seek the cooperation of the opposition parties. Premier Kan expected his Diet members to offer their wisdom and to seek common ground by using the *jukugi* technique, or the art of discussion, to move things forward. By deepening the Diet discussion, lawmakers would understand the differences in their opinions, and would try to discover the best common ground for the state.

Jukugi was officially brought to the policy discourse by the Education Ministry in April 2010. Suzuki Kan, the deputy education minister under the DPJ government, adopted a strong *jukugi* initiative as the introduction to the formal policy-making activities. As part of educational reform, *jukugi* aimed to transmit the opinions of concerned laymen to the education policy-making process at the state level, which was dominated exclusively by the top officials of the Ministry. Actually, the grassroots discussion space was equally located in an experts' committee of the Central Council for Education, which was an advisory body for the education minister, according to a magazine article published by the Education Ministry's Lifelong Learning Policy Bureau (MEXT 2011c, 3).[9] The *jukugi* development is indeed a part of administrative reform, which aims to achieve transparent governance, a key stance in the DPJ government, and the creation of a new education culture in Japanese society.

Jukugi is derived from the combination of two Japanese words—*jukuryo* and *tōgi*. A major Japanese lexicon, *Kōjien*, defines *jukuryo* simply as deliberation, or seriously and deeply considering something, and *tōgi* is a discussion based on a meticulous examination of a problem, as in a deliberate review. Combining these two words, *jukugi* means ample, satisfactory, and thorough contemplation, perusal, or careful consideration of a matter. The Education Ministry defines *jukugi* as a process of problem solving and policy making through *jukuryo* and *tōgi* (MEXT 2011c, 3). The process consists of concerned individuals gathering in the public realm to cooperate and collaborate, seeking common ground, moving things forward, and reaching an agreement among different stakeholders. There are five key steps to creating an active *jukugi* space:[10]

1. All concerned individuals, including parents, teachers, and local residents—if the discussion topic is related to education—get together and sit around the table. At that time, each individual has a short (one-minute) self-introduction, in which the person relates him- or herself to the topic in some manner. In addition, one facilitator and one presenter are chosen from the discussion fellows. The facilitator is expected to strictly manage the allocation of time.

2. Collect and share information and comprehend the state and structure of challenges through lively discussions. Technically, the topics each individual wants to bring to the discussion table should be written on pink sticky notes. Each note should have only one item and should be specific and concise, with one keyword also included in the note. One person can produce multiple notes.

3. Reinforce comprehension of the situation, identifying the responsibilities of each stakeholder. The facilitator encourages discussions among the participants, sorting out (grouping by using color markers) the pink notes on an A1-size white paper.

4. Elicit solutions through the discussions, aggregating everyone's wisdom and energy. At this time, solutions will be written on blue sticky notes. Again, each note should have only one item. Meanwhile, the facilitator confirms a specific solution.

5. Derive the various respective roles, working together intensely to resolve challenges with awareness, respect, and inspiration. The presenter concisely shows the discussion results and provides a feasible solution.

These practices of *jukugi* may be attributed primarily to Jürgen Habermas' work on deliberative democracy (Habermas 1996). Deliberative democracy includes various types of political, administrative, economic, and social institutions in both the public and private spheres. Based on double-track logic, discussions start when formal institutions thematize issues, with informal deliberation taking place outside the institutions and becoming public opinions, which then influences institutional deliberation. The formal administrative institutions play a role in making such issues authoritative.

Deputy education minister Suzuki (2010, 9) mentions that the *jukugi* process has a three-layer structure. First, it is officially conducted at the National Diet; second, it is developed online. Its website—*Jukugi kakeai* (http://jukugi.mext.go.jp)—was launched by the Education Ministry on April 17, 2010. The virtual *jukugi* functions as an intermediary between the state and the individual and facilitates decision-making processes and public opinion formation in a multistream model. In the process of *jukugi*, informal opinion formation turns into public opinion in civil society, which in turn becomes "communicative power" (Habermas 1996, 136), as the expression of citizens' political autonomy. Habermas gives a rationale for this second step, claiming that, instead of administrative power in Weber's sense, "[c]ommunicative generated legitimate power can have an effect on the political system insofar as it assumes responsibility for the pool of reasons from which administrative decisions must draw their rationalizations" (ibid., 484). In fact, communicative power involves a concept of power based on a collective agreement; "[communicative power] expresses consensus achieved through the mechanism of citizens' discursive political will formation on the moral legitimacy of general norms of action" (O'Mahony 2010, 54). Thus, communicative power generated through Japan's civil society "can insert moments of democratic accountability into the system world" (Murphy and Fleming 2006, 51). Third and finally, *jukugi* is developed through real *jukugi* or on-site dialogue. This process of interactive *jukugi* can be developed in the noninstitutional dimension, including the intimate sphere, mobilizing social learning through the transformation of preferences. It contributes to the formation of social infrastructure between various individuals.

The *jukugi* discussions have indeed been conducted in a hybrid manner, with online *jukugi* being quite active. Amid no physical constraints (of either time or place), the online community encourages dialogue on any issue regarding Japanese education through the sharing of messages by anyone interested in the issues. The process has four phases: first, key questions are suggested by deputy education minister Suzuki; second, both Ministery officials and parties involved with the issue participate in the discussion; third, responses from the general public are sorted by Ministry officials as facilitators, who are also expected to supply information, including examples and relevant data; and fourth, the *jukugi* discussions are published online in real time. As of February 21, 2011, for example, nineteen questions had been suggested by deputy education minister Suzuki. The questions included the following:

- How can we further shape concrete strategies that will make research funding easier to use?
- How can we strategize our sports promotion policy?
- What should school assessment guidelines be like?
- What should twenty-first-century schools that utilize information technology learning look like?
- What measures do we need for reinforcing Japanese universities?

As responses to these questions, 14,409 comments were posted. Some 22,000 people have registered in the government-sponsored online community, and there have been 1.79 million pages viewed; participants were from all forty-seven prefectures in Japan as well as from overseas, and they include teachers (40 percent), school volunteers (15 percent), researchers (12 percent), parents (11.5 percent), education bureaucrats (6 percent), and students (5 percent) (MEXT 2011c, 4).

In 2010, one proposal on the improvement of teacher quality (MEXT 2010b) was compiled from 3,128 opinions generated from one *jukugi* community and submitted to deputy education minister Suzuki. In the beginning, Suzuki had posted two questions: What abilities are required of teachers, and how can teachers acquire them? (from April 17, 2010, to May 9, 2010); What specific measures should be implemented to improve the quality of teachers? (from April 17, 2010, to May 9, 2010). The thirty-one-page proposal points out that practicability (*jissenryoku*), expertise (*senmonsei*), and sociability (*shakaisei*) are the three key components required of teachers. In a discussion about how teachers can be more involved with children, the proposal also claims that administrative work currently assigned to teachers should be reconsidered, instead of just increasing the number of teachers. The proposal was ultimately submitted as a discussion reference to the Central Council for Education. This online development in policy making can indeed be considered a new effort by the DPJ government to expand Internet-based communication with fellow citizens, as Matsuura (2010) points out.

Real *Jukugi*

In October 2010, I had a chance to observe one on-site or real *jukugi* in Kudan, central Tokyo. Entering the conference room designated by Education Ministry officials, I first saw a group of mostly middle-aged men wearing grey or black suits sitting toward the front. The room was fairly quiet, and nobody talked to anyone else. I found seats for the general audience in the back of the room. There were still about ten minutes left before the session started.

This observation opportunity had been advertised just five days earlier on the Education Ministry website and was open to the general public. Preregistration with name and affiliation was required. The return receipt had to be presented for entering the conference room. During fiscal year 2010 (April 2010–March 2011), real *jukugi* gatherings were conducted seventy-one times across the country.[11] A wide variety of people from sixth graders to adult professionals participated, with a total number of five thousand participants (Suzuki 2010, 21). The real *jukugi* I observed was part of a nationwide series, and this was the first time for me to observe *jukugi*. The audience included nearly fifty people and some members of the mass media. A couple of Ministry officials were standing on each side of the room, holding digital cameras.

I sat in a front-row seat in the audience section. In the envelope distributed to the audience at the entrance, I found a list of participants. I realized that the thirty-three middle-aged participants were all top officials (in other words, directors) of the boards of education at the municipal level, only one of which was a woman. It seemed that they had been in a training session over the last couple of days in Tokyo, which was organized by the Education Ministry and that this real *jukugi* was scheduled as the last part of their training. The overall agenda for the real *jukugi* on that day was on how to improve "community schools" (new institutions the Japanese government is introducing to its public school system; these are discussed in chapter 5). Actually, I realized all of the participants were invited from municipalities where community schools had already been introduced and had some success. The list of participants' names also indicated how many community schools exist in each of their municipalities.

During the session, the thirty-three participants first listened to a presentation by an Education Ministry official about how to proceed with the real *jukugi*. The information given was almost the same as what was presented in the previous section: the five key steps to create an active *jukugi* space. Then, the participants were divided into five groups. The groups had already been decided by the officials, considering a geographical balance. Each group included senior directors who had rich experiences in terms of introducing community schools. Each group went into separate rooms, having seventy minutes to discuss an assigned issue around a discussion table. The audience was allowed to follow them and to encircle the discussion to listen. I went with group A, which discussed the role of the school council in the community school system. Mr. Endo, an Education Ministry official (chief of the lifelong learning policy, someone I had interviewed before), was sitting at the head of the discussion table as a facilitator, with another bureaucrat assisting him and seven directors of the municipal board of education participating. Their *jukugi* proceeded exactly in line with the five-step template presented earlier in this chapter. The participants first introduced themselves, which took about ten minutes. Second, Mr. Endo pointed out that the school councils in the community school system are not functioning well and posed a question to the directors concerning what school councils should be like. The directors then had ten minutes to introduce the realities they face at schools by writing on pink sticky notes. Then the group moved to an explanation time for approximately fifteen minutes. All of the participants talked about their experiences, using the notes.

Notes on challenges:

- Local people still don't know exactly what a community school is. (three notes)
- There is a big gap of understanding about community school among the local population.
- Community schools need teachers who are good communicators.
- It is difficult to find appropriate members for the school council. (two notes)
- The same council members stay for a long time.
- The school council focuses more on holding school events with the local community than on administration.

- Teachers' involvement is limited since they are transferred after a certain number of years. Currently, six years is the maximum term for a teacher at any one school.
- Ordinary local people cannot participate fully in the community school system.
- The principal should play a strong role in decision making on the school council.
- Even teachers cannot fully understand the community school.
- Some teachers complain about the administrative burden related to the community school.

At this moment, one senior director in the group mentioned that the school principal should have a prominent role in the school council, claiming that "[t]he role of school principal is key to succeeding in the community school project; in the community school system, the management rights exercised by the school principal should not be denied."

4.2. *Jukugi* demonstration by education officials; proposing problems, October 12, 2010.

He recommended that a local board of education could generate detailed management rules. Further, he mentioned that it would be important to look at the local community, instead of focusing on school. Locating the school in the local community would be a basic way of thinking.

As a third step, the education bureaucrat/facilitator categorized the notes, with the director participants, as well as the audience, looking on. The categorization was relatively smooth. Mr. Endo seemed already to have a lot of experience as a *jukugi* facilitator. Actually, Mr. Endo was a major advocate of *jukugi* with deputy education minister Suzuki, and I assumed that since April 2010 when the Education Ministry had adopted *jukugi* as a policy, he had been accumulating facilitator experiences at the real *jukugi* sites sponsored by the Ministry. This stage took only a total of ten minutes, as the director participants were also watching the process of categorization. The facilitator raised three points as categories:

1. School council's operation

2. Local community—changing people's consciousness

3. Teachers—additional burden

4.3. *Jukugi* demonstration; categorizing ideas using sticky notes, October 12, 2010.

Meanwhile, an experienced director was very helpful in the categorization process. Actually, he was asked by Mr. Endo to comment on each category, so he did, noting first that it is important for teachers to go into the local community. Participating in local events is something people naturally expect of teachers. He emphasized, "There are no easy ways to make changes." Second, what we should keep in mind is establishing networks with local people so that they know about efforts to build up a community school; and third, the teachers' burden can be avoided if teachers share information and collaborate in their work. During his comments, other directors were silent, and some took notes.

As a fourth step in the process, under some pressure, the directors were asked to present solutions by using blue notes. Mr. Endo asked the participants to make their notes specific and feasible, based on their own experiences. This solution-seeking process took twenty minutes.

Notes on solutions:

- Local people need to train teachers (since teachers move a lot).
- Local people should explain what community schools are to the teachers.
- Schools need to give full information to the local community about what they want to do and what they achieve.
- It is important for teachers to look at their schools from the outside.
- Teachers need to study community-oriented social education.
- Teachers should participate in community development in a more active manner.
- It is important to have a coordinator between the school and the local community.
- It is possible to have retired teachers as advisors for the school council.

The short discussion emphasized that dynamic interaction between the school and the local community would benefit both of them.

Five minutes before the end, a presenter had to be selected from the director participants. Nobody volunteered for the role, so Mr. Endo nominated the one female participant in the group. She was asked to

The New Public Commons 93

4.4. *Jukugi* demonstration—a concluding poster, October 12, 2010.

report the discussion results to other conference participants. In reviewing the discussion, one director proposed as a key solution that the school councils should introduce the *jukugi* process to their discussion. It would be the only way the council members would actively participate in the discussion needed to identify solutions. This idea was picked up by Mr. Endo as a major solution. Further, another director pointed out that experienced researchers would be helpful for activating the discussion at the school councils. In so doing, the quality of council members could be improved in some manner. This was another solution.

As the fifth and final stage, the groups reassembled, and each group was given five minutes for presenting the group's discussion results; this presentation was repeated five times. The abovementioned two solutions were reported by the female director from the group A. A primary recommendation from each group was to bring the *jukugi* technique, which they had just experienced, to real problem-solving activities at school. Most agreed that doing so would be the best way to solve the difficulties they faced. Meanwhile, nobody asked questions, nor did the conference organizers ask any questions of the participants. Apparently, the crucial intention for which the Education Ministry scheduled this *jukugi* discussion was so that the participating directors could take their *jukugi* experience as a knowledge generation model to their hometowns and reproduce the same *jukugi* space across the country. The participants were expected to play the role of facilitator in their discussions, imitating Mr. Endo. One *jukugi* participant told me that what the Education Ministry did was indeed provide a *jukugi* template for enhancing discussion on education policy making at the local level, and he mentioned to me his intension to use it in real discussions. In so doing, the discussion template would be distributed in a very effective manner to the countryside through the power of the local education board. The same kinds of *jukugi* participants, or I would say "knowledge-constructing" subjects, are going to be produced and reproduced nationwide, and ultimately, they are expected to support the New Public Commons as active participants. Meanwhile, the series of presentations was never attempting to generate only one solution as a wrap-up. All opinions were respected, no single opinion was denied, and actually, they confirmed that there were no definite answers in their discussions.

New Public Commons as a New Growth Strategy

Interestingly, in the political discourse at the time, the expansion of the ratio of public participation in the New Public Commons was located in the context of a new growth strategy, which was decided by the Kan administration in June 2010 (Cabinet Office 2010a). Since the Japanese economy had been persistently sluggish over the past two decades, the strategy aimed to achieve a strong economy by boosting new demands through insights gathered from the private, nonstate sector. In terms of numbers, the target economic growth was real Gross Domestic Product (GDP) growth of 2 percent, on average, in real terms (taking inflation into account) by 2020. More specifically, the government strategy project consisted of eight fields: environment, healthcare, energy, tourism, local community revitalization, science/technology, employment/human resources, and finance. The New Public Commons was especially promoted in employment and human resources, and the policy document claimed that 50 percent of Japanese citizens would eventually be involved with the development of the New Public Commons through some kind of civil society organization such as an NPO, as opposed to the current 26 percent (Cabinet Office 2009). Further, the government was considering systems to support small nonprofit corporate entities to make it easier for them to operate, while taking into account the consistency of overall systems (New Public Commons Roundtable 2010b, 3). In fact, the New Public Commons policy mentioned that the government would need to design a tax system so that ordinary citizens could benefit; it also would need to review the financial system that supports nonprofit entities, where the active operation of entrepreneurial minds would be inevitable (Cabinet Office 2009). In July 2011, the Japanese government introduced a new tax system: a new tax credit status can be given to NPOs. The new tax incentive would give tax credits of 40 percent of the national income tax and 10 percent of local income tax.[12] NPOs—the likely key actors in the New Public Commons—should benefit from such a reduction and other favorable treatment.

The new growth strategy, which placed great confidence in the neoliberal governance, emphasized the principle of markets as well as the shifting of the role of public administration to private sectors. Since the 1980s, Japan has, through a host of means, been following the example of Anglo-Saxon countries in introducing neoliberal reforms that seek to blur the original distinction between the public and private sectors. According to deputy education minister Suzuki, who strongly advocates the New Public Commons as well as *jukugi*, Japan now promotes a community solution, which means that the concerned parties jointly take the initiative to resolve problems by transferring the role of public administration from a "leave it to the government as well as the market" mentality to themselves and getting positively involved (Suzuki 2010, 10). Under the New Public Commons, the government is indeed trying to make the field of public social services, which has been monopolized by administrative agencies, open to NPOs, placing importance on the citizens' active involvement in public services (New Public Commons Roundtable 2010b, 6).

Under such neoliberal circumstances, as Carol Greenhouse mentions in her work, "it [neoliberalism] is reconfiguring people's relationships to each other, their sense of membership in a public, and the conditions of their self-knowledge" (Greenhouse 2010, 2). The New Public Commons is a vehicle for reforming relationships with citizens and other sectors involved in operations of national and local government. Here, an important neoliberal premise is that "knowledge-constructing" subjects, like the *bunka borantia* and *jukugi* participants, are self-directed individuals. The Japanese neoliberal state needs such disciplinary "knowledge-constructing" subjects, who are armed with the new knowledge or civic knowledge, to maintain its new rationality of governance: the New Public Commons. In so doing, the state intends to manage what I call "governmental risk," as introduced in chapter 1. Through the interactions between the "knowledge-constructing" subjects and the state, knowledge, which is discursively defined as legitimate, forms the basis for the operation of a neoliberal government. Ultimately, the "knowledge-constructing" subjects are becoming an integral part of the solid consolidation of the neoliberalism that has replaced welfare statehood, thereby celebrating the virtues of self-responsibility and self-managed risk. They are becoming independent, entrepreneurial selves who construct the necessary knowledge for positively participating in the society and strategically surviving the neoliberal politics.

It has been mostly argued that, in a historical institutionalism framework, the Japanese state in the post–World War II era has been an "activist state" (Pharr 2003), successfully institutionalizing only specific kinds of civic-sector groups that significantly support a national ideology. Japan civil society specialists have documented that the Japanese state plays a significant role in molding its civil society (cf. Schwartz and Pharr 2003; Pekkanen 2006; Ogawa 2009a; Haddad 2010; Avenell 2010a). The current emergence of the *bunka borantia* described in this chapter can be situated within this conventional "activist state" argument, since their activities contribute significantly to the neoliberal political administration through their collaborative engagement toward the formulation of a state discourse concerning the New Public Commons. The Japanese state has helped to generate the entrepreneurial self through the nation's lifelong learning strategy, and it has developed "new human resources in a bid to promote their participation in accessible social activities" (New Public Commons Roundtable 2010b, 5). While solidifying their activities at the grassroots level, the *bunka borantia*, armed with their newly acquired civic knowledge, could prove to be solid partners with the government. While also locating *jukugi* in the "activist state" argument, I would claim that *jukugi*, a nationwide phenomenon, generates a certain kind of disciplinary subject who can contribute exclusively to producing positive solutions for changing society in an effective manner under the New Public Commons ideology.

The New Public Commons, supported by "knowledge-constructing" subjects like the *bunka borantia* and *jukugi* participants, creates new dynamisms of ideas, roles, and money in Japanese society (cf. Yorimoto and Kohara 2011; Okuno and Kurita 2010). One mayor who introduced the *bunka borantia* in citizens' public halls told me that working with such volunteers would be a good chance to bring about a change in rigid public administration and pointed out that public officials are nowadays expected to serve as coordinators for such citizen activities. In addition, a career bureaucrat in charge of facilitating *bunka borantia* or culture volunteer issues at the national level interestingly pointed out that the state's promotion of the New Public Commons ultimately helps the civil society sector raise money for public purposes; it aims to change the way in which money is circulated in society when Japanese governments at various levels try to tighten their budgets.[13] Meanwhile, when I was revising this manuscript in winter 2013, I realized that the New Public Commons was still an active policy, even though the LDP came back into power after the December 2012 election, replacing the DPJ. In fact, the policy making related to the New Public Commons was very active at the local level; prefectural governments were pushing the policy forward through funding NPOs, which were greatly contributing to the formation of the New Public Commons. Concerned, independent citizens, or "knowledge-constructing" subjects, who are armed with civic knowledge, firmly and flexibly lead the ongoing neoliberal societal restructuring, while challenging the existing systems, and they have increasingly become the center of the New Public Commons as the new growth strategy.

5

The Japanese "Community School"

Revival of Communication

On children and youth

- Over the years, communication among members of nuclear families has considerably decreased.
- Children even tend to eat alone.
- In recent years, children have often been taught that they must not speak to adult strangers.
- Children refrain from becoming personally involved with others because they are afraid of being hurt in the process.
- How quickly one receives email responses is thought of as a measure of the depth of a friendship.
- Some parents demand too much from their children's schools.
- Some children cannot communicate with other children from different age groups.
- In the past, we would often hear spontaneous greetings from students when we visited a school; however, in recent years, we no longer hear such greetings.
- Moreover, students do not even greet each other. (Suginami Board of Social Education 2009, 4)

This list comes from a report by the board members of social education in Suginami, a ward in the western Tokyo district. The report, titled *Yaritori no fukkatsu* (Revival of Communication) highlights several realities that Japanese children now face. The board members consider communication to be a key to resolving such critical situations. The members think that enhancing communication would contribute to the generation of the New Public Commons—a sociopolitical imagery currently promoted by the ruling DPJ government. As mentioned earlier in this book, the new public space can serve as a foundation for solidarity, which, in turn, can enable conscientious citizens to improve society while functioning in a sphere in which people in general, or those interested in a specific cause, can voluntarily participate (New Public Commons Roundtable 2010a).

The board members attribute the phenomenon mentioned above primarily to the collapse of local communities (Suginami Board of Social Education 2009, 4). In a local community, people from different generations and backgrounds mingle, and because of this, the report claims, the local community plays a particularly significant role in socializing children. Socialization is the process through which people emulate the way of life within their society. Several decades earlier, perhaps until the 1970s, when Japan was working toward a prosperous economy, children played a lot within their neighborhoods; they greeted their neighbors, were guided and instructed by the adults as necessary, and were even scolded by their neighbors. Indeed, a certain local space existed where children and adults interacted dynamically. In fact, children were nurtured in their communities. This process of socialization was what I experienced as I grew up. The local community was a key agent of socialization, along with the family, school, peers, and so on. Such socialization is supported by the rationale that through participation in the community, young people can generate bonding, bridging, and vertical social capital that can help to build more socially cohesive communities (cf. Kisby 2009). Young people need to belong somewhere in their society; there is a strong desire to form and maintain enduring positive interpersonal attachments (Baumeister and Leary 1996).

Today, such local communities are facing the risk of collapse in Japanese society. The traditional community, which has been based on a dense human network, has now evolved into mostly nuclear families, who are connected by much looser social ties. The members of the Suginami Board of Social Education point out the following additional concerns about the local communities they have observed:

On local communities

- Our community has lost its mom-and-pop shops. The number of convenience stores has increased, and these stores interact with customers only according to rules in service manuals.
- We adults do not even greet each other in our neighborhoods; we hesitate to relate to others.
- The opportunities for gatherings within the community, such as those for seasonal festivals, have decreased; we no longer have occasions to come together.
- Some adults were never scolded or reprimanded during their childhood. Hence, they are unable to scold or reprimand their children or others.
- Some adults focus only on being happy in their individual lives. They are not interested in making the effort to help others achieve things.
- Public manners have deteriorated; in fact, we hardly care about others in a public space. (Suginami Board of Social Education 2009, 5)

Hiroi Yoshinori (2009), an expert on public welfare, argues in his bestselling book *Revisiting Communities* (roughly translated) that after World War II, the Japanese people created a solid human relationality on the basis of communities, including local neighborhoods, families, and companies. These communities were the foundation of their everyday lives. However, over the past couple of decades, such relationality among human beings has gradually disappeared. Moreover, local communities have collapsed owing to the increasing socioeconomic divide, nowadays popularly termed *kakusa*, among the Japanese population. Meanwhile, individuals are becoming isolated from one another. Hence, Japanese society needs to create a new type of community to nurture independent individuals so they can more easily survive in this difficult and complicated contemporary world. How can the local community be reconstructed as a "device of socialization" (*shakai ka no sōchi*) (Suginami Board of Social Education 2009, 3)?

This chapter demonstrates how Japanese society is making an effort to rebuild its local communities through the institutionalization of the "community school" system. Community schools have been initiated since the early 2000s; their number has gradually increased at the grassroots level across the country. These schools have been functioning as centers for community solutions (cf. Kaneko 2002; Imamura et al. 2010), which means that the concerned parties jointly take the initiative to resolve problems in their communities. Therefore, local public schools are considered the centers of community reconstruction. Furthermore, the placing of schools at the center of local communities is a conscious move to integrate formal school education and nonformal, community-oriented social education—the cornerstone of Japan's new lifelong learning in the 2000s. En route to institutionalizing the community school at the grassroots level, the revival of communication between children and adults is crucial. It requires a process whereby adults try to incorporate children socially into the local communities.

The Japanese "Community School" System

Shortly after World War II, the United States brought the idea of the "community school" to Japan in a move to democratize teaching and develop student-centered schools (Sato 2010). Certainly, such a school system stressed the importance of learning within the local community. The schools served as both a teaching institution and a center of community life, mobilizing local resources. However, the movement gradually lost momentum because parents began worrying about the falling academic levels of their children. Japanese economic development required standardized subjects who could work efficiently. Therefore, formal school education concentrated on the production of such subjects in a school-oriented meritocracy. Such community schools did not necessarily connect with the local communities. In addition, after the late 1970s, as Japan achieved a higher level of economic development, serious demoralization began to seep into the schools, including bullying, classroom disruption, and increasing juvenile delinquency. Under these circumstances, the partnership between schools and families began to draw more attention. Teachers and parents realized that partnerships limited to schools and families would not be effective; therefore, local communities came to be included in this bilateral collaboration. This addition was also encouraged by the emergence of volunteer activities in Japanese society following the Hanshin earthquake in 1995 in Kobe, where disaster-relief volunteers played a significant role in redeveloping communities. Consequently, the

Japanese people started becoming more conscious of their own communities. In the meantime, the concept of "communities" became the basis for hope in policy improvement (Okumoto 2008). Okumoto pointed out that positioning communities as key to the national education policy should be an explicit part of official documents, particularly after the second half of the 1990s.

In the early 2000s, half a century after the idea of community schools first entered Japanese society, the idea was reintroduced. Kaneko Ikuyo, a professor at Keio University, and Suzuki Kan, the deputy education minister of Japan in 2010 and Kaneko's former colleague, published a book on community schools (Kaneko et al. 2000). Modeled on the United Kingdom's system of a board of governors as an administrative structure for the school, a community school was introduced primarily as a new educational institution that would enhance the involvement of parents as well as of local communities in school management. One of the important messages conveyed in the book was that the rigidity of the existing hierarchical school system had stifled the pursuit of creative and diverse educational goals. The Education Ministry sits atop the current education structure, with prefectural and municipal boards of education at the next tier and local schools at the bottom. In contrast, under the community school system, self-governing community schools organized by local community members would have considerable authority over school management issues, including teacher appointments and budget decisions, through discussions with community members.

In December 2000, the community school concept was first proposed at the National Commission on Educational Reform (*kyōiku kaikaku kokumin kaigi*), an advisory body to the Prime Minister; Kaneko was a member of the Commission. The panel was established in March 2000 under the administration of Prime Minister Obuchi Keizo, and the final report was submitted to his successor, Mori Yoshiro, as a set of recommendations on educational reform. In the final report, the community school was declared "a new school for the new age" (National Commission on Educational Reform 2000). It introduces the new school system as follows:

> Parents hope that their children feel safe going to school. For this [goal], schools must not lead an isolated existence. They must exist together with the parents and local communities. Whether or not a school becomes a good one depends on its community. It is necessary to have the viewpoint that

the community creates the school, and the school creates the community.

Promote the establishment of new types of schools (such as "a community school").

Diverse educational opportunities should be provided to make it possible to establish new types of schools. Japanese educational communities need to be revitalized by promoting new challenges and attracting entrepreneur-minded people into school education.

Proposal

Based on the unique need in each community, the possibility of establishing new types of public schools ("a community school") by cities, towns, or villages should be studied. In such schools, communities should take part in school management. In this system, cities, towns, or villages will recruit school principals, examine suggestions made by supporters, and establish schools. School principals will appoint school management teams and manage schools, possessing the right to employ teachers. School management and operational results will be regularly examined by community school councils, set up at each school by the cities, towns, or villages. (National Commission on Educational Reform 2000)[1]

Within four years, in 2004, the first of such schools was introduced into the Japanese formal school system. These schools are officially called "community schools" in Japanese (as the English words are directly used as the official name; some call them *chiiki shien gakkō* using Japanese). As of April 1, 2010, the year when I conducted fieldwork for this book, there were 629 community schools across the country, mostly elementary and junior high schools; there were 36 kindergartens, 428 elementary schools, 157 junior high schools, 3 high schools, and 5 schools for the disabled (MEXT 2010c), and the number was expected to increase annually.

In my neighborhood, Suginami in Tokyo, as of April 1, 2010, 14 schools (8 elementary and 6 junior high schools) were registered as community schools from among a total of 66 schools (43 elementary and 23 junior high). The number of community schools has been annually increasing in the ward; in 2011, 2 more (an elementary and a junior high school) were added. Typically, each community school has a council (*gakkō un'ei kyōgikai*), a group that tackles important issues. The school council plays the following four major roles: (1) approving the management appointed by the principal, (2) presenting opinions on the management to the principal as well as the local board of education, (3) presenting opinions on teacher appointments, and (4) evaluating school management and disclosing information to parents.

In 2005, one of my neighborhood junior high schools (the equivalent of grades 7 to 9 in the United States) registered as a community school; a year later, it reopened as a community school. Located in a popular residential area along the Kandagawa River, the school had about three hundred students and nine classes (three classes for each grade). A community school project, designated by the local board of education, usually has a four-year term, and the school had entered its second term. In the fall of 2010, eleven people were involved in the school council. The council was headed by a senior researcher of a think tank specializing in education policy in Tokyo. Since this community school was the first of its kind in the municipality, the researcher, a man in his fifties, was directly appointed by the municipality's board of education in 2005 to help with this community school project. The remaining ten local people's profiles are given below.

- Two women (one in her sixties and the other in her forties) from the local committee of youth guidance workers (*seishōnen shidō iin*) were appointed. The elder of the two women was invited to be the deputy chair of the governing body. The children of the younger woman were then students at this junior high school. Both women had originally been active in their neighborhood associations and were local youth committee members. The younger woman was also the coach of the girls' basketball team at the school.
- The local sports club organizer, who was a graduate of the school and was then in his early seventies, was also invited. The sports club was one of the oldest of its kind in Japan and is considered to be one of the most successful local sports clubs. Because the sports club used the school grounds and gymnasium, it provided the students with opportunities to play sports with the local residents.

- Two women from the PTA were appointed; one was the current chair, while the other had held the post previously, and both were in their forties.
- A local mom-and-pop shop owner, who was in his sixties and who was a graduate of the school, was involved.
- Another graduate from the school was in his sixties; he was a friend of the local sports club organizer.
- A local YMCA member, who was in his sixties and a friend of the mom-and-pop shop owner, was also invited.
- Two college professors living in the local community were appointed.

In addition, seven teachers supported the operations of the school council. These included the principal, two vice-principals, and four regular teachers. The teachers were assigned to supervise the school affairs, academic curriculum, career guidance, and administrative matters.

The school principal assumed the overall responsibility for selecting the council members. The ten members were each paid six thousand yen (fifty-eight dollars) per monthly council meeting attended. The money was funded by the local board of education. In September 2010, two of the ten council members resigned from their posts for reasons due to their age. In January 2011, the posts were advertised on the school website as well as at the municipal board of education. The requirements were that applicants should live, work, or study in Suginami and that they should be older than twenty. In the application form, applicants were asked to fill out their activity experiences in the local community, including those with PTAs, youth guidance workers, welfare commissioners (*minsei iin*), and volunteer probation officers (*hogoshi*). In addition, the applicants were required to submit an eight-hundred-word essay expressing their views on the relationship between local communities and school management. On the basis of the essay and the interviews, in March 2011, the school council selected the two new members from the candidates that were short-listed by the school principal. The new members had rich local experiences; one was a mom-and-pop shop owner, and the other was a retired elementary school principal living in the local community.

Ikiru Chikara (Zest for Living)

My neighborhood junior high school council usually held its monthly meeting on the last Thursday of the month at 4:00 p.m. The meetings were held at the school library and were open to the local public; no advance registration was required. The discussion records are available on the school website. The meeting, always facilitated by the head of the council, lasted for a couple of hours. Interestingly, the discussion always commenced with somebody from the local community saying, "Today I received a really good greeting from our students as I came in through the school gate. That was pretty nice." Somebody would then respond, "Yes, I also received very cheerful greetings. I was happy to receive them, too." In fact, a major ongoing topic of discussion at the school council was how to enhance communication between adults and children in the local community, as well as the ways in which adults could facilitate such communication. The discussion reminded me of the "Revival of Communication" report (Suginami Board of Social Education 2009), which recommends intentionally setting up places to create direct interactions between adults and children. Joint efforts would be made by developing links among schools, families, and communities. In other words, people from the local community would come into the school, and the students would go into the local community. Several efforts have been made to arrange such activities (see also Sato 2008; Kainose 2010). For example, local people can volunteer to teach science or English classes, or they can have lunch with the students and converse with them. The students and local people can attend short lifesaving-training courses together. In addition, the students can regularly participate in cleaning activities in their community, as organized by the local neighborhood associations. They can also gain internship experiences in locally owned shops. Local residents can join the students on school excursions. Here, my argument is that the underlying philosophy of these joint efforts by the community could contribute to an educational ideology represented as *ikiru chikara* (zest for living), which ultimately translates into the ability to survive in the contemporary world. That is also one major component of the state-sponsored "comprehensive knowledge" for which I argued in chapter 3.

Ikiru chikara is a keyword used in the current (recently revised) teaching guideline (*gakushū shidō yōryō*) from the Education Ministry (MEXT 2009b). The term itself was originally introduced in 1996 in a policy proposal by the Central Council for Education:

> We believe the most relevant thing for children, however much our society has changed, is to acquire the ability to solve problems independently, to learn and think by themselves, to judge the value of situations, and to act. Further, by establishing a disciplined mind, children need to cooperate

with others and take care of others. We believe that these are the important factors for the development of well-rounded children. Of course, it is also important to have a sound and healthy body. We term these abilities *ikiru chikara*—the ability to survive in this dynamic and changing contemporary world. These abilities should be well balanced and nurtured. (Central Council for Education 1996, section 1, chapter 3)

The term *ikiru chikara* is already more than a decade old. The concept mentioned above was actually embodied in the teaching guideline previously announced in 2002. This guideline expressed an intention to develop this ability through an integrated studies program (*sōgōteki na gakushū*), which was designed to increase teacher autonomy and augment student interest in learning (cf. Bjork 2009; Cave 2009). The implementation of this program was part of the controversial *yutori* (low-pressure) pedagogic policy. However, the current teaching guideline (MEXT 2009b), which is actually titled *Ikiru chikara*, pushes the concept to the fore.

I found a small fifteen-page booklet on the new teaching guideline in the application packet for the public elementary school in which I tried to enroll my six-year-old daughter. The booklet (MEXT 2010d) seemed to be prepared specifically for applicants' parents. Looking over the booklet, I realized that the term *ikiru chikara* was used repeatedly, and I found two very interesting developments. One was a 10 percent increase in the number of class hours compared to the previous guideline. This change stemmed primarily from Japan's performance on the 2003 OECD-sponsored academic test (Takayama 2008), or the Program for International Student Assessment (PISA), where from 2000 to 2003, Japan fell from first to sixth place in mathematical literacy and from eighth to fourteenth place in reading literacy. Second, and more interestingly, the enhancement of communication abilities was presented as the highest priority over all school subjects. It was not limited to the Japanese language. Guidelines were established for each subject that were aimed at developing abilities that would lead to the proper expression and accurate comprehension of subject matters.

Japanese language:

The subject aims to develop the ability of students to document and report what they experience. Students are expected to present their experiences properly and to document them in a detailed manner by using the knowledge that stems from actual experiences.

Social studies:

The subject aims to develop the ability of students to read documents and interpret social issues. Students are expected to explain what they understand, and furthermore, to exchange their thoughts with fellow students.

Mathematics:

The subject aims to develop the ability of students to think rationally by using language, numbers, numerical formulas, figures, tables, and graphs. Students are expected to prepare the reasoning and to explain it to their fellow students.

Science:

The subject aims to develop the ability of students to explain everyday phenomena by using scientific words. Students are expected to develop hypotheses, conduct observations and experiments, and analyze the results.

Fine arts:

The subject aims to develop the ability of students to express their impressions about art works properly and to criticize and comment on each other's work. (MEXT 2010d, 8)

Apparently, there is an intense focus on communication across all the subjects. Enhancing such communication abilities could be considered a key component of *ikiru chikara*. Communication is an inevitable skill, wherein one properly presents oneself to the society in which one is a member. By enhancing communication abilities, each student is ultimately expected to make serious efforts to become an independently learning subject who actively participates in his or her society. In fact, such abilities lead to the enhancing of self-directed learning activities, which enrich life's quality at any stage. This indicates that Japanese schools function as a primary space to support self-achievement and to generate networks for individual learning. Japanese schools are no longer a place where students primarily pursue the knowledge and skills to support economic development.

In the "Revival of Communication" report, under the new teaching guideline, the role of the local people is to offer "logistical support" to their schools (Suginami Board of Social Education 2009, 9). In other words, the role of the community is to create a coordination system that makes such teaching and learning possible and to mobilize local resources—such as people, information, and locations. The report claims that "[e]ducation is not completed only at school. The ultimate purpose of education is to nurture the members of society and to generate such education; cooperation from outside the school is necessary" (ibid., 9). Opening up the school to the local community means that the dynamism of communication can start between children and local adults. The children will then have a number of opportunities to be directly involved or conversant with local adults, not merely their parents and teachers. They are expected to become involved with others by using the communication techniques that they learn daily in class. Generating these experiences through the initiatives taken by local adults is one of the most effective ways of reviving communication; it could also reconstruct solid local communities. Throughout these processes, the children are socially included in the local community.

Integrating School Education and Social Education

The recent emergence of the community school system can be directly attributed to the policy proposal by the national councils on education policy making in the late 1980s and 1990s, which emphasized the generation of strong links between schools and local communities (see chapter 2). Furthermore, the Lifelong Learning Council (1996) began using the term *gakusha yūgō* (literally, "integration of school and society") and implying that the Council was actively trying to integrate formal school education and nonformal social education, which was the cornerstone of Japan's new lifelong learning. In fact, the institutionalization of the community school in the Japanese public education system in the 2000s can be located in the intersection of school education and social education (see appendix 1).

When the Fundamental Law of Education, Japan's educational charter, was revised in 2006, one newly added article defined the significance of traditional social education in all Japanese education:

Article 12: Social Education

(1) The national and local governments shall encourage education to be carried out in society, in response to the demands of individuals and the community as a whole.

(2) The national and local governments shall endeavor to promote social education by establishing libraries, museums, citizens' public halls; and other social education facilities; opening the usage of school facilities; and providing opportunities to learn, relevant information, and other appropriate means.

Indeed, as briefly mentioned in chapter 2, Japanese social education faded in the 1980s; more individual-based, leisure-oriented lifelong learning offered at private culture centers gained momentum. However, the current refocus on social education reflects a solid grassroots demand for galvanizing the local community through grassroots learning activities— the original purpose of state-sponsored social education. Furthermore, article 13 of the revised charter mentions the generation of collaborative efforts by various stakeholders to support schools.

Article 13: Partnership and Cooperation among Schools, Families, and Local Residents

Schools, families, local residents, and other relevant persons shall be aware of their respective roles and responsibilities regarding education, and shall endeavor to develop partnership and cooperation.

Following article 13, the Education Ministry launched the School Support Community Headquarters (*gakkō shien chiiki honbu*) in 2008, a project aiming to generate a formal link between schools, families, and communities for jointly raising children in the local community. The Education Ministry's Lifelong Learning Policy Bureau took a strong initiative in this project, juxtaposing it to the community school system led by the Elementary and Secondary Education Bureau (*shotō chūtō kyōiku kyoku*). As of May 2010, 2,528 Japanese schools across the country had become part of this project (MEXT 2010e).[2] In my neighborhood in Suginami, all the elementary and junior high schools have school support communities that mobilize volunteers from the local communities. A parent volunteer told me that positive synergy was being generated between the schools and the communities. The synergy created a new dynamism of human network in the local community. Since 2009, furthermore, the Social Education Division of the Lifelong Learning Policy Bureau has implemented another policy supporting children—the provision of after-school activities (*hōkago kodomo puran*) at local schools—with 9,280 schools participating in the national project as of April 1, 2010 (ibid.).

Once again, by mobilizing the local people as volunteers, the policy is aimed at enhancing educational abilities in the local community. In tandem with these policy efforts, the Social Education Law was revised in 2008, and social education officers in each municipality, if requested, now advise schools about their links with social education and local communities.

In the fall of 2010, these policy moves culminated in the creation of a New Public Commons type of school—with an initial budget of 200 million yen ($1.9 million) (MEXT 2010f). The Japanese DPJ government now advocates a New Public Commons under which not only the government but also citizens, NPOs, private businesses, and other parties play an active role in providing daily social services in a spirit of mutual assistance, as I argued in chapter 4. In the budget policy proposal devised by the Education Ministry, a New Public Commons school is described as "a location where all children acquire *ikiru chikara* when collaborating with local communities" and as "a location that galvanizes local communities" (ibid.) Interestingly, the budget proposal clearly defines local communities as not only traditional territory-based communities but also as all parties concerned with local children, including residents, students, universities, lifelong learning facilities (i.e., libraries, museums, etc.), local shops and industries, neighborhood associations, NPOs, and local governments. All these parties are expected to be involved with the operations of the local school.

The key rationale here is that this type of New Public Commons school would provide both adult learning and community solutions. In general, the local adults would be involved with the local children's growth. *Ikiru chikara* would be generated for children through their communication with the local adults. Similarly, for the adults, such involvement with the children at local schools would also lead to their own learning. The local schools would be a place of learning for adults such as teachers, parents, and local residents. In fact, teaching is learning. Local volunteers would be expected to participate in teaching as assistants to regular teachers in classrooms and after-school clubs, and they could also be guest teachers if they have specialized in particular fields. Their learning would be generated through their teaching preparations and reflections after teaching. The local school is also expected to play a significant role in adult education. Ultimately, such local collaborations would revitalize the school as a center of community solutions, contributing to the generation of the New Public Commons. In fact, a motivation to better the local school could lead to a motivation to better the local community. Various stakeholders in the community are expected to gather at the local school and to reconstruct their community by sincerely playing their own roles.

I also want to add one observation from my fieldwork: one of the key phrases I often heard from my informants and interviewees was *kodomo wo man'nakani oku* (putting children at the center [of all community activities]). In actuality, this concept coincided with the refocused movement of social education in the national education policy making of Japan in the 2000s. Japanese social education originally targeted adults. However, since people have been worrying about the collapse of the traditional local community, Japan's social education is now re-engineered toward "putting children at the center." Obviously, the current emergence of the community school presents a major paradigm shift in the Japanese school system. On this point, Sato (2003) argues that school education and social education should be well integrated for the sound development of children, claiming that these two types of education should not be separated but presented together as one educational theory and practice. Hence, these two types of education—in other words, formal, school-based education and nonformal, community-based social education—are interlinked.

A Varied Landscape

The Japanese community school is still in its early stages. In fact, only 629 schools have been registered as community schools (as of April 1, 2010), six years after such schools were introduced. When I was completing this book in August 2014, I confirmed that the number reached 1,919 (as of April 2014), more than triple the level five years earlier (MEXT 2014); there were 94 kindergartens, 1,240 elementary schools, 565 junior high schools, 10 high schools, and 10 schools for the disabled. However, more than 30,000 schools (elementary and junior high schools) exist across the country, and some might say that the development is very limited. Further, the community schools are concentrated only in some regions, including Kyoto, Okayama, Tokyo, and Yokohama. They are not yet a national phenomenon, and a comprehensive evaluation of the new school system has yet to be disclosed. Meanwhile, the teachers are struggling to adjust to the new system, and one teacher confided in me saying that his work, which is mostly administrative, has almost doubled since his transfer to a community school.

I was in Hirosaki, a rural part of Aomori Prefecture in which social education is firmly rooted within the local population, for part of my multisite fieldwork. I inquired of my informant about the idea of a community school. She told me that it would not be necessary to introduce the community school system in her municipality because everyone already took it for granted that all the local schools were community schools. She said, "For a long time, we have been placing our schools within the local communities. Our schools were originally community schools." This point was confirmed during my fieldwork in eastern Tokyo where I have worked during the past decade. "Kawazoe," a pseudonym used in my ethnography (Ogawa 2009a), is an old district in Tokyo that people call *shitamachi*. Owing to the dense human network in the local community, I never actually heard the people mention the phrase "community schools." Instead, the local schools were always at the center of their daily lives, and the local people have been active in different educational projects as volunteers. The schools were already open to the community and the people. Thus, the areas where the idea of community schools has been discussed and successfully introduced might be limited mostly to those where there had been a remarkable collapse of the community and school education.

One of the practical justifications behind why local adults choose community schools is that the students' academic standards are raised. According to the results of the recent national academic achievement test (National Institute for Education Policy Research 2009), students' average scores were higher when local volunteers were involved in educational activities through a form of community school. In fact, such students' academic scores were more than five points higher than the national average. Interestingly enough, I observed that the test results were propagated when the Education Ministry sponsored a national conference on community schools in mid-September 2010 in Yoyogi, Tokyo. The conference targeted the general public, mostly including groups of parents who were considering the establishment of community schools in their local communities. I should also mention another reason behind the active promotion of community schools: Japanese schools have been suffering from student violence. The total number of cases hit a record high of 60,913 cases in fiscal year 2009 (April 2009–March 2010); the cases of physical violence targeting teachers and fellow students amounted to 44,309 cases, and the violence appeared mostly in junior high schools (43,715 cases) (MEXT 2010g). These numbers demonstrate that Japanese schools can no longer be managed only by teachers; they need help from the outside or from local adults, providing yet another honest excuse for the introduction of community schools.

The Suginami neighborhood is a nice residential area in Tokyo. The average scores of the local schools in academic standard tests are always among the top ranks in Tokyo's twenty-three wards. However, even this community might be collapsing. A neighbor told me that she hesitated to send messages to her neighbors via the notice circulation board (*kairanban*), a communication tool often used in Japanese neighborhood associations, because she did not know her neighbors. I myself have experienced the same hesitation. Further, there was a big divide among the children—some attended elite private junior high schools and others, regular public schools. Considering this reality, many local elementary schools were designated as community schools, and the local schools gradually gained momentum. After graduating from elementary school, however, many children who went to private junior high schools lost the solid connection with local adults that they had experienced in elementary school. Sadly, the social inclusion project, sponsored jointly by the state and the local community, has not been completed.

Community schools are probably a good development, and the number is likely to expand across the country in the near future. By introducing a neoliberal market principle or shifting the control of schools from the government to local communities in public education, these communities can now explore mutual assistance under the New Public Commons ideology. Reflecting the ideology, the "community school" is likely to become a major form of Japanese schools. In fact, the findings of one survey showed that Japanese people believe their local schools to be the most significant component of the local community and the center of any community activities (Hiroi 2008). Indeed, public schools are equally distributed across Japan, and such schools can gather all the social resources required for reconstructing local communities. The establishment of the "community school" can be located as a policy action that manages the risks of governance or what I call "governmental risk" for the state. By studying at such schools, which are deeply rooted in the local community, children will learn how to survive in this difficult and complicated neoliberal world through their communication with local adults, and the local community will once again be a key "device of socialization."

Thus far over the last three chapters, I have documented accounts on what I call "governmental risk." In the next two chapters, I will discuss the other risk: socioeconomic risk, primarily employing Beck's notion of individualization. I document two cases: vocational training for nurturing social entrepreneurs and competency-based career education programs for students, both of which are new and important parts of lifelong learning. My ethnographic accounts will demonstrate the ways in which socially vulnerable people, such as men of less education with limited skills and young students, are strongly encouraged to acquire new knowledge and skills and to produce their own "biographies" while coping with enhanced anxiety and insecurity in contemporary society. Their learning is a risk-hedging activity, which directly responds to the new employment style informed by neoliberal markets.

6

Becoming a Social Entrepreneur

Why Don't You Initiate a New Style of Working?

In a persistently sluggish economy, lack of employment is a major social problem. However, even in this type of economy, some people leave their jobs because their employment fails to provide meaning. Often, some people feel they are not doing exactly the kind of work they would like to do. We seek to help these kinds of people find worthwhile jobs within social enterprises that aim to contribute exclusively to the local community and economy. Why don't you consider working in these types of social enterprises as social entrepreneurs?

Social enterprises are considered the third sector after the government and commercial businesses. This course is funded by the Ministry of Health, Labor, and Welfare. It explores the potential for social enterprises to create a new job market in the local community.

This great opportunity will allow you to contribute to your local community by using your accumulated knowledge and skills. If you are interested in participating in this course, please contact Hello Work.

—2010 public job placement office recruiting poster

"Hello Work" is a public job placement office (*kōkyō shokugyō anteijo*).[1] The above quote appeared on a recruiting poster advertising a vocational training course (see the recruitment flyer shown in photograph 6.1). This course targets the increasing number of unemployed individuals who are

6.1. Recruiting poster for the vocational training course to nurture social entrepreneurs who support the New Public Commons, provided by the Aomori NPO Center.

trapped in the persistently sluggish Japanese economy. This vocational training course is intended to nurture social entrepreneurs who will support the New Public Commons, a policy discourse currently advocated by the DPJ government. This training course, which was funded by the national government, was established in the summer of 2010.

The vision of the "New Public Commons," which I discussed in chapter 4 as a neoliberal social restructuring process, was originally presented by the New Public Commons Roundtable, held in June 2010 during Premier Hatoyama Yukio's administration. This policy discourse, which aims to establish a vibrant civil society in which people support one another, is based on the following definition:

> The "New Public Commons" comprises venues of cooperation established by and among stakeholders who hope to create a society filled with mutual support and vibrancy. In this way, individuals, citizen groups, local organizations, businesses, and governments can work together to achieve social benefits for the community and to improve economic benefits by increasing productivity. The cooperative efforts of Roundtable participants to establish the rules and roles required for the creation of this type of platform resulted in the creation of the "New Public Commons." (New Public Commons Roundtable 2010a, 5)[2]

The document further states: "This is not a new idea. In fact, the concept of a "public commons" has long thrived in Japanese communities, although this concept is in danger of becoming a thing of the past. Therefore, the concept has been revised and adapted to accommodate present circumstances with the goal of rebuilding the bonds among people and communities" (ibid., 1).[3] I argue that this policy discourse calls for individuals to obtain special knowledge and skills through training. Japanese society must produce individuals who will exclusively work as social entrepreneurs to support this public sphere. These individuals would be expected to engage in social activities and to prioritize the creation of social, rather than economic, returns (ibid., 4). In tandem with the New Public Commons promotion, announced in spring 2010, the Ministry of Health, Labor, and Welfare began funding special vocational training courses with the goal of producing social entrepreneurs who would support the New Public Commons. I observed the very first course, which was managed by a local NPO support center located in the rural Aomori Prefecture on the northernmost tip of the main Japanese island. Later that year, similar courses were introduced in other prefectures, including Niigata, Chiba, and Aichi.

In this chapter, I discuss emerging trends in vocational training in contemporary Japan, referring to what I call "socioeconomic risk" in chapter 1. Vocational training has been a key component in the lifelong learning activities that help individuals gain the knowledge and skills required to adapt to the demands of the labor market. Traditionally, the Japanese government has funded and organized vocational training programs. Meanwhile, the recent DPJ government has attempted to address unemployment among middle-aged and elderly workers by encouraging them to retrain as social entrepreneurs who will contribute to the New Public Commons—a sociopolitical imagery promoted by the DPJ government—while supporting themselves economically. Between May 2010 and April 2011, I regularly attended the newly created vocational training course held in Aomori. Based on a combination of ethnographic findings and policy-document analyses performed at various levels, my primary research interest was to explore the experiences and feelings of course participants and organizers in the new vocational training courses that were designed to support the New Public Commons. In particular, I examined the grassroots interactions of the macropolicy discourse on the New Public Commons (cf. Shore and Wright 1997; Goodman 2002; Shore et al. 2011). A major finding of my research reveals that, in reality, ordinary people and, primarily, the socially vulnerable unemployed were encouraged to enroll in these training courses. They have been asked to "voluntarily take risks" (Lyng 1990, 2004) by becoming social entrepreneurs. These risks are disproportionately experienced by social groups consisting of less-educated individuals and individuals who possess poor and/or outdated skills. Indeed, risk taking is a central proposition of late modernity, a term that refers to a particularly advanced phase of the modernization process that is characterized by unpredictability and rapid flux (Giddens 1991). The neoliberal paradigm requires individuals to become more entrepreneurial, celebrating the virtues of self-responsibility and self-managed risk. This paradigm continues to attack the welfare-state model, because its costs are considered too high. In addition, the prevalence of excessive security set against risk can lead to the suppression of individual entrepreneurship and responsibility (O'Malley 2004).

Here, I first provide an overview of Japan's traditional vocational training programs. Then, I argue that, from a vocational training perspective, the current policy measures implemented by the DPJ government failed to address the problem of unemployment following the economic crisis that developed from the collapse of Lehman Brothers in 2008. The remaining sections present an ethnographic account of the new vocational training courses that was designed to help individuals establish social enterprises supporting the New Public Commons. Social enterprise, which originally emerged in Europe, is relatively new in Japan. The DPJ government has been introducing this concept as a means to revitalize society. However, this chapter argues that ordinary people are being asked to assume the "socioeconomic risk" when they become social entrepreneurs. I demonstrate this using narratives collected during my observations of the first course provided for the new vocational training program.

Vocational Training in Japan

Traditionally, Japanese vocational training was provided by employers when lifetime employment was widespread and when workers were employed in the same companies for their entire careers, until they reached the mandatory retirement age of sixty (Miura et al. 1992). Employers were generally convinced that vocational training yielded good returns, because their workers made long-term commitments to their companies. In addition, improvements in workers' abilities were expected to provide further development for companies. However, this practice does not work as well nowadays, because lifetime employment is becoming somewhat obsolete. As mentioned earlier, more than one-third of all Japanese workers became part of the flexible or nonregular workforce (MHLW 2011). Meanwhile, public entities have played significant roles in the provision of vocational training. Since 1958, the Vocational Training Law (*shokugyō kunren hō*) has supported citizens' efforts to develop the knowledge and skills required for new jobs.[4] The business owners of small- and medium-sized companies who cannot afford vocational training costs take advantage of public training opportunities. These opportunities are also open to others, such as new graduates, the employed, the unemployed, and the disabled. Public vocational training facilities—which are jointly supported by the government at various levels and by what is currently known as the Employment and Human Resources Development Organization of Japan (*koyō nōryoku kaihatsu kikō*)—have been in use since the 1960s.[5] Ten polytechnic colleges (*shokugyō nōryoku kaihatsu daigakkō*) and one polytechnic junior college (*shokugyō nōryoku kaihatsu tanki daigakkō*) have been established.[6] Programs are primarily focused on courses related to electrical and mechanical engineering and architecture. These colleges offer several two-to-five-day courses, or sixty hours, of lectures and on-the-job training (OJT). These short-term courses are provided to employees who work at small- and medium-sized companies in order to help them acquire advanced knowledge and skills that are applicable to their current jobs. Moreover, the colleges offer courses to newly graduated students and the unemployed. Similar training is also provided at local vocational training centers (*shokugyō nōryoku kaihatsu sokushin sentā*), which are popularly referred to as "polytech centers" in the local prefectures. As of November 2010, sixty-two polytech centers had been established across the country. A man who runs a family-oriented steel factory and enrolls his employees in the program informed me that this training opportunity is very important to small businesses similar to his own, because employees can learn state-of-the-art techniques. The business owners pay tuition for their employees. However, the tuition costs are relatively cheap compared to the costs for employers to provide the training themselves. According to the available statistics, there are forty-two thousand workers employed in small- and medium-sized companies across the country who participated in public training programs in fiscal year 2009 (April 2009–March 2010). Of those participants, 98.3 percent expressed satisfaction with the courses (Employment and Human Resources Development Organization of Japan 2010). The Japan Vocational Ability Development Association (*chuō shokugyō nōryoku kaihatsu kyōkai*), which is affiliated with the Ministry of Health, Labor, and Welfare, also provides similar vocational training programs and career guidance.

In addition to the provision of training courses for employees who work in small- and medium-sized companies, the current public vocational training courses also target the unemployed. Both local polytechnic colleges and local vocational training centers offer free short-term (primarily six-month) training courses aimed at developing vocational abilities. They also provide consultations focused on career development for attendees. The courses held at these centers primarily include basic engineering, IT, and accounting. For example, the polytech center located in Saitama Prefecture, near Tokyo, offered twenty-four courses in basic engineering between April 2010 and March 2011. The center continuously offers courses aimed at developing different skills. Courses last six months, if they are held daily (9:20 a.m.–3:30 p.m.). On average, two new engineering courses are introduced every month. Approximately 450 participants are trained and retrained during the year. Simultaneously, two courses, focused on computers and accounting, are taught every three months at two local, specialized training colleges (*senmon gakkō*) that have been entrusted with developing the program. Course participants are expected to pass qualification exams offered by the Japan Chamber of Commerce and Industry (*Nihon shōkō kaigisho*). In total, 120 participants are expected to be retrained and to pass these exams during the year. A newspaper report on public vocational training stated that building maintenance was a popular course (*Yomiuri Shimbun*, September 17, 2009). The course provides the skills required for the maintenance and repair of air conditioners. It also offers the basic knowledge required by the qualification exam for boiler engineers. Another newspaper article highlighted the popularity of these types of courses by quoting a comment made by a forty-three-year-old man who had recently lost his job as a plumber (*Hokkaido Shimbun*, May 14, 2009): "I want to obtain some qualifications because I know that people who do not have any are the first target for layoffs in a bad economy. I was contemplating jobs related to elderly care. However, young people would be preferred for such jobs. Keeping my age in mind, I believe I can continue with a building-maintenance job for as long as I wish." In 2009, ninety-six thousand people attended courses offered by these types of public vocational training facilities; almost 70 percent of course participants obtained jobs within three months of completing training (Employment and Human Resources Development Organization of Japan 2010). In contrast, the national ratio of job offers to job seekers dipped to a record low of 0.42 in August 2009 (MHLW 2009), which indicated that only four out of ten people could be employed.

After the Lehman Shock

The collapse of Lehman Brothers in September 2008 plunged the global economy into a prolonged recession. The Japanese economy was no exception. In the summer of 2010, more than 3 million individuals were unemployed, and 17 million workers were left without full-time work. In fact, according to a Labor Ministry survey released in August 2010 (MHLW 2010b), 288,000 nonregular workers lost, or were expected to lose, their jobs between October 2008 and September 2010. At about the same time, in a presidential campaign speech provided at the western exit of Shinjuku Station in Tokyo, Prime Minister Kan Naoto promised his audience that his party (the DPJ) would make extensive efforts to remedy the grim economic situation by bolstering job security. One of his most impressive assurances was his strong intention to create jobs: "Employment comes first, second, and third [in the government's policy priorities] (*Ichi ni koyō, ni ni koyō, san ni koyō*)." I was one of the members of the crowd that gathered in the strong sunshine to hear Kan's public speech.

Between fall 2008 and fall 2010, the Japanese government compiled employment stimulus measures six times as part of its efforts to develop comprehensive fiscal stimulus packages. Unlike the former LDP administration, the national government no longer liberally spent money on public works or infrastructure projects because it was saddled with a mounting budgetary deficit. Rather than aiming for short-term effects, the new DPJ government has, with its various policy measures, focused on sustainable development of the Japanese economy and society. For example, the government's stimulus packages include billions of yen for the development of environmental measures, such as forest road improvements, the promotion of energy-saving home appliances, and investment in energy-efficient housing.

Within these stimulus packages, employment also serves as a key issue. Taxpayers' money, which amounts to 950 billion yen ($9.2 billion), has been used to create jobs and pay for human-resource training. In fact, the Japanese government has now begun to implement an active labor market policy. It intervenes in the labor market to help unemployed individuals find work. As an emergency job creation measure, the government eased requirements for companies in relation to the receipt of government subsidies to maintain employment. In other words, the government helps young people find jobs by providing financial incentives to companies that are able to offer employment. The program offered a maximum of 160,000 yen ($1,500), over three months, to companies for each employment trial completed in 2010 (MHLW 2010c). Meanwhile, the government urgently attempts to ensure stable employment for young people, especially new college graduates. The core of the support policy focuses on promoting employment in small- and medium-sized companies that lack human resources. By increasing the number of job counselors at universities and Hello Work job placement offices, the government hoped to raise awareness among college graduates about employment at firms that possess significant growth potential. It was hoped that this strategy would encourage the overall revitalization of the nation's industries. Furthermore, the government prepared an emergency fund for job creation in nine specific areas: elderly care, childcare, industrial innovation, tourism, the environment, agriculture and fisheries, education, information technology, and disaster relief. In addition to medical care, the elderly care, tourism, the environment, and agriculture sectors were considered to have growth potential. An economic analyst for *Asahi*, a major Japanese daily newspaper, stated that the injection of taxpayers' money into the nursing and daycare sectors alone could lead to the creation of innovative technologies or the development of ideas that would contribute to economic growth (*Asahi Shimbun*, September 9, 2010).

In the stimulus packages, the government's most distinctive and novel measure is the creation of a new demand for employment through the development of social enterprises, because conventional businesses are less likely to hire additional people without a significant improvement in economic outlook. Furthermore, social entrepreneurship currently plays a significant role in re-establishing the growth and generation of community stability, as well as the improvement of sustainability in rural regions where, as Matanle and Sato (2010) point out, citizens face an ongoing decline in populations and industries. Social enterprises (*shakai-teki kigyō*) can be simply defined as financially independent civic activities that maintain social aims ranging from voluntary activism to corporate social responsibility. The notion of a social enterprise first appeared in Italy in the late 1980s, a few years before it emerged in the United States (Defourny and Nyssens 2008; cf. Thompson and Doherty 2006). Currently, it has become a global phenomenon (Kerlin 2010). Defourny and Nyssens (2008) note that, in the United States, the term "social entrepreneur" has been emphasized by American philanthropic foundations and other organizations that support individuals who launch new activities dedicated to social missions. Meanwhile, in Europe, the emphasis has more frequently been placed on the collective nature of social enterprises, as well as on their associative or cooperative forms.

Social enterprises are relatively new in Japan. In all likelihood, more time will be required to identify what constitutes a typical Japanese social enterprise.[7] The current developments in response to the New Public Commons discourse appear to have generated a new trend: Japanese social enterprises that consist of collaborative projects between the government and civil society. In fact, historically, the Japanese state has played a significant role in molding civil society actors (cf. Schwartz and Pharr 2003). Thus, the expansion of Japanese social enterprises could be aligned with existing scholarships.

According to the Japanese Ministry of Economy, Trade, and Industry (METI), about eight thousand people are currently engaged in social enterprises in Japan. These businesses boasted an annual turnover of 240 billion yen ($2.3 billion), as of 2008 (METI 2008). The figure might appear small in comparison with the annual turnover of British social enterprises, which amounts to GBP 27 billion (about 5.2 trillion yen, $50 billion).[8] However, social enterprises are expected to become highly significant due to their ability to generate local employment, to support and revitalize local communities, and to contribute to economic growth. Hence, in the stimulus package released on December 8, 2009, the government funded an additional 7 billion yen ($68 million) to generate jobs in social enterprises in the 2009 fiscal year supplemental budget. Twelve proposals, primarily from NPOs, were selected from competitive funding applications. Each NPO received 3 million yen ($29,000) in start-up funds.[9]

The vocational training course I observed was developed as part of this policy effort. The Ministry of Health, Labor, and Welfare established a special fund, in the amount of 40 billion yen ($390 million), in the 2009 supplemental budget to develop specific vocational training programs in collaboration with the Japan Vocational Ability Development Association. Most of the vocational training programs were rather conventional. They emphasized the provision and improvement of knowledge and skills required to work in computers and accounting, as well as the skills needed to acquire jobs with growth potential, such as elderly care. For example, based on this funding, sixty-two such courses were scheduled for December 2010 at the vocational training center in Saitama Prefecture.[10] Meanwhile, money was also allocated for a special course designed to produce social entrepreneurs who would support the New Public Commons as part of the new initiative in the framework of vocational training courses. As the conventional job market continued to shrink, the unemployed began to explore new opportunities.

The Knowledge and Skills Required to Support the New Public Commons

One weekday morning in mid-September 2010, ten men were seated together for their 9:30 a.m. class. All wore grey business suits. The men were probably in their late forties or early fifties. They resembled tired *salarymen*. All of the men concentrated on the lecture and took notes. This took place during a vocational training course designed to support the New Public Commons. I was in the back row of the classroom. The course was held in a local NPO support center in Aomori Prefecture.

The ten men attended the course based on arrangements made by the local Hello Work job placement office. Thus, they had apparently recently lost their jobs. During the time they were on the job market, the last quarter of fiscal year 2009 (January–March 2010), the ratio of job offers to job seekers in Aomori Prefecture equaled 0.29, the second-lowest figure, after Okinawa Prefecture, among all the Japanese prefectures (MHLW 2010d). Therefore, only about one in four participants would obtain a job in the rural prefecture. At that time, the national ratio of job offers to job seekers equaled 0.45. However, these ten men were paid to enroll in this special vocational training course, which focused on nurturing social entrepreneurs. They would be paid an allowance of 120,000 yen ($1,100) per month if they attended 80 percent of the courses during a ten-month period (May 2010–March 2011).[11] Additionally, they could borrow 80,000 yen ($770) from the state per month. If their job hunting was successful after completing the course, they would only have to repay half of the debt. Furthermore, tuition was free. In the difficult labor-market situation, attending this training course was the only available choice that would enable them to get "income." Apparently, they would not have autonomously selected this opportunity. Yet, they had no other choice. The 200,000 yen ($1,870) they would receive was close to the average monthly salary in Aomori, which amounts to 222,400 yen ($2,100). The average monthly salary in Aomori was the lowest in Japan at that time (MHLW 2010d).[12]

According to demographic data released by the NPO secretary who organized the program, the average age of these ten men was forty-seven. The NPO support center had only two requirements when it recruited participants: the applicants were required to be on the job market, and they were required to live in the local prefecture. Originally, twenty positions were available, and sixteen people applied for the course. Of those sixteen, thirteen passed the interviews, and twelve, including one woman, registered for the course. After a month, one man left because he decided to take over his family business. The woman moved out of the prefecture when her husband received a job transfer.

The participants had previously worked at various jobs. The majority had been salaried employees. A few of the men definitely resembled managers. I also identified one taxi driver and one truck driver. One man stated that he was working in the *pachinko* (i.e., gambling) industry. These middle-aged men faced difficulties in finding jobs primarily because of their age. One of the men, who had applied for a position with an age limit of forty, stated, "I was even told by the job interviewer that I only had three months to go before turning forty." He had applied to three dozen companies during the past year. However, he was continually rejected, primarily because of his age. Furthermore, Mr. Sawada, one of the course organizers, told me that none of the younger participants had ever worked as regular employees. After graduation from school, they all worked at nonregular or temporary jobs. Nonregular workers were the underemployed; those pushed into a work style of casual labor.

These ten men were actually learning how to transform their work methods. Their classroom was called the "incubation room." Mr. Sawada stated:

> After the course finishes, we will follow up with those participants who intend to work for social enterprises such as NPOs. We will focus on those participants who hope to contribute exclusively to their local community. Thus, as social entrepreneurs, they need to gain and accumulate new knowledge and skills related to ways to establish and, more importantly, operate NPOs in their local community. . . . Even if they choose to work in regular, commercial-based businesses, we hope they will eventually collaborate with local NPOs.

The course included seven training agendas, considered the "basic knowledge and skills" required for involvement in civic activities with social aims. Participants were expected to gain knowledge, skills, or experience in the following areas:

1. Public interest activities and civil society;
2. Planning, project management, and fundraising;
3. The local prefecture, including local history, folk art and crafts, food, festivals, and traditional performing arts;
4. Social welfare, including the life of the disabled and the elderly;
5. Community development and primarily collaboration with the government and local businesses;
6. Use of the library as a source of information; and
7. Career consulting, business manners, and IT skills.

The total time allotted for lessons was 1,000 hours. This included 550 hours of lecture and 450 hours of OJT at local NPOs and the main prefectural library. Every weekday, from Monday through Friday, 9 a.m. to 5 p.m., participants attended class in the building that housed the local NPO support center, which was located in the central district of Aomori City. Local leaders, primarily NPO practitioners, were invited as lecturers and facilitators. Because some of the course participants lacked computer skills, the program even allotted time for classes in basic computer training.

The lecturer and facilitator of the course I attended was Mrs. Shimada, a retired civil servant in her early sixties. She was successful in her career development. She had always been the first woman to work in her assigned roles. In her last position, she served as head of the citizens' public hall in her municipality, a core public institution of lifelong learning activities in Japanese society. On the first day of the workshop, Mrs. Shimada lectured during five fifty-minute sessions. She primarily emphasized the importance of networking (*tsunagari*): "If you encounter someone you don't know, you have an opportunity to network, an opportunity to move ahead. . . . Even though the area you are assigned to work in is completely new, you need not worry. If you are connected to someone and that person is knowledgeable in this area, it would help you greatly. If the person does not have adequate knowledge, you could ask her if she knows someone else who does. This is how I myself have connected with people." Mrs. Shimada also pointed out that community development was not a solitary enterprise: "You need to be connected to as many people as possible. . . . One tip for success is to get the local government involved in your project. You can approach this from your side as a citizen. The government is definitely a resource for you. It has talented human resources and rich information. Why don't you use them to your advantage?"

On the second day, Mrs. Shimada began the workshop by asking, "What do you imagine needs to change to make your community more active? How do you aspire to make your community more fun?" Mrs. Shimada wrote the phrase, *Machi wo asobu* (Liven up the town), on the whiteboard. The ten men were divided into two groups of five (I later joined a group). The men were expected to create a presentation by the end of the day. Before beginning the group activity, Mrs. Shimada mentioned two important techniques to ensure smooth work: "First, respect others' opinions, and do not deny them, because we must respect our diversity; and second, do not explore others' histories because these histories have nothing to do with what we are doing today." The members of my group rearranged the tables and chairs to create a worktable for the discussion. They began brainstorming by writing their ideas on sticky notes. To create the presentation, they arranged the notes on a piece of paper. The presentation was entitled "Our Theme Is the Park." Each man contributed his aspirations for the Shin-Machi area (the location of the NPO center).

> Mr. Yamamoto, in his fifties: I want to open a farmers' market and buy lots of agricultural and fishery products from local farmers and fishermen.
> Mr. Mori, in his forties: Should we work jointly with the neighborhood association and organize a sports festival? It might be fun to use this city's main street for a one hundred-meter race.
> Mr. Suzuki, in his twenties: I want to open a shop and sell goods from Akihabara, Tokyo. This would be a unique shop. It could become the center of pop culture in this prefecture. It would be fun!
> Mr. Abe, in his forties: I would like to run a small zoo in this town. If children come, their parents will accompany them. A number of people will visit and spend money on this otherwise sluggish shopping street.
> Mr. Saito, in his sixties: Yes, I like the idea. It might create new jobs here, which is very important for this community. . . .

During the workshop, the participants were expected to present their aspirations or ideas, regardless of their feasibility. Participants then had to explain the reasoning behind these aspirations. Mrs. Shimada often reminded the groups that they needed to specify who could be mobilized for, and who would collaborate in, the achievement of these aspirations: "You will become the so-called 'key persons' or coordinators in your community. Think about the people in your community and discover those from whom you could seek help." Participants were constantly questioned about what they hoped their fellow members might achieve. They were also required to explain their reasoning.

It became clear that the goal of the workshop was for participants to gain new knowledge and skills that would enable them to work in the New Public Commons (discussed in chapter 4). In the past, the Japanese economic system has always been based on the idea of meritocracy. Japan has begun to shift away from a school-oriented meritocracy (which dominated after World War II) towards what Honda Yuki, an educational sociologist, calls a "hyper-meritocracy" (Honda 2005, 20–34). Meritocracy is a social system in which responsibilities are assigned to individuals based on their talents and abilities. Conventionally, meritocracy has been standardized into the basic abilities, acquired by individuals at school, that can be quantified through examinations for the purposes of comparison. Although this style has dominated Japan's modernization since the Meiji era, the quality of knowledge that is required in a postmodern society differs greatly. This new knowledge is not quantifiable; it includes diversity, novelty, creativity, strong motivation, and the ability to network and collaborate with different stakeholders. Contemporary society needs creative people who can spontaneously act with a complete sense of self-responsibility (Japan Federation of Economic Organizations 1996, 41–42). However, I noticed that the knowledge and skills of the workshop's participants, which were originally built under the school-oriented meritocracy, would be considered obsolete today. Due to the significant changes that have occurred in the labor market, the participants lost their jobs and were forced to retrain themselves. They had to acquire specific, and new, knowledge and skills that would help them address the challenges of this new world.

Becoming a Social Entrepreneur: A Challenging Opportunity

As previously indicated, the ten men who attended the training course were required to participate in OJT for about half the time. In early November, Mr. Koyanagi, secretary general of an NPO located in Hirosaki (the third major city in the prefecture), organized a ten-day OJT program for the ten participants. As part of my fieldwork, I met with Mr. Koyanagi to learn more about his NPO's background. Mr. Koyanagi's NPO was established in May 2005 and actively focuses on children and family issues within the community. Mr. Koyanagi's NPO has three missions: (1) childcare support, (2) community development, and (3) learning support. A total of 136 individuals, drawn primarily from the local community, are full members of the NPO. As of November 2010, 8 of these individuals were employed as paid staff members.

When questioned about the NPO's focus, Mr. Koyanagi simply stated, "We aim to reconstruct the local community by 'putting children at the center [of all community activities] (*kodomo wo man'nakani oku*). I believe this will lead to the solution of several of today's social problems." The NPO's brochure claims:

> Children, as well as their parents, have become isolated in recent years because people do not communicate well with one another. We are surrounded by enormous amounts of digitalized information. In addition, children are exposed to digital games. We feel it is necessary to create a place where children can physically experience social activities. The local people support this type of place. . . . The government also provides childcare support. However, it would be great if we could actively provide additional support for childcare on the citizens' level. This effort will benefit our children.

In 2009, the NPO opened a public space, the Toy Square, in the center of the community. This tiny, fourteen-square-meter, space was located on the first floor of an office building. Its development was part of an attempt to diminish the desolation of the city center. A number of "mom-and-pop" shops had closed, due to the aging of their managers. About 170 locally made wooden toys were collected so the town's children could play while their mothers interacted with one another. The space was also available to the elderly. Users were charged an entrance fee of one hundred yen (ninety cents) for each visit. Mr. Koyanagi explained: "We try to enhance the communication between children, adults and children, and adults and other adults. This sort of communication would enhance the childcare capabilities of the entire local community. We believe this, in turn, will enhance the elderly care capabilities of the local community. We directly address problems such as childcare, aging, and community renovation."

Since its establishment as a business entity, the NPO has based its efforts on two ideals. The first goal is to achieve financial independence. Mrs. Takano, a board member, told me: "One thing we can be proud of is that we never ask the government for money. . . . We collect money by ourselves, mostly through membership fees. We also write funding proposals to foundations and sell originally invented goods such as wooden toys." The second ideal is to create employment opportunities within the local community while solving social problems at the citizens' level. To operate this NPO, four staff members were hired (two full-time and two part-time) on a three-year contract. Their wages were covered

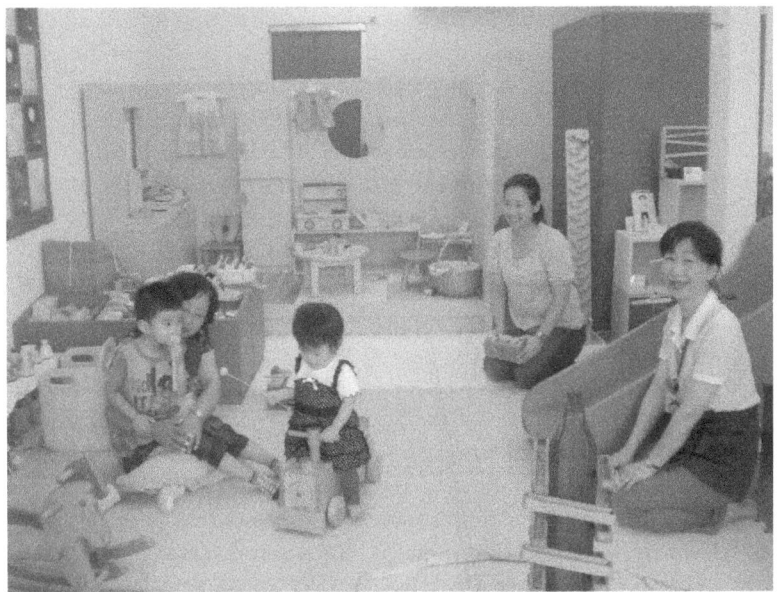

6.2. Local people gathering in Toy Square, August 2010.

by the state-sponsored emergency job creation program described earlier in this chapter. Mrs. Takano added, "We need to earn 50 million yen ($480,000) by ourselves so we can hire eight staff members. Currently, we have successfully earned this amount." Mr. Koyanagi also observed that "[we] should solve our problems . . . at the citizens' level, instead of solely depending on government solutions. Solving social problems is not necessarily a territory exclusively dominated by the government."

It became abundantly clear during the special vocational training course that the course focused on the promotion of social enterprises. This goal was mentioned repeatedly. The course organizers obviously believed that social entrepreneurship was the type of employment these ten men should engage in upon completing the course curriculum. Ideally, they would become social entrepreneurs in their own local communities. Mr. Sawada, one of the course organizers, explained the concept of social enterprises to the course participants:

> In Japan, social enterprises began to gain attention a decade ago, around the year 2000. . . . In the UK, interest in social enterprises has increased because the government and

NPOs have joined to promote the establishment of social enterprises. . . . Social enterprises are required because of the increase in diverse social problems, such as the acceleration of demographic aging, the collapse of the community, and because of changes in both work and lifestyles. It has become difficult for the government and conventional businesses to find solutions. We need people who can work together to discover new ways to solve these social problems. Social enterprises try to shed light on social problems that are not easy to solve. Furthermore, these social contributions will cause the development of new ways of working and will improve lifestyles.

Mr. Sawada cited a special report on social enterprises, provided by Japan's Ministry of Economy, Trade, and Industry (METI 2008). He listed the three main characteristics that a social enterprise should possess: sociality (*shakaisei*), business sense (*jigyōsei*), and innovativeness (*kakushinsei*). First, the business's primary purpose must be to solve social problems. Conventional, commercial-based businesses primarily aim to make profits. They change their business interests based on economic and social situations. However, social enterprises must maintain their business interests. In so doing, they can obtain support from various stakeholders. Second, good business sense is essential, because social enterprises contribute to society by providing goods and services in return for fees. Profits make the business sustainable. Third, social enterprises sell original goods and services to solve social problems. Therefore, innovativeness must be the driving force for changing our society.

Once the series of lectures on social enterprises was completed, the ten men began their OJT at Mr. Koyanagi's NPO. The program emphasized that the participants would learn all about the workings of the NPO as a social enterprise operating in the local community. This was important because the ten men possessed no practical experience working in NPOs. They possessed even less knowledge about how to establish NPOs. On the first day, Mr. Koyanagi asked the men to spend the entire morning observing the secretariat meeting, so they could gain a clearer idea of the NPO's exact nature. An informational session was held in the afternoon. On the second day, they were invited to see the wooden toys in Toy Square and to communicate with the visiting children and their mothers. On the following days, Mr. Koyanagi scheduled "fieldwork," consisting of visits to several local sites so that the participants could find inspiration for and discover hints about their future businesses. One day, they visited Kuroishi, which is in Aomori Prefecture. During this visit, a staff member of an NPO in Kuroishi described some interesting developments related to social enterprises in Kuroishi:

> In the late 1980s, the Japanese government under former Prime Minister Takeshita Noboru distributed 100 million yen ($970,000) to 3,081 Japanese municipalities. Kuroishi bought a pair of *kokeshi* dolls created from gold and silver. (A *kokeshi* is a type of Japanese doll that is usually made from wood.) Kuroishi is well known for producing these dolls. Around that time, the Japanese media often ran a story about 100-year-old twin sisters named Kin and Gin, which translates to mean "gold and silver." Taking advantage of the sisters' popularity, the city used grant funding to build a new museum for the gold and silver *kokeshi*. The goal was to attract tourists. This idea looked successful at first. However, the tourists never returned and local tourism gradually lost its momentum. Two decades later, the city sold the pair of *kokeshi* to a businessman in an auction. Today, however, the city has regained its momentum for two reasons. Several local volunteer-based NPOs similar to us have played significant roles in the community's redevelopment. A decade ago, we thought our neighborhood's *Komise-dōri* would attract tourists. The 300-meter-long shopping street retains its currently-unspoiled Edo period state. A number of small stores, literally translated as *komise*, stand in a row along the street. Old Japanese-style houses stand in eye-catching rows along with old wood shops and sake breweries. Further, the city is nowadays experiencing a nationwide boom in *B-kyū gurume* (B-grade gourmet), which is cheap and delicious comfort food served home-style. Kuroishi's original "soup yakisoba" (stir-fried noodles dipped in a soy sauce-based soup) has gained popularity in the annual national B-grade gourmet festival. These two projects were planned deliberately. Their success is the result of our serious efforts to collaborate with the local government.

The staff member's explanation of ways to galvanize the local community, in which he emphasized that the local people themselves must be actively involved, provided just one example of the many excellent opportunities through which the ten men could learn real-life stories of social enterprise activities during their OJT.

However, the participants looked bored during the presentation. More specifically, it appeared that they did not understand what the staff member was saying. Only a few of them took notes. None of them asked questions. Mr. Koyanagi and Mrs. Takano shared this impression. Mrs. Takano expressed her anxiety about the men's lack of a strong drive to learn. She noted that she had been observing this behavior since the secretariat meeting: "On the OJT, being a passive listener can be frustrating. These men are expected to become social entrepreneurs in the future, right? Being a social entrepreneur is not an easy task. Honestly speaking, I was even wondering what they would actually want to do as social entrepreneurs. Why are they taking this special vocational training course? I think the taxpayers' money could be used in other ways." Later, during a brainstorming session on social enterprises, one of the participants expressed his opinion about the program to his fellow group members:

> I know I am expected to learn about social enterprises, NPOs, etc. . . . all of this is completely new to me. I know I am expected to fully understand the organizational entity and become a social entrepreneur. During the past five months, I believe I have learned a lot. However, realistically speaking, I have no idea how to convert my ideas into money. I have to support my family. This course is going to end in four months. How will my family and I survive after this course ends? At this moment, I cannot envisage the future. I wish the course could be extended a little longer.

During the brainstorming session, this man expressed an interest in developing a business that would decrease youth unemployment in his local community. However, the idea was still too vague to be developed. Understandably, the man was overwhelmed by the reality that awaited him.

Taking Risks to Survive in the New Labor Market

"Taking a risk" (*risuku wo toru*) is a phrase I frequently heard during my fieldwork on Japan's lifelong learning. The use of this phrase was quite common when the focus was placed on vocational training. An important part of Beck's theory of a risk society involves individualization. This concept suggests that individuals must produce their own biographies in the absence of fixed and obligatory traditions (Beck and Beck-Gernsheim 2002). In fact, Beck refers to this type of biography as a "reflexive biography" (Beck 1992, 135) or a biography that is self-produced, rather than socially produced. Further, in today's world, a person is obliged to become individually engaged in the changing demands of various social institutions, such as the new labor market. Indeed, being a social entrepreneur is one of the most challenging endeavors a person can embark on, because it involves the individualization of risk. Social entrepreneurs must understand and manage risks. The inevitable setbacks must be overcome. As a result, the outcome is always expected to generate new value for customers, "whether it be financial, social, aesthetic, or environmental capital, or a combination of more than one" (Thompson and Doherty 2006, 361). Mr. Koyanagi, a social entrepreneur himself and the organizer of the course's OJT, stated:

> Social enterprises are necessary so that we can change our society. We could say "No" to the reality we face. Then, we could try to change it. This is our mission. However, this mission involves risks. The business might not be stable. The business might not always be successful. A strong possibility exists that things will not go well. Nonetheless, I want to challenge this by taking the risks involved in social entrepreneurship. . . . Our NPO has always been involved with a dynamic sense of innovation and social entrepreneurship. I believe this is the real thrill for social entrepreneurs.

A similarly brave discourse on risk was offered at a public conference on university education and youth unemployment, held in Tokyo in fall 2010. During the conference, one panelist asserted the necessity of risk taking by observing: "[C]urrent students always try to avoid risks. Risks should be personally managed. University education does not encompass ongoing changes. Taking risks is challenging, but it is also rewarding. Why don't you manage risks? What is required now is the preparation of an environment, including a safety net, to support people who take and manage risks." During a national conference for NPO practitioners in fall 2010, a panel was set up to discuss social enterprises. During the panel discussion, a successful Japanese social entrepreneur introduced the term "risk." His business imitated the British Big Issue, a program that offers homeless and vulnerably housed people the opportunity to earn legitimate incomes. When the audience asked this entrepreneur to define risk management, he replied: "Social enterprises always face risks. Risks surround us. However, rather than dwelling on risk avoidance, I think about what I can do and about what kinds of businesses I can develop with my limited resources. To manage risks, everything must be out in the open. We should always consider whether risks are unavoidable based on our missions." This panelist had been invited to the conference. In all likelihood, the audience members, who were primarily men and women in their late forties and early fifties, aimed to become social entrepreneurs. The audience members listened seriously to his comments.

One major limitation of this risk discourse is that not every individual can take risks all the time. Nor can all individuals efficiently manage risks. People such as Mr. Koyanagi will take risks and write their own biographies. Mr. Koyanagi has become sufficiently empowered to consider an NPO as an opportunity to achieve social entrepreneurship in which creativity and innovation are fundamental characteristics. The state expects the ten men who participated in the new vocational training course in Aomori to take and manage risks as social entrepreneurs because the state funded the course. Two decades ago, these middle-aged Japanese men operated in society's mainstream. They represented what Hidaka (2010) calls "Japanese hegemonic masculinity" in the post–World War II period. However, they landed in a socially vulnerable class that was located outside the majority because they lost their jobs due to corporate restructuring. During my observations of these ten men, it appeared that they had lost their confidence and self-esteem. They needed money to live and support their families. Rather than being asked to take risks, they required real vocational training that would help them secure jobs and earn money for living. Currently, they cannot afford to take any of the risks associated with establishing social enterprises.

In Japan, when people lose their jobs, the majority of them usually crash to the bottom of society. Yuasa Makoto, a social activist, describes this phenomenon as *suberidai shakai*, the "slide society" (Yuasa 2008). In marginalized local areas, such as Aomori Prefecture, employment opportunities are extremely limited because corporations are concentrated in metropolitan areas such as Tokyo. Fortunately, in Aomori, the family system remains solid. People can ask their family members for help. They will not become homeless, as often happens to people in Tokyo and Osaka. Young-Jun Lee, a local economist at Hirosaki University, has proposed a way of life, the Aomori Model, which allows people to pursue a more relaxed way of life because they are supported by their large families.[13] People living in rural Aomori can pursue lifestyles that differ from the lifestyles of people living in Tokyo. Thus, those who live in Aomori can survive in a dense human network. Most own their homes and are not required to pay rent. Most of the families maintain agricultural businesses. They do not require full salaries. They can share their work and, in so doing, expand employment opportunities in the local community. The ten men participating in the course may not slide to the very bottom of society, because they have the support of their families in rural Japan.

The Japanese government has injected billions of yen into efforts to nurture social entrepreneurs. The people trained in government-funded vocational training programs are expected to establish NPOs to support the New Public Commons for Japanese locals. However, the policy mistakes the means for the end, as Mrs. Takano noted during the OJT. Under the old system, people established social enterprises because they wished to improve the current situations in their community. In other words, people established their mission before searching for funding. However, under the government's current policy, which promotes the New Public Commons, funding (even funding for vocational training) is the first priority. The search for a mission follows.

In late November 2010, the government agreed, in its supplemental budget for fiscal 2010, to provide 8.8 billion yen ($85 million) over two years for nurturing social entrepreneurs. These funds were appropriated exclusively for supporting the New Public Commons. According to the project guidelines distributed by the Cabinet Office (2010b), the primary objective for this funding was the development of an environment that would encourage positive participation in the "public" realm. Individuals' participation should contribute to the efficient supply of public social services. Further, the guidelines stated that NPOs must finance their own operations and work independently of the government. Ultimately, they must generate employment in their local communities. In particular, the government considers the generation of jobs in fields such as elderly care to be one of the most urgent needs in a society that has a rapidly aging population. To obtain funding, NPOs must follow several guidelines. Mission setting, the most important factor in the establishment of social enterprises, would be influenced, more or less, by government-funded schemes. However, the mission-setting process should arise from grassroots efforts. It must be developed based on individual needs that are generated during everyday lives, rather than on mere policy discourse, such as the New Public Commons. In its acceptance of this large sum of money from the government, the Japanese civil society may risk its independence from state control. An NPO practitioner once honestly stated: "The government is entrusting many projects to NPOs or social enterprises that require the hiring of people under the New Public Commons framework. However, we are not prepared to accept these people. Why can't NPOs efficiently provide social services and replace the roles of governments that are more organized and talented than us?" The 1998 NPO Law was passed more than a decade ago. However, the social role of Japan's NPOs remains in its infancy. Rather than entrusting ordinary people to start risky social enterprises, the government should provide these individuals with solid, sustainable, and well-envisioned vocational training programs. Social entrepreneurship is indeed beneficial to Japanese society. Therefore, special training courses should become permanent projects, rather than time-limited projects.

In March 2011, the vocational training course held in Aomori ended. Of the ten participants, three found full-time, one-year contract jobs in a community revitalization project that the local government had entrusted to the NPO that developed the vocational training course. One man obtained a full-time food-delivery job that was unrelated to vocational training that supported the New Public Commons (he was actually hired during the middle of the course, and subsequently quit the course). Six failed to receive job offers upon graduation. Initially, they felt encouraged, but in reality, they were forced back into a dismal job market. However, in April, the NPO hired two of the men, because the government entrusted that NPO with two new community-development projects. Further, after a huge earthquake hit eastern Japan on March 11, 2011, two other men found jobs as coordinators for disaster-relief volunteers in the neighboring prefecture. Ultimately, the two remaining participants, one of whom was the youngest man in the cohort, failed to find jobs. This man informed me that he could not afford to take any risks. Therefore, he could not become a social entrepreneur at that moment, even though he was still in his early 30s. He stated: "Probably one of the most tangible benefits in this vocational training course was my ability to obtain a driver's license that permits me to transport disabled individuals. I believe this license will be useful in my job search because I can physically present the license card to my future employer." The job market remains tight. In the meantime, the unemployed are simply expected to thoroughly take advantage of public vocational training that enhances their employability by securing *tangible* benefits. This remains the only way to survive during this uncertain and unpredictable time.

Postscript

One and one-half years after the great earthquake, during the summer of 2012, I revisited Aomori. At that time, I was greatly interested in discovering the ways in which the new political discourse—the New Public Commons—was being interpreted and put into practice at the grassroots level. In particular, I was concerned about the future of the participants I had witnessed in the newly created vocational training courses that aimed to support the New Public Commons. I observed many course participants between 2010 and 2011. Their graduation ceremony was scheduled for March 15, 2011, and I had planned to attend. However, my flight to Japan was canceled because of the earthquake. This was disappointing, because I had wanted to follow up and confirm participants' plans after completing the course.

I traveled to a closed-down school, located in the countryside of Aomori, with Mr. Sawada and a local NPO practitioner. Mr. Sawada's NPO had begun a community redevelopment project in the closed school. The NPO organized an art exhibition. Riding in the car driven by Mr. Sawada, I saw Mr. Yamamoto, one of the participants in the vocational training course who had left midway through the course, when he was hired as a full-time food-delivery person. He was watering the athletic field in the bright sunshine. He looked very happy.

I ate vegetable curry rice for lunch with Mr. Sawada at a small restaurant attached to the former school. The restaurant was also operated by his NPO, as part of the community redevelopment project. I told Mr. Sawada, "I recall that the vocational training course for the New Public Commons had ten participants." I asked him, frankly, "Are you still in touch with any of them?" As I have documented earlier in this book, all of the participants were middle-aged men who possessed low levels of education and limited skills. Even though some had found jobs, those jobs were short-term and contract-based. Mr. Sawada responded, "Actually, I am in touch with only two: Mr. Yamamoto and Mr. Nakai." He continued, "We hired Mr. Nakai. He is now in charge of the administrative tasks at a local support center for the New Public Commons. We have been entrusted by Aomori Prefecture with the operation of the support center." He continued:

> That vocational training course continued for two years. It ended this past March (2012). However, honestly speaking, the second year did not turn out well. We came to realize that, among course participants, there were a certain number of people known as *watari,* people who continuously participated in different kinds of vocational training courses because they were unable to find jobs. They had no particular motivation for or knowledge about the New Public Commons or even about NPOs. Yet, they kept coming to us because they were paid if they attended the program. They came to our course because they had no other choices. They were almost forced to take the course by the officials at the local employment center. In this type of situation, it became quite difficult for us to continue the course.

He did not mention Mr. Yamamoto. A short time earlier, I was told a similar story by Mrs. Takano, an NPO practitioner who offered OJT training as part of the aforementioned vocational training course that promoted the New Public Commons. She told me:

> We declined the OJT opportunity for the second year. We were unsure of the participants' motivations. In fact, it was quite difficult to communicate with them. What they needed was to develop their basic communication skills, including how to listen, talk, and understand one another. Now, instead of focusing on this type of middle-aged men, we accepted several college students as interns. I believe their experiences at an NPO will contribute to their careers in the future.

As of April 2012, the national government has stopped funding the vocational training course aimed at promoting the New Public Commons. The course is no longer offered. Instead, the money was shifted to reconstruction efforts related to the great earthquake. During my fieldwork in the summer of 2012, I often heard the term *fukkō shien,* or reconstruction support (related to the great earthquake), rather than *atarashii kōkyō,* or the New Public Commons. During the past decade, at my other field site, SLG, an NPO that promotes lifelong learning in an eastern Tokyo community, has received less aid money from the local government for the promotion of lifelong learning than was originally expected. This was because the government had to spend more money on the construction of earthquake-resistant public school buildings in case another earthquake hits Japan. The art exhibition I mentioned earlier was also part of the reconstruction support efforts. The exhibition featured arts and crafts made by evacuees from Fukushima Prefecture.

After lunch, I had a chance to speak with Mr. Yamamoto. He recognized me and stated: "Well, I started a new job. It did not work out. I quit the job in February 2011 after spending four months there. Actually, I was consulting with the local employment office on the day of the earthquake. I am still looking for a job. I have asked Mr. Sawada for an employment opportunity with his NPO. However, I am not sure how that will go." Mr. Yamamoto was unemployed. He had participated in the community redevelopment project as an unpaid volunteer. I had the impression that Mr. Yamamoto was one of the most active men in the vocational training course I had observed. He seemed to absorb a lot of the new knowledge and skills related to NPOs, the community, civil society, and the New Public Commons. All of these facts were new to him. While listening to Mr. Yamamoto, I reflected on Mr. Sawada's comment. He had stated: "I think it would be ideal if they could work with us and use skills based on what they learned in the past or based on the new knowledge and skills they acquired in our course. Otherwise, I hope they can use what they have learned in the future, at some stage of their life."

7

New Knowledge for Youth

Suicide among Young People

On March 3, 2011, Japan's National Police Agency (*keisatsu chō*) released data containing the number of suicides that occurred during 2010. In one year, 31,690 Japanese people committed suicide, about 80 people each day (National Police Agency 2011). Shockingly, 424 of these 31,690 people stated that their failure to secure employment was their primary motive for committing suicide. In addition, 153 of these individuals were in their twenties. Of those young people, 46 were seniors at universities. The number of young people who committed suicide was twice the number of suicides that occurred in 2009. These numbers represent the tip of the iceberg; they only represent the published, "successful" suicides.

As Cox and Koo (2006, 6) point out, a relatively strong correlation exists between employment insecurity and suicide in Japanese society. They consider the urge to commit suicide to be a cultural psychology that regards job loss as a particularly heavy burden. This phenomenon casts a strong light on two aspects of Japanese society. First, Japanese people are more likely to interpret job loss as a personal failure, rather than considering it a normal event that can occur in an economic system. Second, Japanese people may feel more pessimistic about finding new employment in an economy that fails to engage in robust job creation. Between 1953 and 2003, each single percentage-point increase in the cyclical component of the male unemployment rate led to a 5.39-percentage-point increase in the cyclical component of the male suicide rate.[1] This effect is thirty-eight times larger for Japan than it is for the United States (see also Osawa et al. 2013).

Suicide is a major social problem in contemporary Japan. Over the past decade, the annual number of suicides has remained above thirty thousand. Ways of decreasing this number have become an item on the national emergency agenda. Prime Minister Kan Naoto of the DPJ advocated for the creation of "a society with the smallest amount of unhappiness" (*saishō fukō shakai*). In addition, the Japanese government established the Council on Comprehensive Measures to Prevent Suicide (*jisatsu sōgō taisaku kaigi*). The government has "set up every conceivable consultation window at various ministries" and has "been providing consultations to address the concerns of each individual with care at the closest point of interface" (Prime Minister Kan's Blog 2011). The Japanese government designated March as Suicide Prevention and Awareness Month (*jisatsu taisaku kyōka gekkan*), which coincides with the end of the school year.

The phenomenon of seniors who are enrolled at universities failing to acquire steady employment after graduation is not new to Japan, nor is it purely a Japanese phenomenon (Furlong and Cartmel 2007). Japanese society already produced its so-called "lost generation" (*rosugene sedai*) of youth during the "hiring Ice Age" (*shūshoku hyōgaki*), between the mid-1990s and the early 2000s, after the bubble economy collapsed (*Asahi Shimbun* 2007). In 2003, a survey revealed that only 55.0 percent of university graduates found employment immediately after graduation. This figure represents a record low (MEXT 2003). Today, these graduates continue to work in part-time, contract, and temporary positions. Further, Japan is at risk of developing its second lost generation of youth because the still-fragile economy is recovering from the worst recession in sixty years. The recession began in 2008, when Lehman Brothers filed for bankruptcy. Prior to his graduation in March 2010, an informant of mine applied to thirty-five firms, ranging from big manufacturing companies to start-up ventures. He failed to receive any offers of employment. In April, he decided to remain enrolled in a university and to continue searching for a job. This tactic is being employed by an increasing number of students in order to avoid becoming *freeters* (young Japanese workers trapped in unstable, low-paying jobs).

During my fieldwork, I learned that only 68.8 percent of the students who graduated from universities had acquired jobs by December 1, 2010, shortly before their graduation in March 2011. This was the lowest level recorded since 1996 (MHLW and MEXT 2011).[2] Japanese companies hire a massive number of new graduates every April. Often, they make employment offers one year prior to graduation. They provide opportunities for stable, career-track jobs. If students are unable to secure jobs prior to graduation, they will, in all likelihood, accept precarious employment or become part of the working poor (see Genda 2001; Inui 2003; Sato and Koizumi 2007; Kobayashi 2008; Obinger 2009). The development of Japan's first lost generation was primarily attributed to the neoliberal "structural changes" (*kōzō kaikaku*) that began to occur in the Japanese business industry in the mid-1990s. The Japan Federation of Employers' Associations (*Nikkeiren*), an influential Japanese business lobby, proposed a strategic human-resources policy to increase firm competitiveness (Japan Federation of Employers' Associations 1995). They advocated for the generation of a flexible workforce within the Japanese labor market that would allow firms to adjust labor costs at their convenience. This proposal suggested three types of employment status: (1) long-term employees who comprise an organization's core, (2) highly specialized professional employees hired on limited-term employment contracts, and (3) a flexible workforce to perform simple and routine work. About fifteen years later, this proposal was actually enacted. In 2010, 38.7 percent of workers—more than one-third of all Japanese workers (MHLW 2011)—became part of the flexible workforce. Another business lobby, the Japan Association of Corporate Executives (*Keizai dōyukai*), recently devised a new employment model based on three pillars. They suggested (1) increased job availability through job-content-based contracts entered into by firms and individuals, (2) enhanced employability based on the assumption that the labor market is fluid, and (3) firms' acceptance of a variety of working styles (Japan Association of Corporate Executives 2008, 17–18). Because Japan's traditional, company-based employment system is in a state of collapse, the business lobby has asserted that each individual must become an equal partner with his/her employer, taking responsibility for his/her choices from among several job options. Each individual must take responsibility for the consequences of those choices (ibid., 17; see also Takenaka and Nanbu 2010). The current neoliberal regimes indeed rely on self-governance, which allows individuals to accept additional responsibility for themselves by celebrating the virtues of self-responsibility.

Brinton (2008), whose research primarily focuses on graduates or dropouts from nonelite high schools, points out that Japanese students are insufficiently prepared to make the transition from school to workplace. Meanwhile, an article published in *Yomiuri Shimbun* (July 22, 2010), a Japanese national daily newspaper, criticized the roles played by Japanese schools at different levels, particularly with respect to the content of university education. The article stated that Japanese university education should place greater emphasis on enhancing students' employability by teaching the actual meaning of work and helping students decide which type of job they desire. University education must help students gain the skills and abilities required to perform their desired jobs. A report recently submitted to the education minister revealed that 31 percent of university freshmen have never thought about their future careers (Central Council for Education 2011, 14). This fact is quite concerning to the HR personnel working in Japanese firms. My informant, an HR manager of an electronics manufacturing company, related the following incident: during a job interview, an applicant for a system-engineer position stated that his part-time experience involved working at an *izakaya* (Japanese-style bar). The HR manager was unsure if the applicant had ever given serious thought to obtaining relevant job experience.

I have observed that Japanese students frequently encounter difficulties when they make the transition from the school environment to the work environment. In fact, these difficulties seem to be unrelated to whether students graduated from prestigious universities or nonelite high schools. The education in Japanese schools does not address ongoing social changes, particularly labor-market changes. Indeed, the Fundamental Law of Education failed to mention the term "vocation" (*shokugyō*) in its articles until it was revised in December 2006. However, over the past two decades, the Japanese education system has begun to consider the significance of vocational education (*shokugyō kyōiku*). I argue that, as employment styles change, the knowledge imparted to students by the Japanese education system must also change. New knowledge involves competency-based skills and experiences. It encourages youth to make active commitments to their own society. In discussing these forms of education, this chapter first highlights "career education,"[3] a course only recently introduced in Japanese schools at the elementary and secondary levels that aims to enhance students' employability by helping them acquire four key "basic and versatile competencies" (*kisoteki han'yōteki nōryoku*) (Central Council for Education 2011, 25–26). Second, this chapter demonstrates that universities have also attempted to offer new knowledge and skills aimed at helping students secure future employment. Furthermore, the chapter locates the recent development of career education in Japan within the European argument focusing on social exclusion. I argue that Japanese career education has been developed in the context of attempting to help young people manage the new risk or what I call "socioeconomic risk" in chapter 1, which has emerged as a negative result of the neoliberal economy. Finally, I argue that career education is an effective tool that can be used to promote the social inclusion of youth. It could also serve as a foundation for developing the citizenry of contemporary Japan.

"Career Education"

The term *kyaria kyōiku* (career education) first appeared in 1999, in a Japanese policy document submitted by the Central Council for Education to the Education Minister. Career education in Japan appears to be similar to "recurrent education," a concept disseminated by the OECD during the 1970s. It was a strategy for lifelong learning that stressed alternative and recurring sequences of education (Griffin 2009, 265). Meanwhile, the Japanese advisory body first used the term when it attempted to improve the connection between school and society, as well as between primary/secondary and higher education.

> A need has arisen to implement career education that will begin at the elementary school level, and continue in line with each stage of a child's development. This would help provide a smooth transition between school and society, and between different levels of schooling. . . . Families and local communities should work in partnership with schools to implement "career education." A focus should be placed on experience-based learning. (Central Council for Education 1999)

The authors created this report because they had witnessed the rapid increase in the number of *freeters* during the 1990s. The number has again increased over the past decade, reaching a record high of 2.17 million in 2003. Recent data has revealed that, in 2010, 1.83 million *freeters* were working in Japan (MHLW 2010e). The 1999 report highlighted the need for career education that would begin at an early stage of education. This would enable Japanese youth to identify their job interests and make the necessary preparations for their future careers. Further, career education should be focused on work ethics. The hope was that the program would whet students' appetites for work and stem the rising tide of despondent youth.

It is incorrect to assume that Japanese schools lacked any form of vocational training prior to these efforts. Since the 1960s, academic and career counseling (*shinro shidō*) has been provided to students. In particular, guidance is provided to students prior to their graduation during the junior and/or senior year of high school (cf. Miyazaki 2007, in particular 45–48). However, the counseling did not function well, due to the school-oriented meritocracy operating in Japan. Japanese firms expected students or job applicants to demonstrate strong trainability, which was primarily measured by students' success in competitive university entrance examinations. Firms believed that students' success in these examinations was proof of their balanced thinking, memory skills, and ability to manage tough situations, skills that are regarded as indispensable for surviving the difficult corporate world. Firms would hire new graduates who did not yet possess any professional skills. Firms would then train these new graduates, periodically moving staff among different departments and offering on-the-job training.

During the 2000s, career education became a key component in Japan's youth policy. In 2003, the Japanese government launched the Young People's Independence and Challenge Plan (*wakamono jiritsu chōsen puran*). The implementation of this policy was a joint effort by the Cabinet Office, in collaboration with the ministries of education, labor, and economy. This represented the first and most comprehensive youth policy scheme developed after World War II, strengthening the linkage between education and employment. The plan highlighted four priorities: supporting social independence, supporting youth who are particularly in need, adopting the view of youth as active members of society, and stimulating free and open discussions in society. For example, the Ministry of Health, Labor, and Welfare formulated youth policies that were focused on social security. In 2004, the Education Ministry began to actively promote career education by providing 140 million yen ($1.3 million) to fund it (National Institute for Education Policy Research 2011a, 4). It also organized two national forums to publicize the significance of career education. Over the next four years, it introduced the work experience program, first in junior high schools and then later in senior high schools. The program had a total budget of 1.1 billion yen ($10 million) (ibid.). According to a countrywide survey conducted by the National Institute for Education Policy Research, 94.5 percent of junior high schools and 71.1 percent of high schools implemented work experience programs in their school curricula (National Institute for Education Policy Research 2010).

This positive approach to career education received additional support when the Fundamental Law of Education was revised in December

2006. The revision included the phrase "Foster an attitude that values labor while emphasizing the connections between *vocation* and daily life" (emphasis added by the author) as one of the educational objectives (article 2 of the Fundamental Law of Education). Furthermore, the Basic Plan for the Promotion of Education (*kyōiku shinkō keikaku*), a ten-year plan created after this revision, clearly defined the role of career education: "We will promote career education that will begin at the elementary school level by building collaborative partnerships with governments at various levels and with private businesses, PTAs, and NPOs. The goal will be for children to establish solid views of work and society. In addition, career education will equip children with self-awareness related to their own future paths for careers and life" (MEXT 2008b, 18). To implement this plan in a more precise manner, the Central Council for Education established a special task force on career education at the behest of the Education Minister. The task force was asked to identify "the 'basic and versatile competencies' required for students to make smooth transitions from school to work" (MEXT 2008c), which would become the focus of the career education program. As Fujita (2011, 43–44) points out, this consultation represented a significant change in the Education Ministry's awareness of issues. The focus was limited to improving youth unemployment, a significant change from when career education was first introduced in 2004. The later effort included an investigation of the "full strategy of systematic career education."

In January 2011, the Central Council for Education submitted a final report on career education to the education minister (Central Council for Education 2011) that clearly defined the meaning of "career" in the following manner: "When an individual experiences several roles in his/her life, he/she attempts to discover the value of his/her own role and his/her relationship with others. The networks and accumulations of knowledge generated through these types of experiences would nowadays be considered a 'career'" (Central Council for Education 2011, 17). Unlike the previous definition, which emphasized work ethics, the new career education was strategic and comprehensive. The report emphasized the introduction of more practical vocational studies in secondary education (at junior high and high school levels). The report even proposed the creation of a new type of school that would specialize in providing practical vocational training during the later stages of secondary education (Central Council for Education 2011, 42–59). Moreover, the report recommended further promoting career education from early childhood (but not limited to elementary school or earlier) through higher education. It particularly focused on children's development of the fundamental abilities and attitudes that would lead to social and vocational independence. The Council defined four fundamental areas as the "basic and versatile competencies" (Central Council for Education 2011, 25–26):

1. Competency to build human relationships

   This competency is meant to help individuals understand different opinions. Based on their understanding of others' opinions, individuals are expected to communicate their own opinions. Furthermore, in addition to their complete understanding of their roles in society, individuals are expected to cooperate with others and to participate in and contribute to society in a positive manner.

2. Competency of self-understanding and self-management

   This competency is intended to help individuals identify what they can do, what they feel is important, and what they want to do. By developing mutual relationships with others in society, individuals are expected to act independently, based on their positive understanding of their future possibilities. They are also expected to control their thoughts and feelings and to continue to learn for their personal development.

3. Competency of problem solving

   This competency means that individuals can identify problems, analyze them, and solve them. Individuals are expected to develop their problem-solving abilities by following detailed, appropriate schedules.

4. Competency of career planning

   This competency is designed to help individuals understand the meaning of "working." Individuals are expected to identify "working" in the context of a complete understanding of their anticipated roles in society and their relationships with others. Individuals should spontaneously develop their own career paths by choosing appropriate information related to different ways of life.

The National Institute for Education Policy Research initially devised eight areas to be included in the career education program (National Institute for Education Policy Research 2002). These included self-understanding, communication, searching for information, job comprehension, grasping roles, project implementation, decision making, and problem solving. These eight components were refined to the four fundamental areas, as presented above. They have recently been renamed the "basic and versatile competencies."

When the Central Council for Education finalized the policy proposal in November 2010, I had the opportunity to interview Ms. Aoki, an independent female business consultant who taught career education in a rural area of Aomori Prefecture, Japan. Prior to that time, regular teaching staff (or subject teachers) taught career education in schools. However, because the Japanese government had begun to actively promote career education, some schools attempted to hire professional career consultants. Ms. Aoki had been hired by several local high schools as an adjunct teacher specializing in career education. When I asked her to describe the biggest obstacles facing young people, Ms. Aoki identified their limited communication skills. She said, "Each time, my first question to the students is, 'Tell me about yourselves.' However, they never describe themselves well." Meanwhile, I remember another occasion when the director of an NPO that supports youth job training in Osaka also cited students' limited communication skills. In October 2010, at a national forum on youth labor policy in Tokyo, the NPO director stated: "Honestly, I was surprised that they couldn't talk about themselves. Therefore, we first encourage them to write something about themselves. This can include "what I like," "what I have done up to now," and "what I want to do in the future." We believe writing to be an important step in the process of identity confirmation." Ms. Aoki's teaching materials included a handout titled "Self-comprehension or Who I Am." To help students complete the handout, she always proposes that they interview one another and talk about themselves in a frank manner. Ms. Aoki suggests that they answer questions such as "What do you like?" "What don't you like?" "What do you want to be?" and "What do you not want to be?" She stated: "What I like and what I don't like . . . I remember these were popular topics when I used to talk to my parents during my childhood. [I assumed she was in her late 40s.] Apparently, the students' inability to communicate can be attributed to their lack of communication with their family members."

Consequently, developing communication skills is one of the several major issues addressed in the career education program. According to a recent survey conducted by a Japanese business lobby (Japan Business Federation 2010), communication skills are the second-most important aspect emphasized by Japanese firms during the hiring process; the most important aspect is achieving independence. Interestingly, the ongoing career education program attempts to develop communication skills by building strong links with families, as well as with local communities (Central Council for Education 2011, 96–97). Families must consistently support a child's career development, foster his/her independent thinking and behavior, and sustain his/her motivation. Meanwhile, the local community was described as "a cradle of career development" by a guideline leaflet on career education that was distributed to local boards of education throughout the country (National Institute for Education Policy Research 2011b, 10). In fact, the local boards are expected to mobilize a number of local actors. According to the guidelines, children are expected to engage in interactions with their family members and with neighbors in their local communities prior to starting school. During primary school, children are expected to participate in events organized by their local communities. They are also expected to visit workplaces in order to learn about actual work. At the secondary school stage, children are expected to participate in work-experience opportunities and internship programs sponsored by local mom-and-pop shop owners, small business managers, NPO practitioners, and so on. In fact, local communities are becoming major providers of career education (Mimura 2010, 10). Schoolteachers often experience difficulties when providing instruction related to real-world vocations, because they possess limited knowledge. It would be ideal if teachers could collaborate with members of the local community who possess rich experiences to support youth development because there are practitioners and experts working in various areas of employment in each community. It is important for local people to commit to the career education programs developed by local schools. In addition to providing career education courses as regular school subjects, these efforts have primarily been embodied by the recently institutionalized efforts of "community schools" provided at the elementary and secondary levels. (I discussed this issue in depth in chapter 5.)

Changing Trends in Universities

Universities also play a significant role in the provision of new knowledge and skills that help students secure future employment. On July 22, 2010, the Science Council of Japan (*nihon gakujutsu kaigi*) published a report that addressed quality assurance in university education, based on each discipline (Science Council of Japan 2010).[4] The report answered the following questions: What do the bachelor's degrees offered by Japanese universities signify? What types of abilities should be guaranteed by bachelor's degrees earned at Japanese universities? (ibid., 1). The head of the Education Ministry Higher Education Bureau posed these questions in May 2008. The Council proposed that the following four specific components should be taught in Japanese universities: (1) knowledge and understanding (*chishiki, rikai*), (2) versatile competencies (*hanyōteki ginō*), (3) attitude and intentionality (*taido, shikōsei*), and (4) integrated learning experiences and imaginative thinking (*tōgotekina gakushū keiken, sōzōteki shikōryoku*) (ibid., 1). These components are currently referred to as *gakushiryoku* (standards for bachelor's degrees). The purpose of university studies is not solely for students to acquire certain types of knowledge; students should also gain the skills required to adapt themselves to society's actual requirements. Since the end of World War II, Japanese universities required students to take four years to complete their bachelor's degrees. They take courses in both general education (*kyōyō kyōiku*), during the first two years, and specialized education (*senmon kyōiku*), during the last two years. Nonetheless, one policy proposal (Central Council for Education 2008b) suggests that both general education and specialized education should enable students to develop a common knowledge bank. In other words, the content of the knowledge produced at Japanese universities should be standardized. *Gakushiryoku* should be recognized as an important part of this knowledge standardization (cf. Kusumi et al. 2011).

For over a decade, Japanese universities have faced major challenges amid intensified international competition directed at the development of a full-fledged knowledge-based society and aimed at the implementation of several reforms (see Goodman 2001, 2010; Poole 2003; Fuwa 2009; Burgess et al. 2010). In 2004, all of Japan's public universities were transformed into university corporations, which converted them into administrative bodies operating independently of the Education Ministry. This reform was intended to remove government control of public universities by introducing competition and flexibility. It provided universities with discretionary powers and employed the public management concept (Christensen 2011). Each university now works to build its autonomy. Each produces a midterm plan that details its educational and research activities over a six-year period. For this purpose, the National University Corporation Law (*kokuritsu daigaku hōjin hō*) was legislated in July 2003. The ongoing reform examines the content of university education and the knowledge it imparts to students. The focus was not specifically placed on the subjects taught. Rather, it was placed on learning outcomes. In fact, university education's content is changing; it is now trying to directly correspond to the dynamic social changes and difficulties faced by university graduates when they seek employment. With respect to total admission capacity, by 2007 universities in Japan admitted all of their applicants, because spaces outnumbered applications two years earlier than expected (Central Council for Education 2005). Japanese universities are no longer academic institutions aimed at nurturing elites.

In fall 2010, I attended two sessions of a public symposium that addressed the connection between university education and work. It was held in Yasuda Hall at the University of Tokyo. The symposium panelists included university professors, managers of human resource departments at Japanese firms, entrepreneurs, and popular critics. About one thousand people attended the symposium. Most attendees were middle-aged men. There were also a few women and students who attended. One graduating student from a private university in Tokyo was included among the symposium panelists. He offered the audience his honest opinion:

> With respect to the job-hunting process, I want to tell you that we university students are faced with three difficulties: increased stress, uncertainties, and anxiety. I spend lots of money on transportation to attend job interviews. I also sacrifice a substantial amount of my study time. We begin job hunting in the summer of the third year—one and one/half years prior to graduation. Often, we can't attend classes because we must prioritize our job searches. My university supports my job-hunting activities. They assist me when I encounter technical issues such as how to complete job applications. However, I find it very difficult to discover information that is *realistic* (emphasis added by the speaker).

In my opinion, his use of the term "realistic" demonstrates his annoyance with companies' expectations for students' work performance and their preparation prior to employment. Moreover, why should students be forced to engage in these types of tiresome job-hunting activities? Should they sacrifice their study time in the bargain? These years are probably some of the most precious years of their lives.

While listening to some of the discussions between panelists, I began to realize that university education in Japan does not address ongoing social changes. The knowledge provided to students should more directly connect with the real world. It should connect to the labor market in particular. This symposium was scheduled after the release of the Science Council of Japan's report, mentioned earlier in this section, on the quality assurance of university education, based on each discipline. Ironically, the symposium panelists never referred to the quality assurance of disciplines in their specialized education. The prime topics of discussion, to cite a key term, included the "basic attainments" (*kihonteki na soyō*) that should be pursued by all students. These basic attainments stress the methods that students should use to study subject matter and emphasize students' use of knowledge in real-life settings. These basic attainments also include students' development of communication skills. A panelist, who is employed as a professor at a nonelite university, stated: "I teach economics. However, when I think about my students' futures, I don't need to stick to macroeconomics, microeconomics, or whatever it is. Most of them will become salespersons after graduation. Therefore, instead of studying the traditional classifications of economics, it would be more relevant for my students to gain a basic knowledge of sales." On the other hand, a professor employed at an elite university stated: "What Ph.D. students are developing is "material" for thinking. What we aim for is to help them develop transferable or generic skills as professional researchers." In fact, as one panelist revealed, with respect to job hunting in Japan, students who earn doctoral degrees from prestigious universities are unable to secure jobs. The academic job market is indeed too tight. Further, Japanese firms prefer not to hire individuals who hold doctoral degrees because their areas of interest are too specific. Hence, these individuals lack the potential to be trained. Both types of students, who are positioned diametrically opposite one another on the education spectrum, are extremely anxious about the realities that they face.

The type of knowledge provided by universities can be changed. In fact, it is changing. A panelist employed by a local public university stated: "Some of my students try to establish social enterprises in their local communities. By bringing the university closer to the local community, we could revise our university mission. Universities need to be sustainable. For example, universities could collaborate with local NPOs. They could provide space for activities organized by NPOs. Ultimately, the knowledge imparted at universities is expected to contribute to students' activities." Another panelist, an entrepreneur, pointed out that universities must provide courses that reflect contemporary times. Students should not be required to attend courses if they can comprehend the course content solely by reading the required materials. In this case, it might be better to create additional active partnerships with the private sector, so students can gain a better understanding of the demands of the real world. Courses that are endowed by the business community would provide one way to open universities to society.

Toward Social Inclusion

This book represents my attempt to create an account of risk in Japan. I have observed Japan's new initiative, which focuses on lifelong learning within the context of the protection provision for people who risk social exclusion, which I briefly touched on in chapter 3. Once again, lifelong learning encompasses all of the aspects of learning that begin in infancy and continue through the adult years. Providing a new type of knowledge in schools as a form of career education, for example, should be considered as an attempt to protect students from social exclusion. In other words, this new form of knowledge production could be considered to be a process aimed at the social inclusion of youth.

Briefly, "social exclusion" was originally a French concept that was expanded into EU policy making (Percy-Smith 2000; Bhalla and Lapeyre 2004; Daly 2006; Humbert and Sato 2012). This concept has now attracted attention in Japan. It represents the opposite of social integration, because it stresses how important it is that an individual joins society. According to a Laidlaw Foundation report (Barata 2000), the term "social exclusion" originated in France in the early 1970s, during a period in which poverty was increasing.[5] The term was developed in response to the problems that arose from attempts at sustaining social integration and solidarity (Barry 1998). The term became popular in 1974 with the publication of the work of the then secretary of state for social action, René Lenor. His work demonstrated the necessity of improving the conditions of those individuals who did not benefit from economic growth, by introducing a higher degree of social justice into economics and by giving growth a human face. These actions would eliminate the dangers inherent in social inequalities, as well as in the various forms of social exclusion. At that time, the term was used to describe the physically and mentally disabled and the socially maladjusted.

However, the meaning of "exclusion" has substantially changed in Europe. The definition now reflects the economic and social changes that swept across Europe during the 1980s. According to a report released by the Laidlaw Foundation (Barata 2000, 2–3), these changes resulted in (1) the shifting nature of jobs, (2) changes in family styles, and (3) the retrenchment of the welfare state. First, the emergence of the social exclusion framework coincided with significant changes occurring in the employment structure throughout Europe. The industrial sector faced severe losses that affected traditional manufacturing industries and unskilled labor (Bynner 1998). The new methods, used to organize work around flexible, just-in-time production, led to lowered wages and undermined the traditional forms of career progression. Second, an increase in child poverty was identified as a widespread concern. Some groups of children in particular were identified as the most affected by economic and social changes, including children whose parents suffered from long-term unemployment or survived on low wages and children raised in single-parent families (Mierendorff 1998). Third, welfare-state retrenchment, as well as inadequacies in social insurance, resulted in increased rates of child and family poverty and higher social exclusion across many European countries (Sorensen 1999). Moreover, social expenditures could be blamed for the depressed economic growth (Evans 1998). Individualization was a significant sociocultural trend influencing European policy (Kloprogge 1998).

In Europe, during the early 1990s, social exclusion became linked to the inadequate realization of social rights. In 1992, the European Commission defined "social exclusion" as "[certain individuals'] inability to enjoy social rights without help. These individuals suffer from low self-esteem, inadequacy in their capacity to meet their obligations, the risk of long-term relegation to the ranks of those on social benefits, and stigmatization, which, particularly in the urban environment, extends to the areas in which they live" (European Commission 1992, 10). Furthermore, social exclusion refers to the multidimensional factors that result in disadvantages in the areas of income, health, education, access to services, housing, debt, quality of life, dignity, and autonomy (Cheetham and Fuller 1998). In the 2000s, the so-called Lisbon strategy, which was developed following an agreement in Lisbon, Portugal, in March 2000, gave social exclusion a much fuller identity. The Lisbon strategy actively sought to develop a coordinated policy on poverty and social inclusion that involved applying the open method of coordination. In other words, it followed common guidelines (Council of the European Union 2000). Daly (2006) points out that the Lisbon strategy's central ideology—economic performance and social cohesion—is not mutually exclusive. However, it can be mutually reinforcing, based on the culmination of attempts to raise the position of social policy on the EU agenda. Daly implies that social exclusion has developed into a template that is used for social policy making in the EU.

During the late 2000s, after this European discourse had occurred, *shakaiteki haijo,* a Japanese translation of social exclusion, became a buzzword among Japanese policy makers and academic circles. Its use developed in the context of efforts aimed at gaining a better understanding of contemporary Japanese society. The concept was introduced as a modern way of addressing these issues, as new forms of poverty stemmed from long-term unemployment, socioeconomic precariousness, social polarization, and disintegration (see Miyamoto 2002; Nakamura 2006; Abe 2007; Fukuhara 2007; Iwata 2008, 2010; Iwata and Nishizawa 2008). The contemporary trend could primarily be attributed to labor-market dualism (i.e., the increasing proportion of nonregular workers, who are paid significantly less than regular workers), as well as to other factors, including the aging of the workforce (OECD 2006). Iwata (2010) identifies the emergence of social exclusion in Japan as part of the ongoing process of globalization, as well as a part of the transition to the neoliberal economy that has occurred since the 1980s. In the West, the social-exclusion phenomenon appeared in the 1970s, directly after two energy crises occurred. This phenomenon appeared later in Japan, however, in response to the bubble economy that developed in the late 1980s when Japan experienced a labor shortage. Globalization, which I describe as the enhancement of interconnectivity beyond national borders, shook the traditional mode of mass production in the manufacturing industry, altered the stable employment system that supports production, and, consequently, affected the mass-consumption system. Instead, the contemporary world is dominated by information technology. Because of the development of new technology, flexible production methods are being invented and new styles of flexible working explored. Service sectors, such as finance, are becoming prominent. Capital, supported by neoliberal ideology that shifts the responsibility of risk management in economic institutions from the state to markets, moves globally towards new markets. To support this mode of production, the labor market is consequently being liquidated and reorganized. On the one hand, a limited number of highly educated and very skilled individuals are working as core employees. On the other hand, the majority of employees are becoming marginal, flexible, or nonregular workers. This labor-market dualism has created a bifurcation in the Japanese population. This was recently described as *kakusa,* or "the socioeconomic divide." Japanese society is being divided into winners (*kachigumi*) and losers (*makegumi*).

The losers are becoming the targets of social exclusion. Many young people fall into this category, as mentioned in chapter 3.

In 2009, the Science Council of Japan issued a report addressing social inclusion, or *shakaiteki hōsetsu* (Science Council of Japan 2009). The report stated that social-inclusion policy should be implemented based on mid- or long-term perspectives. The report placed the current phenomenon of social exclusion within the larger scheme of today's social changes, such as globalization and the postindustrial society (ibid., 5). This is not a temporary phenomenon arising from the global economic crisis that began in 2008. The collapse of the conventional working style of lifetime employment and the consequent emergence of nonregular/temporary workers and increased youth unemployment are global issues. The socioeconomic divide and the working poor in Japanese society are derivative phenomena that developed due to these changes. These factors are known as *atarashii shakaiteki risuku* (the new social risks) (ibid., 1). This term reminds us, exactly, of Taylor-Gooby's (2004, 2–5) argument of the "new social risks" that people face due to socioeconomic changes that occurred following the transition to the neoliberal economy. These changes were primarily revealed in the labor market. The associated risks tend to affect younger people, because they are new to the labor market and are required to establish places for themselves within it. Young students cannot efficiently take on or manage risks. They are also socially vulnerable (cf. Miyamoto 2002) to all kinds of risks in the society they are about to enter. To effectively solve the problems we face, several policies related to the prevention of social exclusion, including education, employment, housing, and social security (national health insurance and pension) must be carefully combined. Furthermore, policies should be formulated that support a variety of family styles, including single parents and elderly couples. In early 2011, the Japanese government established a special assignment team to promote social inclusion, operating under the direct supervision of Prime Minister Kan Naoto. The team initiated a comprehensive policy framework on social inclusion. The team pointed out that one social risk could trigger an additional risk; in other words, the unavailability of learning opportunities can generate unstable employment. This fragility can cause bad health, unemployment, and even the loss of housing. It may eventually cause social exclusion (Cabinet Office 2011c, 1). The team also noted that these types of social risks would be amplified following the March 11 earthquake that hit eastern Japan (ibid., 5).

The career education program introduced in Japanese schools and the new type of knowledge, referred to as "basic attainments," produced at universities are believed to represent key measures in the management of expanding social exclusion, or what I call "socioeconomic risk" in chapter 1. Because career education programs promote the acquisition of new knowledge specifically represented as the four key competencies (building human relations, self-understanding and self-management, problem solving, and career planning), they can be considered a major tool for promoting social inclusion among young people. Ultimately, the proposed goal of obtaining these competencies in the context of career education can be achieved based on the *ikiru chikara* (zest for living) that can be developed, beginning in elementary school, in the Japanese education system, as I discussed in chapter 5.

The production of these competencies can be supported by lifelong learning activities developed by civil society institutions, including local communities and local community-oriented NPOs. Both of these entities are significant resources for these types of learning activities. Moreover, universities (which can be categorized as one of the civil-society actors) should play a significant role in developing these competencies as well. A number of Japanese universities, particularly several private universities, have begun to offer positive vocational guidance. In fact, with respect to private universities, their graduates' success in gaining employment can be directly linked to university management. Applicants refer to the rates of employment among graduates; therefore, operating career support centers is becoming a major business for universities. For example, Meiji University and Ritsumeikan University—private universities located in Tokyo and Kyoto, respectively—are known for their good career-support systems. Meiji University is currently enrolling its largest number of applicants yet for its undergraduate program. In April 2011, the Japanese government introduced "career guidance" or *shokugyō shidō* as a graduation requirement for all Japanese universities, regardless of whether they are public or private.

Meanwhile, I would argue that the new curriculum primarily requires students to adjust themselves to an ongoing reality through their acquisition of the four key competencies. In the labor market, they are simply asked to be *flexible* subjects or *convenient* subjects for employers. However, I claim, what students really should do is resist this reality. To do this, they require knowledge allowing them to empower themselves as laborers. "Basic and versatile competencies" in the career education program could be beneficial to survive in the contemporary neoliberal world; further, the new knowledge should include a basic understanding of labor laws and rights. Basic labor rights are clearly guaranteed under articles 27 and 28 of the Japanese Constitution. Article 27 defines the right and the obligation to work, as well as standards for wages, hours, rest breaks, and other working conditions. Article 28 guarantees the right of workers to collectively organize, bargain, and act. These articles are powerful and concrete tools when people reflect on their current situation, and they provide a basis for taking action against these conditions. Furthermore, the labor rights, as well as the right to life (article 25) and the right to education (article 26), are important social rights in contemporary Japanese society. Indeed, students must learn to be much more critical of the issues that now confront them. In fact, youth should take a strong initiative in determining how they work, one that reflects the severe realities they face. A current phenomenon observed in Japanese society is the abusive employment practices of the so-called black companies (*burakku kigyō*)—a new term referring to employers that hire a large number of new college graduates, assuming many of them will quit sooner or later due to the harsh working conditions, including unpaid work, extended overtime, low wages, and continuing harassment (cf. Konno 2012). Such harsh working conditions are becoming common, justified in the name of global competition—a key characteristic of the neoliberal era. Meanwhile, becoming familiar with labor-related laws and laborers' rights through labor education (*rōdō kyōiku*) is indeed a useful means of empowering themselves to survive in or to strongly resist such difficult and unfair labor conditions. In particular, they must learn how power is currently structured around them and comprehend how social exclusion, as well as inclusion, processes work. One way of realizing this is to raise their voices and take action against it. Otherwise, their working conditions will never improve, and their actions will lead to the revision of the entire employment system.

Developing Citizens

Lastly, implementing policy for the production of new knowledge through career education, which I have discussed in this chapter, ultimately aims to create Japanese citizens (*shimin*) who will support civil society in an active manner. Indeed, with respect to the Japanese discourse on civil society offered over sixty years ago, Kuno Osamu, a philosopher and critic, pointed out that a strong link exists between citizenship creation and vocations. He claimed that *shimin* possess a strong consciousness that they employ as vocational ethics (Kuno 1960, 10; Ogawa 2009a, 149–150). In fact, about one-third of the report on the quality assurance of university education, released by the Science Council of Japan (2010) and mentioned earlier in this chapter, discusses the significance of civil society and the generation of citizens through university education: "Rather than listing the minute knowledge required by each specific subject, we [university teachers] should try to provide students with foundational knowledge that will be relevant to them as vocational professionals, as well as citizens, throughout their lives" (Science Council of Japan 2010, 3–4). This statement is in alignment with the 2005 proposal that was issued by the University Council under the Central Council for Education. The proposal states that the fundamental purpose of contemporary university education is to nurture its "citizens for the twenty-first century" (*21 seiki gata shimin*). It defines a citizen as "someone who has a broader liberal arts education and a specialty, who supports society in a positive manner and who possesses a higher sense of publicity and ethics, who tries to improve society" (Central Council for Education 2005).

Citing one relevant example, the abovementioned policy proposal statements offered by the two councils in Japan actually remind us of the citizenship-education programs offered in higher education in the UK. Citizenship means "membership in a political grouping of some sort, but it is widely recognized that there are tensions between the political-legal language used in describing this membership and the symbolic-affective dimensions of citizenship" (Arthur 2005, 1). Citizenship education equips people with the knowledge and skills necessary to play active roles in society as informed, critical citizens. In fact, citizenship education is a nationwide project. In 2002, citizenship education was introduced into the national curriculum as a statutory subject offered at the primary and secondary levels in the UK (National Curriculum 2011). The Citizenship Foundation in the UK relies on a comment made by Bernard Crick in 1999: "Citizenship is more than a subject. If taught well and tailored to local needs, its skills and values will enhance democratic life for all of us, both rights and responsibilities, beginning in school and radiating out" (Citizenship Foundation 2011). Further, at the level of higher education, some universities now specifically refer to the significance of citizenship in their education strategies. For example, James Arthur of Birmingham University noted that, in reference to his university's citizenship education curriculum, "Educating for academic skills alone is not sufficient in helping graduates prepare for civic commitment or to understand their responsibilities as members of a community. Civic engagement is now an essential learning goal for institutions throughout higher education" (Arthur 2010; cf. Arthur and Bohlin 2005). Civic education in higher education was also designed to enhance employability, as well as to recognize personally transferable skills, during a time when unemployment, as well as underemployment, rates among university graduates continue to grow. In fact, the knowledge and skills developed in citizenship education—such as communication abilities, working with others, and problem solving—can transform individuals' lives in a solid manner, increasing their social mobility and social inclusion. Both of these factors are vital to the improvement of an individual's employability.

Meanwhile, a report issued by the Science Council of Japan (2010, 24) also included the term *shimin kyōiku* or citizenship education. The report claimed that citizenship education is not a subject; rather, it is an ideology that should be addressed in all subjects. The Young People's Independence and Challenge Plan of 2003, which was mentioned earlier in this chapter, is considered a basic blueprint, at the policy-making level, for citizenship education in Japan. Further, the new Fundamental Law of Education, which was revised in 2006, also encouraged this trend. The aims of education are stated in article 1: "Education shall focus on the total development of personality, strive for the rearing of people who are sound in mind and body, who shall love truth and justice, esteem individual value, respect labor, have a deep sense of responsibility, and be imbued with an independent spirit, to serve as builders of the peaceful state and society." In addition to the emphasis on social and moral responsibility, Japan's citizenship education is framed by active social involvement. Article 2 of the revised educational charter states that education should encourage "public spirit that leads to independent participation in the construction of society, together with the development of an attitude of wanting to contribute to its growth." Japan actually reflects citizenship education that emphasizes social and moral responsibility, as well as community involvement (Qualifications and Curriculum Authority 1998), from the UK, where neoliberal politics is more advanced. To implement this type of educational ideology in a more strategic manner, the 2010 proposal that was produced by the Science Council of Japan mentions citizenship education in the context of enhancing the quality of university education. The Council's report defines citizenship as "an attitude and behavior that attempts to solve social public agendas with people who possess different backgrounds and standpoints" (Science Council of Japan 2010, 28). Further, the report states that the meaning of citizenship can change over time. What we need most in neoliberal Japan is flexible thinking and improved communication abilities. It is particularly important to communicate with people from different sociocultural backgrounds and with people from different age groups, in order to revitalize local communities that are not linked to kin and territory (ibid., 37). Japanese universities are, in the upcoming years, expected to broaden the horizons of citizenship in contemporary society. In all likelihood, the most reasonable expectation is that students, as well as faculty, will make solid commitments to the real world through the production of knowledge.

This new knowledge is crucial to achieving young people's inclusion in society. Armed with the four key competencies that are developed in the career education program, Japanese youth are currently expected to enter society as citizens. Citizens in our contemporary society should have specialized vocations. They are expected to use the knowledge and skills they have developed in their vocations when they commit to society. In the past, the Japanese educational system may not have seriously considered nurturing citizenship through vocation. However, Japanese schools are currently attempting to achieve this goal through the introduction of "career education," under the policy framework of lifelong learning. I consider this a strategy crafted by the neoliberal state to develop certain types of required human resources for its own benefit. In other words, the state hopes to develop conscientious neoliberal citizens who will remain active in their own local communities and who can independently survive in the stagnant labor market.

Afterword

Kizuna

It is the summer of 2011 as I am finishing this book in Stockholm, Sweden. In recent news articles from Japan, I have frequently come across the Japanese word *kizuna*. In simple terms, it means bonding or embracing solidarity in the community.

On March 11, 2011, the Great East Japan Earthquake hit the Tohoku region in eastern Japan. This massive earthquake, unprecedented in Japan and one of the biggest recorded in world history, triggered a more than twenty-meter tsunami that battered Japan's east coast, killing many people and sweeping thousands of people, cars, homes, and buildings away. Many people have not been found. One town in Kesennuma in Miyagi Prefecture, which was totally wiped out by the tsunami, was where my wife had lived as a teacher when she was in her early twenties. Therefore, the disaster was a personal tragedy for my family.

The subsequent radiation leakage from the nuclear power plant in Fukushima Daiichi has brought further uncertainty to the Japanese people, forcing thousands to evacuate their familiar neighborhoods, which are now tainted with radiation. This anxiety is not showing any signs of ending; in fact, the Fukushima incident brings to mind the Chernobyl disaster of 1986. Nuclear fear is now spreading across and beyond Japan. In Europe, particularly in Germany and Italy, the Fukushima case ignited a social movement for nuclear nonproliferation, and efforts are underway to close down nuclear power plants. Encouraged by such positive sentiment outside the country, Japanese grassroots protest demonstrations are calling for the phasing out of the use of nuclear energy. However, Japanese politicians have not shown any strong intention of closing nuclear power plants, even though the country is at grave risk.

Post-3/11, Japan faces two risks: first, the real risk generated by the natural disaster (the earthquake), along with the man-made, technology-based nuclear radiation leak from the Fukushima Daiichi nuclear power plant; and second, the socially constructed risk that has emerged in the neoliberal era. In this book, I primarily discuss the latter, showcasing it as (a) governmental risk for the state and (b) socioeconomic risk for individuals. As Japan tries to manage all of these, I believe that *kizuna* will be at the center of forum discussions, and developing *kizuna* will be at the core of the solution.

As we pray for Japan, the spirit of *kizuna* will bring us together for reconstruction efforts. I have heard that so far, nearly forty-five thousand people have volunteered in various reconstruction efforts while working closely with local governments and communities. The number of disaster-relief volunteers this time is likely to outnumber the approximately 1.3 million volunteers for the Hanshin earthquake in 1995—the sheer number of volunteers in the first year led the Japanese media to call it a phenomenon. Calls for volunteers are constantly circulated through Internet-based social media such as Twitter.

In the meantime, a flyer I recently received (MEXT 2011d) says, "Learning (or *manabi*) will provide the power (or *chikara*) for reconstructing new local communities after the earthquake." Actually, this is a quote from the advertisement for this year's *manabipia*—the annual national festival for promoting lifelong learning, sponsored by the Education Ministry (discussed in chapter 2). To paraphrase, new knowledge generated through our own lifelong learning activities can be a powerful, rich source for reconstructing a new society. We need to realize that Japan's efforts toward developing a new initiative on lifelong learning, the very topic explored in this book, are now simultaneously progressing along with the earnest efforts at reconstruction after the 3/11 disaster. Lifelong learning is indeed discussed in the context of disaster reconstruction, as demonstrated in the flyer mentioned above.

The rationale here is that knowledge generated from lifelong learning can be the core of reconstruction efforts in local communities. We are first expected to be armed with the new knowledge, what I call "comprehensive knowledge" (chapter 3). We are then expected to generate something positive by practicing such knowledge in the local communities where we belong. Nikolas Rose points out precisely what Japan is now exploring:

> [C]ommunity is not simply the territory of government, but a *means* of government: its ties, bonds, forces, and affilia-

tions are to be celebrated, encouraged, nurtured, shaped and instrumentalized in the hope of producing consequences that are desirable for all and for each. (Rose 1996, 355, emphasis in original)

To support this kind of community, comprehensive knowledge is necessary. The new knowledge required nowadays is not quantifiable knowledge as measured by the school-oriented meritocracy. It is not produced merely by formal school education. What we are expected to acquire as knowledge is presented primarily as competencies in problem solving, communication, constructing human relations, project management, and career planning. The Japanese are now positioned for the emergence of a new ideology of lifelong learning, for being trained and retrained over their lifetimes in order to develop these competencies, which eventually contribute to community solutions. These competencies are *ikiru chikara* (zest for living)—necessary to survive contemporary times.

We can look back on the history of Japan's lifelong learning in the post–World War II era by revisiting the early postwar period. In the late 1940s and 1950s, the tradition of social education was started as an education alternative for the poor who could not attend upper-level schools (high schools and universities). Social education is still an active grassroots activity across Japan as a convenient source of learning, carried out mostly in public citizens' halls, libraries, and museums. In the economic growth era of the 1960s and 1970s, the lifelong learning concept was actively introduced from Western countries; it aimed primarily at reducing the Japanese tendency to be too diploma-oriented. After the 1980s, lifelong learning came to be discussed in the context of leisure as the Japanese enjoyed economic affluence; hence, private, leisure-oriented learning became another key feature in Japan's lifelong learning. Since the 1990s, lifelong learning has been discussed in terms of skill development in the context of a knowledge economy. Furthermore, the international policy making that promoted lifelong learning in the late 1990s buoyed positive sentiment toward lifelong learning in Japanese society. This book has explored the series of new policy developments that occurred primarily in the late 2000s and their interactions with the grassroots through ethnography. One of the major arguments in this book was that lifelong learning is promoted as a method of governance in new modes of governmentality shaped by neoliberal principles; practicing lifelong learning is a risk-hedging activity for individuals in updating their knowledge and skills to directly respond to the new employment style informed by neoliberal markets.

Japan's lifelong learning has not been entirely visible compared with the formal school education system. However, it is a significant and unique form of learning. I myself discovered lifelong learning when I was conducting fieldwork on Japan's civil society in the early 2000s. I chose to do research on NPOs, new civil-society organizations that had been institutionalized under the NPO Law in 1998. As a case, I selected SLG (pseudonym), an NPO that promotes lifelong learning in eastern Tokyo. I documented the microactivities of community-oriented lifelong learning, as facilitated by local volunteers, in the form of ethnography in my book, *The Failure of Civil Society?* (Ogawa 2009a). SLG is one of the biggest lifelong learning NPOs in Japan, in terms of both membership and funding. Among local residents, 130 have registered as unpaid volunteers, and they plan courses on various subjects, administer courses in order to facilitate participants' learning, and also collect and provide information on learning opportunities to local residents via the Internet, local cable TV, and newsletters. SLG offers more than one hundred courses a year, and some 10,000 local residents in total take courses as part of their lifelong learning activities.

The Failure of Civil Society? documented my action research (cf. Greenwood and Levin 1998). My project consisted of trying to solve actual problems in the process of implementing the community-oriented lifelong learning program. My interactions with SLG participants did not consist of simple knowledge transference from my side as a professional researcher. Instead, in order to enhance the quality of our organizational life, we jointly produced knowledge for making changes within the organization to support "a more just or satisfying situation for the stakeholders" (Greenwood and Levin 2007, 4). Actually, it was a daily struggle to explore what kinds of lifelong learning we would offer to the local community. The organizational mission of SLG was to promote learning for local residents by the local residents themselves. Their learning covered a variety of issues, such as local history and culture, career development, foreign languages, liberal arts, information science, after-school activities, arts and crafts, and sports and dance. Their learning was not an individual matter, however. SLG is indeed envisioning a new way of community revitalization via learning. In line with the mission of learning, local people who had certain kinds of special knowledge became teachers, and local people were expected to learn under their guidance; they learned from each other. Such grassroots learning interactions functioned as a medium through which people came to know each other well or deepen *kizuna* within the local community. Ultimately, their teaching was expected to enhance the quality of local public life. In other words, promoting such community-oriented learning would contribute to integrating the currently socioeconomically divided Japanese population; this learning managed what I called governmental risk by promoting local solidarity.

My research commitment to SLG was an experience that developed trust, one key aspect of an ethnographer's—that was, my own—way of experiencing life, as James Peacock points out (Peacock 2001, 137). Ten years after starting the research at SLG, I have no intention of ending my commitment as an action-oriented researcher, strengthening and confirming trust—I would say *kizuna*—with my research collaborators. In the initial stage of my research, I tried to facilitate the process primarily by taking a strong initiative. However, I expected that my role would be gradually transferred to my research collaborators, and I did successfully accomplish this transition. Mr. Iwata, one of my research collaborators, became a member of SLG's board of directors in the spring of 2009. He organized a symposium in October 2010 to celebrate the tenth anniversary of SLG's establishment. The major discussion at the symposium centered on what kind of learning the group would explore as a community-oriented lifelong learning NPO and in what way SLG could distinguish itself from other providers of lifelong learning. However, the answer seemed obvious: SLG was always trying to focus on the local community in their learning program. Their learning was intended to contribute to their community in many positive ways. The symposium, which was opened to the local public, provided a good opportunity for SLG participants to reflect on their organizational mission as well as their own *kizuna*, which they tried to develop with local people through offering learning.

In my continuing observation, SLG manages to survive; the volunteers are still active, keeping a tight relationship through generous funding from the municipal government, which amounts to some 150 million yen ($1.4 million) annually. SLG currently employs twenty people from the local community and provides employment opportunities for the local people amid a sluggish economy. I believe SLG can be regarded as a typical Japanese NPO, which major daily *Asahi Shimbun* (January 30, 2009) calls a GoNPO (*gonpo*). GoNPO is an abbreviation of government-led NPO. *Asahi* points out that one of the major trends seen in Japanese NPOs is that the local government plays a key role in establishing and operating them. According to the Cabinet Office's research from 2008, approximately 55 percent of civil society organizations' revenues are from their various projects with the government, 28 percent from governments' subsidies, 5 percent from donations, and 5 percent from membership fees (Cabinet Office 2008b). Further, activities conducted by civil society organizations such as NPOs are replacing the government in the role of providing social services the government no longer could, nor was willing to, provide. As a result, the government could provide the same social services at no or discounted cost through the mobilization of volunteers. My case, SLG, is directly in line with this observation.

Since my involvement with SLG, my interest in lifelong learning has gradually increased, and the increased interest and accumulated knowledge in the field of lifelong learning motivated me to write this book. While continuing my research at SLG, I have been involved since 2005 with *bunka borantia* (culture volunteers), during my postdoctoral research (introduced in chapter 4). These workers were key players in local public facilities for lifelong learning, such as citizens' public halls, libraries, and museums. They helped as volunteers in the operation of public facilities through interacting with officials. What they actually intended was to identify and solve problems inside facilities by bringing in citizens' perspectives. The *bunka borantia* network has been expanding across the country. In particular, after the March 11 disaster, the network envisions a new scope of activities. Along with conventional disaster relief volunteers, culture volunteers have started to play a significant role in reconstructing cultural heritage, both tangible and intangible, including arranging local festivals, and I came to be involved with several projects as a trained anthropologist. Confirming *kizuna*, or bonding with disaster victims through reconstruction work, is at the core of our actions. I am currently facilitating the *bunka borantia* network as part of my continuing action research project.

Via the *bunka borantia* network, I visited Hirosaki, a city in northern Japan for the first time in summer 2007. Hirosaki was well-known for its social education tradition, and I was impressed with the ways in which local communities were solidly and successfully developed through grassroots learning activities at citizens' public halls—one of the most traditional public facilities promoting lifelong learning in Japanese society. Working together with neighborhood associations—the most conventional and longest-surviving Japanese civil-society organizations—the citizens' public halls offered various kinds of learning programs targeting all generations in the local communities. For them, this learning intentionally created local places where individuals could meet.

At the same time that I was watching the number of social education course participants hitting a record high in 2008, I was documenting that Japan was establishing a new kind of lifelong learning program as a political technique for managing the risks (both governmental and socioeconomic) for both the state and individuals. Local communities were being reinstitutionalized as sites where such lifelong learning for managing the emerging risks was actively practiced. The policy implementation at various levels, including formal school education and vocation training programs, was conducted in a strategic and comprehensive manner, and I discovered that what people were actually exploring through lifelong learning initiatives might ultimately be enhancing *kizuna*, or more simply, communication among community fellows. Indeed, all of the specific project examples that I have presented in this book—*bunka borantia* and *jukugi* (in chapter 4), community schools (in chapter 5), a vocational training course (in chapter 6), and career education (in chapter 7)—place a special emphasis on enhancing communication skills.

Kizuna is indeed a key word for understanding contemporary Japanese society. It was something that the Japanese lost during the economic development in the post–World War II era, and lifelong learning was identified as a major effort to restore it.[1] During my fieldwork in Japan in 2010, I often came across the term *muen shakai* (no-relationship society), a society without relationships or *kizuna*. The term can even be translated as disconnected, neglected society. The phrase was originally used in a documentary aired by state-run NHK in January 2010, suggesting the increasing isolation of individuals in contemporary Japanese society (NHK 2010; cf. Taylor 2012). In fact, the country's solitude was reaching an alarming level. In the beginning of the 2010s, I heard news reports that the social isolation and hidden poverty of many were revealed in people dying alone in their rooms; meanwhile, missing centenarians and shocking child abuse cases highlighted the weakening of family ties. Every year in this country, there are indeed about thirty-two thousand "solitary death" (*muen shi*) cases where the remains of people who have either committed suicide or have starved or frozen to death are not claimed. The increasing lack of human connection caused by being single, divorced, or unemployed is expanding this group's membership in the disconnected society. I would argue that this reality represents a collapse of the various forms of traditional communities that Japanese society has enjoyed—territory based, corporate based, and kin based. According to the documentary program, the people whose remains were not claimed were nothing special; they were very ordinary people. Where *kizuna* had traditionally functioned as a buffer between society and the individual, under the current uncertainties and with the near extinction of *kizuna*, ordinary Japanese individuals carry some heavy burdens.

Once again, the importance of local communities is being seriously reconsidered in Japanese society. Japan's new lifelong learning has been discussed in this context, and lifelong learning is thus practiced at the center of a community. Local learning is indeed a vital medium for connecting disconnected people. Further, such grassroots learning would strengthen our *kizuna*, and through such grassroots learning, I expect that Japan's civil society will be ultimately strengthened. In fact, "revitalizing civil society and sustaining a critical public sphere" (Murphy and Fleming 2006, 52) are major tasks for lifelong learning. What I have documented in this book is active learning activities at various stages of life developed in local communities—the key realm of Japanese civil society. People are active at local lifelong learning facilities, such as citizens' public halls, libraries, museums, public schools, and NPOs. All activities have been developed under the new policy framework of lifelong learning, and all participants are committed to generating a solid process of social inclusion, targeting the socially vulnerable in their own self-directive local communities. Their learning always strengthens their *kizuna*, and that is the major reason why they are drawn to Japan's new lifelong learning.

Appendix 1

Japan's Lifelong Learning in the 2000s

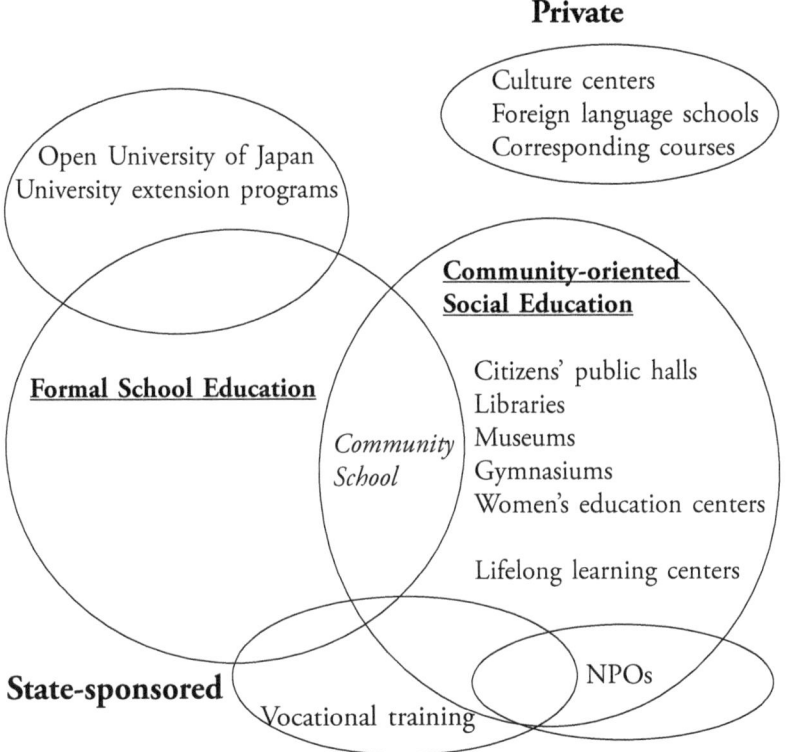

Appendix 2

Major Legal and Policy Developments of Japan's Lifelong Learning (1947–2011)

1947   Fundamental Law of Education

1949   Social Education Law

1950   Library Law

1951   Museum Law

1953   Law for the Promotion of Youth Classes

1958   Vocational Training Law

1961   Sports Promotion Law

1965   Paul Lengrand of UNESCO presented the term *lifelong education*

1966   Central Council for Education report mentioned the concept of a wide-ranging education throughout one's life

1971   Social Education Council report on the arrangement of social education to cope with rapid changes in the social structure

1981   Report on lifelong education by the Central Council for Education

1983   University of the Air opened

1984   Ad Hoc Council on Education established

1985   First Report by the Ad Hoc Council on Education

1985	Vocational Ability Development Promotion Law
1986	Second Report by the Ad Hoc Council on Education
1987	Third Report by the Ad Hoc Council on Education
1987	Fourth (Final) Report by the Ad Hoc Council on Education
1990	Lifelong Learning Promotion Law
1990	Lifelong Learning Council was established
1990	Report on development of a lifelong learning infrastructure by the Central Council for Education
1991	Report on the reform of educational systems by the Central Council for Education
1991	Report on the improvement of university education by the University Council
1992	First report by the Lifelong Learning Council
1996	Report on *Ikiru Chikara* by the Central Council for Education
1996	Report on expanding lifelong learning opportunities by the Lifelong Learning Council
1997	Report on measures to make the best use of results of lifelong learning by the Lifelong Learning Council
1998	Report on social education administration responding to social changes in the future by the Lifelong Learning Council
1999	Report on the encouragement of using learning results by lifelong learning activities by the Lifelong Learning Council
1999	Report on nurturing Japanese children through real experiences in actual daily life and nature by the Lifelong Learning Council
2000	Report on measures to promote lifelong learning, the acquisition of knowledge and skills in the new information technology, by the Lifelong Learning Council
2001	Social Education Law revised
2004	"Community School" introduced to Japanese public education system
2006	Fundamental Law of Education revised; lifelong learning was mentioned for the first time since its enactment in 1947

2008	Report on lifelong learning policy measures to explore the new era, aiming to construct a knowledge-circulating society by the Central Council for Education
2008	Social Education Law revised
2010	Report on the quality assurance of university education by the Science Council of Japan
2011	Final Report on career education by the Central Council for Education

Appendix 3

List of Civic Knowledge Sources

Mission

- Conduct the mission you want to accomplish.
- Share your mission with other people, and adhere to it to achieve success.
- Try to find government officials who share your mission.
- Keep in mind that successful cases always start with a clear mission.
- Remember that your mission will be the foundation for success for every type of action in your project.
- Think about the core factor of your motivation. That could be a mission.
- Share your mission with the next generation.
- Include a sense of community development in your mission so that local residents can join in your project.
- Remember that successful missions can be supported by current trends.

Management

- Think about how to best develop your activity.

- Develop both short- and long-term plans for your activity.
- Think about how local residents can become involved in your activities.
- Update your planning abilities regularly.
- Keep local residents informed of your plans so that they can understand and support your activities.
- Recognize and understand that volunteers will be disoriented if your activity's mission is not clear.
- Reflect on what you are doing at all times to enhance your management ability.

Continuity and Sustainability

- Never give up.
- Remember that continuity itself can be a strength.
- Do not hurry. It takes a long time to accomplish something.
- Collaborate with local residents. Your project will be more sustainable if local people support it.
- Mobilize the available resources, including human beings and local practices.
- Collaboration and openness are key factors for your activity's continuity.

Bonding

- Meet new people as your first step.
- Keep in mind that a person with aspirations can always be at the front and center; from there, new activities can be developed in an active manner.
- Interact outside your group to encounter new people and learn what they do.

- Use a mailing list actively to enhance the flow of information.
- Remember that local residents, government officials, and students can all serve as important collaborators for community development.
- Express your interest clearly to people outside of your community, and try to connect your interest to other people's interests.

Networking

- Develop your own network of people who understand what you want to do.
- Remember that networks can be developed beyond generations.
- Connect with people who have similar interests to yours.
- Get to know people with different backgrounds and specialties from yours, as they can become new sources in your network.
- Exchange information within and beyond your network.

Volunteering

- Keep in mind that volunteering can be the first step in community development.
- Change your community by participating as a volunteer in the community.
- Collaborate with volunteers, government officials, and local residents.
- Build trust with your friends and delegate responsibilities to them.
- Think about who will understand your activity.

Coordination

- Designate a person to coordinate volunteer activities.
- Remember that volunteer coordinators play a significant role in managing volunteers' talents and time.
- Keep in mind that volunteer coordinators primarily seek to enhance volunteers' motivations.

Partnership

- Find government officials who are pro citizen activities; they can be sources of information.
- Try to communicate with government officials and involve them in your activities.
- Talk directly to government officials about your mission.
- Develop a common language or focus on shared interests with government officials to achieve your mission.
- Do not wait for the government to approach you; you can initiate a partnership with the government.
- Brush up on your skills as a volunteer to successfully partner with the government.

Notes

Chapter 1

1. The term, "continuing education," can be used interchangeably with the term, "lifelong learning." This term is primarily used in North America. In this book, I employ the term "lifelong learning," which is the literal translation of *shōgai gakushū*.

2. The formal name in English is the Ministry of Education, Culture, Sports, Science, and Technology. In this book, I use "Education Ministry" or its acronym, MEXT.

3. *Shakai kyōiku chōsa* (*Report on Social Education*) is published every three years. I relied on the edition published in 2008, which was available when I was doing fieldwork in Japan. The figures were based on the data collected in fiscal 2007 or April 2007 to March 2008.

4. In this book, "NPOs," refers to nonprofit organizations established under the NPO Law (formally, the Law to Promote Specified Nonprofit Activities; *tokutei hieiri katsudō hōjin*) enacted in 1998 in Japan

5. The formal name of the law in Japanese is *shōgai gakushū shinkō no tame no shisaku no suishin taisei nadono seibi ni kansuru hōritsu* (law concerning the Development of Systems to Facilitate Measures for the Promotion of Lifelong Learning.)

6. EUR 1 equals USD 1.47 in 2008.

7. This approach includes works by Douglas (1966, 1985, 1990, 1992), Douglas and Wildavsky (1982), Ferreira et al. (2001), and Boholm (2003).

8. This approach includes works by Beck (1992, 1995, 1997, 1998, 1999a, 1999b, 2000a, 2000b, 2002, 2005, 2006, 2008, 2009a), Beck et al. (1994), Beck and Beck-Gernsheim (1995, 2002); Dingwall (1999), Adam et al. (2000), Denscombe (2001), Beck-Gernsheim (2002), Elliott (2002), Beck et al. (2003), Matten (2004), Beck and Lau (2005), Beck and Znaider (2006), Beck and Grande (2007), and Bora (2007).

9. This approach includes works by Foucault (1991), Ewald (1991, 1993), Rose (1996, 1999, 2000), Dean (1999a, 1999b), Hacking (1999, 2003), Ericson

and Doyle (2003, 2004a, 2004b), Ericson et al. (2003), O'Malley (1998, 2000, 2003, 2004, 2006). Furthermore, comprehensive scholarship on the analysis of risk includes works by Luhman (1993), Lupton (1999a, 1999b), Taylor-Gooby (1999a, 1999b, 2004), Cohen (2000), Taylor-Gooby and Zinn (2001, 2006), Hood et al. (2001), Adam (2002), Baker et al. (2002), Kemshall (2002), Tulloch and Lupton (2003), Pidgeon et al. (2003), Zim (2006, 2008), Renn (2008), Arnoldi (2009), and Smith (2009).

Chapter 2

1. Shortly after the conference, the concept of lifelong education was introduced to Japanese academics by Hatano Kanji, a participant at the conference. Hatano published a book entitled *Shōgai kyōiku ron* (*Lifelong Education Theory*) in 1972 (Hatano 1972).

2. The term "lifelong learning" first appeared in 1974 when an OECD report on recurrent education was translated into Japanese. The translation was read by policy makers, business executives, and academic researchers. Sawano (2007, 473) points out that many people became interested in this translation, which described how educational systems supported recurrent education in Northern Europe. The translated report considered Sweden a model learning society.

3. I (Ogawa 2009a) intensively documented lifelong learning activities developed by a public lifelong learning center located in downtown Tokyo. The center had been established by the municipal government. Because of budget constraints that arose following the collapse of the bubble economy, which resulted in decreased tax money, the municipal government mobilized local resident volunteers to create lifelong learning courses. After the NPO Law was enacted in 1998, a group of local volunteers gained nonprofit corporate status under the law. The municipal government then formally entrusted the content creation of lifelong learning courses to that NPO. This situation also occurred in the promotion of lifelong learning activities based on the use of the third-sector method, which is introduced later in this chapter.

4. The university's English name was the University of the Air. However, the name was changed to the current name, Open University of Japan, in October 2007.

5. Specifically, these issues included (1) life, (2) health, (3) human rights, (4) human nature, (5) family, (6) consumer issues, (7) community solidarity, (8) community development, (9) transportation, (10) aging society, (11) gender equality, (12) science and technology, (13) information, (14) intellectual property, (15) international understanding, (16) international development assistance, (17) population and food, (18) environment, and (19) natural resources and energy (See LLC 1992, part 2, chapter 4, section 2).

6. Here, I use the names ministries held prior to their reorganization in 2001. In tandem with the ministry restructuring, the advisory councils I mentioned, including the Lifelong Learning Council and the University Council, were integrated as task forces into the Central Council for Education. The Central Council for Education existed prior to 2001. However, it has become a more comprehensive advisory body since that time.

Chapter 3

1. I should mention that the total number of citizenship courses slightly declined in 2011. It was 368,903, down from 469,546 in 2008. The decline was primarily attributed to expanding re-construction costs following the great earthquake on March 11, 2011. However, the ratio of citizenship courses in the entire course offering was still the same level of 7.2 percent, only 0.1 percentage point down from the previous survey.
2. This is the official English translation.
3. The survey is conducted every three years, and the figures for initial income were 0.5263 in 2005 and 0.4983 in 2002.
4. A recent work by Ishida and Slater (2009) shows that this dividedness predates the neoliberal reform in Japan. My point here, however, is that such dividedness has intensified under Koizumi politics.
5. For example, a fifty-year-old man can receive monthly *seikatsu hogo* support, which, for example, in my neighborhood, Suginami, Tokyo, is JPY 135,310 ($1,330) a month, including JPY 53,700 ($525) in rent support (Suginami Ward Government 2011). He can also get a train or bus pass and papers entitling him to medical care. The amount of support depends on municipality.
6. Modeled on the United Kingdom's system of a board of governors (as a governance structure for the school), a community school was introduced in 2004 as a new educational institution, which enhanced the involvement of parents as well as local communities in school management. It is discussed in detail in chapter 5.

Chapter 4

1. Live coverage of the first meeting on the New Public Commons is available at http://www5.cao.go.jp/npc/chuukei/chuukei.html, accessed March 3, 2011.
2. Updated information on the New Public Commons is available on the Cabinet website: http://www5.cao.go.jp/npc/suishin.html, accessed March 3, 2011.
3. This is the literal English translation.

4. Prime Minister Kan mentioned in his policy speech on June 11, 2010, that his government would pursue the Third Way or *daisan no michi*, implying British politics under the Blair administration.

5. Also see Somers (1995), Kymlicka (1996), Rosaldo (1997), Ong (1999), Delanty (2003), Martin (2003), Stevenson (2003), Makino (2005), Gouthro (2007), Lister (2007), Miller (2007), Pawley (2008), Annette (2009), and Taylor-Gooby (2008).

6. Since February 2002, the Agency for Cultural Affairs has published ten newsletters over a period of four years, which have introduced sixty-two activities that were launched by the *bunka borantia* across the country.

7. Anthropologists have documented these volunteering activities, experienced in Japanese society since the 1990s, as ethnographies. The scholarship includes Stevens (1997), Thang (2001), Nakano (2005), and Ogawa (2009a).

8. This was pointed out by Simons and Masschelein (2008), who were citing Kirzner (1973).

9. The monthly magazine, titled *Shōgai gakushū* (*Lifelong Learning*), was published as official media by the Education Ministry between 2008 and 2014.

10. This five-step list is drawn from my own direct observation of *jukugi* on several occasions, combined with information available in MEXT (2011c).

11. The information on the real *jukugi* is continually updated on the ministry's *jukugi* website, available at http://jukugi.mext.go.jp/library_view?library_id=308, accessed February 15, 2011. All of the *jukugi* records, including discussion records as well as pictures, are available on the website.

12. The Japanese national income tax rate has six categories, the highest of which is 40 percent. Meanwhile, the local tax is flat at 10 percent.

13. Personal communication with the bureaucrat on August 24, 2010. In fact, a survey by Osaka University points out that more than half the Japanese NPOs (54 percent) collect no donations. This implies that they depend exclusively on the money provided by the government to finance their operations (Osaka University School of International Public Policy 2003).

Chapter 5

1. This is the English translation by the National Commission on Educational Reform.

2. MEXT (2010e) and MEXT (2010f) are handouts that were distributed at a meeting on school management on December 3, 2010, at the Education Ministry. The meeting was open to the general public for observation.

Chapter 6

1. Until the early 1990s, Hello Work was popularly referred to as *shokuan*, an abbreviation of a Japanese name. The office is operated by the Ministry of

Health, Labor, and Welfare. It has branch offices in most municipalities in every prefecture. Individuals who lose their jobs can register at Hello Work as unemployed workers. The office helps them secure unemployment insurance and assists them with their job searches. Moreover, the office provides information on several public vocational training courses.

2. This is the official English translation done by the New Public Commons Roundtable.

3. This is the official English translation done by the New Public Commons Roundtable.

4. The Vocational Training Law (*shokugyō kunren hō*) of 1958 was replaced in 1985 by the Vocational Ability Development Promotion Law (*shokugyō nōryoku kaihatsu sokushin hō*).

5. Originally called the Employment Promotion Corporation (*koyō sokushin jigyōdan*), it consisted of a special foundation established in 1961 that was sponsored by the national and local governments to promote employment. The corporation aided in the development of workers' vocational abilities by establishing vocational training institutes, managing apartments for laborers, and providing financial support to employees. The corporation was reorganized into the Employment and Human Resources Development Organization of Japan in 1999. Further, it was merged with the Japan Organization for Employment of the Elderly and Persons with Disabilities (*kōrei shōgaisha koyō shien kikō*) in October 2011.

6. Advanced vocational training opportunities can be obtained by pursuing a four-year advanced engineering program offered by the Polytechnic University (*shokugyō nōryoku kaihatsu sogō daigakkō*) in Tokyo. The Polytechnic University was established by the Japanese government in 1961. A high school diploma is required to enroll in the program. Most of this university's graduates go on to become instructors at local polytechnic colleges and polytech centers across the country.

7. Tanimoto (2006), Komazaki (2007), and Tsukamoto and Yamagishi (2008) are the major works written by scholars that relate to social enterprises in contemporary Japan. An introductory book on social enterprises published by the Organization for Economic Cooperation and Development (OECD) was translated into Japanese. It links the ongoing discourse on the New Public Commons. See OECD (2010).

8. GBP 1 equals USD 1.85, and the USD was converted at 103 yen in 2008.

9. Information on the selection is available at the Cabinet Office website: http://www.chiikisyakai-koyou.jp/outline/, accessed November 15, 2010.

10. The course list is available at the website of the Employment and Human Resources Development Organization of Japan, Saitama Center: www.ehdo.go.jp/saitama/kikin/index.html, accessed on November 10, 2010.

11. This amount was provided to householders. A single person received JPY 100,000.

12. The data was calculated on the basis of figures obtained in June 2009.

13. Personal interview conducted on August 9, 2010, in Hirosaki, Aomori Prefecture.

Chapter 7

1. The link for women in Japan was a 1.38-percentage point, a figure that was much weaker than the men's figure.

2. The ministries selected sixty-two four-year universities, both public and private, and twenty two-year junior colleges nationwide to examine the job market for graduating students. The survey revealed that 70.1 percent of male students received offers of employment. This figure declined by 2.9 points. The figure for female students was 67.4 percent, a decline of 5.8 points. Among students who attended state and local government-run universities, 76.7 percent had received offers of employment. This figure declined by 4.0 points. Among students who attended private universities, the figure was a record low of 66.3 percent, a decline of 4.2 points. According to the survey, employment offered to science and engineering students fell by the largest margin ever, a decline of 7.3 points to 71.3 percent. Among students majoring in liberal arts, 68.3 percent received offers of employment. This figure declined by 3.7 points, which represented the largest margin of decline.

3. Most current accounts related to Japanese "career education" include Komikawa (2007) and Honda (2009).

4. The Science Council of Japan comprises 210 members who represent the nation's 830,000 academic researchers who work in all disciplines. It falls directly under the jurisdiction of the Cabinet Office and functions as a national think tank.

5. The Laidlaw Foundation, based in Toronto, Canada, exclusively focuses on positive youth development based on inclusive youth engagement in the arts, the environment, and the community.

Afterword

1. When I was revising this book manuscript in the winter of 2013, Atsushi Makino, a professor of lifelong learning at the University of Tokyo, published an article that also related the current promotion of lifelong learning by the state to community rebuilding efforts. See Makino (2013).

Japanese Glossary

aisatsu (あいさつ) greeting
anpo (安保) the anti US-Japan Security Treaty movement
atarashii kōkyō (新しい公共) New Public Commons
atarashi kōkyō entaku kaigi (新しい公共円卓会議) New Public Commons Roundtable
atarashii kōkyō suishin kaigi (新しい公共推進会議) Council on the Promotion of New Public Commons
atarashii shakaiteki risuku (新しい社会的リスク) new social risks
b-kyū gurume (B級グルメ) b-grade gourmet
bunka borantia (文化ボランティア) culture volunteers
bunka chō (文化庁) Agency for Cultural Affairs
bunka shinkō zaidan (文化振興財団) culture-promoting foundation
burakku kigyō (ブラック企業) black companies
chiiki (地域) local community
chiiki seisaku shitsu (地域政策室) community policy unit
chiiki shien gakkō (地域支援学校) community school
chiiki zukuri shien shitsu (地域作り支援室) community development support unit
chishiki (知識) knowledge
chuō kyōiku shingikai (中央教育審議会) Central Council for Education
chuō shokugyō nōryoku kaihatsu kyōkai (中央職業能力開発協会) Japan Vocational Ability Development Association
daigaku shingikai (大学審議会) University Council
daisan no michi (第三の道) Third Way
freeter (フリーター)
fukkō shien (復興支援) reconstruction support
gakkō kyōiku hō (学校教育法) School Education Law

gakkō shien chiiki honbu (学校支援地域本部) school support community headquarters
gakkō un'ei kyogikai (学校運営協議会) school council
gakureki shakai (学歴社会) diploma-oriented society
gakusei (学制) Education Order
gakushiryoku (学士力) standards for of bachelor's degrees
gakusha yūgō (学社融合) integration of school and social education
gakushū shakai (学習社会) learning society
gakushū shidō yōryō (学習指導要領) teaching guideline
GoNPO (ゴンポ) government-led NPOs
hakubutsukan (博物館) museums
hakubutsukan hō (博物館) Museum Law
hanyōteki ginō (汎用的技能) versatile competencies
hitsuyō kadai (必要課題) necessary/relevant topics
hogoshi (保護司) volunteer probation officers
hōkago kodomo puran (放課後子どもプラン) provision of after-school activities
hōsō daigaku (放送大学) Open University of Japan
ikiru chikara (生きる力) zest for living
izakaya (居酒屋) Japanese-style bar pub
jigyōsei (事業性) business sense
jisatsu sōgō taisaku kaigi (自殺総合対策会議) Council on Comprehensive Measures to Prevent Suicide
jisatsu taisaku kyōka gekkan (自殺対策強化月間) Suicide Prevention and Awareness Month
jissenryoku (実践力) practicability
jōka machi (城下町) castle town
jukugi (熟議)
jukuryo (熟慮)
junkan-suru (循環する) circulate
kachigumi (勝ち組) winners
kairanban (回覧板) notice circulation boards
kakusa (格差) socioeonomic divide
kakushinsei (革新性) innovativeness
karuchā sentā (カルチャーセンター) culture centers
keisatsu chō (警察庁) National Police Agency
kihonteki na soyō (基本的な素養) basic attainments
kisoteki han'yōteki nōryoku (基礎的汎用的能力) basic and versatile competencies
kizuki (気づき) becoming aware of

kizuna (絆) bonding
kodomo wo man'nakani oku (子どもを真ん中におく) putting children at the center [of all community activities]
kokeshi (こけし) a Japanese doll usually made from wood
kokumin seikatsu shingikai (国民生活審議会) Council on National Life
kokuritsu daigaku hōjin hō (国立大学法人法) National University Corporation Law
kokuritsu josei kyōiku kaikan (国立女性教育会館) National Women's Education Center
kokuritsu seishōnen kyōiku shinkō kikō (国立青少年教育振興機構) National Institution for Youth Education
kōkyō shokugyō anteijo (公共職業安定所) public job placement offices or Hello Work
kōminkan (公民館) citizens' public halls
koyō nōryoku kaihatsu kikō (雇用・能力開発機構) Employment and Human Resources Development Organization of Japan
Koyō sokushin jigyōdan (雇用促進事業団) Employment Promotion Corporation
kōzō kaikaku (構造改革) structural reform
kyaria kyōiku (キャリア教育) career education
kyodō (協働) collaboration
kyōiku kaikaku kokumin kaigi (教育改革国民会議) National Commission on Educational Reform
kyōiku kihon hō (教育基本法) Fundamental Law of Education
kyōiku shinkō keikaku (教育振興計画) Basic Plan for the Promotion of Education
kyōyō kyōiku (教養教育) general education
kyūgeki na shakai kōzō no henka ni taisho suru shakai kyōiku no arikata ni tsuite (急激な社会構造の変化に対処する社会教育のあり方について) On the Arrangement of Social Education to Cope with Rapid Changes in the Social Structure
machi wo asobu (街を遊ぶ) liven up the town
makegumi (負け組) losers
manabi (学び) learning
manabipia (学びぴあ) annual lifelong learning festival sponsored by the Education Ministry
minsei iin (民生委員) welfare commissioners
muen shakai (無縁社会) a society without relationships
muen shi (無縁死) solitary death
nejire kokkai (ねじれ国会) divided Diet

nihon gakujutsu kaigi (日本学術会議) Science Council of Japan
nihon shōkō kaigisho (日本商工会議所) Japan Chamber of Commerce and Industry
nihon toshokan kyōkai (日本図書館協会) Japan Library Association
nihon wo tsukuri naosō (日本を作り直そう) reinventing Japan
rikai (理解) understanding
rinji kyōiku shingikai or *rinkyōshin* (臨時教育審議会、臨教審) Ad Hoc Council on Education
risuku (リスク) risk
risuku wo toru (リスクを取る) taking a risk
rōdō kyōiku (労働教育) labor education
rosugene sedai (ロスジェネ世代) Lost Generation
saishō fukō shakai (最小不幸社会) a society with the least happiness
seikatsu hogo (生活保護) livelihood protection
seinen gakkyū shinkō hō (青年学級振興法) Law for the Promotion of Youth Class
seishōnen kōryū no ie (青少年交流の家) Youth Friendship Centers
seishonen shidō iin (青少年指導員) youth guidance workers
seishōnen shizen no ie (青少年自然の家) Youth Outdoor Learning Centers
senmon gakkō (専門学校) specialized training colleges
senmon kyōiku (専門教育) specialized education
senmonsei (専門性) expertise
shokuan (職安、公共職業安定所) old abbreviated version of *kōkyō shokugyō anteijo*
shakai ka no sōchi (社会化の装置) device of socialization
shakai kyōiku (社会教育) social education
shakai kyōiku hō (社会教育法) Social Education Law
shakai kyōiku iinkai (社会教育委員会) board of social education
shakai kyōiku ka (社会教育課) social education section
shakai kyōiku kyoku (社会教育局) Social Education Bureau
shakai kyōiku shuji (社会教育主事) social education officers
shakai kyōiku shingikai (社会教育審議会) Social Education Council
shakaisei (社会性) sociality
shakaiteki haijo (社会的排除) social exclusion
shakaiteki hōsetsu (社会的包摂) social inclusion
shakaiteki kigyō (社会的企業) social enterprises
shikōsei (志向性) intentionality
shimin (市民) citizens
shimin chi (市民知) civic knowledge
shinro shidō (進路指導) academic and career counseling

shin nihon kensetsu no kyōiku hōshin (新日本建設の教育方針) guidelines for education that were aimed at the development of a new Japan
shitamachi (下町) downtown
shōgai gakushū (生涯学習) lifelong learning
shōgai gakushū ka (生涯学習課) lifelong learning sections
shōgai gakushū kyoku (生涯学習局) Lifelong Learning Bureau
shōgai gakushū seisaku kyoku (生涯学習政策局) Lifelong Learning Policy Bureau
shōgai gakushū sentā (生涯学習センター) lifelong learning centers
shōgai gakushū shakai (生涯学習社会) lifelong learning society
shōgai gakushū shingikai (生涯学習審議会) National Lifelong Learning Council
shōgai gakushū shinkō hō (生涯学習振興法) Lifelong Learning Promotion Law
shōgai gakushū shinkō no tame no sisaku no suishin taisei nadono seibi ni kansuru hōritsu (生涯学習の振興のための施策の推進体制等の整備に関する法律) law concerning the development of Mechanism and Measures for Promoting Lifelong Learning
shōgai gakushū shinkō shitsu (生涯学習振興室) Lifelong Learning Development Office
shōgai gakushū toshi (生涯学習都市) lifelong learning city
shōgai gakushū toshi sengen (生涯学習都市宣言) a declaration of lifelong learning city
shōgai kyōiku (生涯教育) lifelong education
shōko kaigi sho (商工会議所) Chambers of Commerce and Industry
shokugyō (職業) vocation
shokugyō kunren hō (職業訓練法) Vocational Training Law
shokugyō nōryoku kaihatsu daigakkō (職業能力開発大学校) Polytechnic Colleges
shokugyō nōryoku kaihatsu tanki daigakkō (職業能力開発短期大学校) Polytechnic Junior College
shokugyō nōryoku kaihatsu sōgō daigakkō (職業能力開発総合大学校) Polytechnic University
shokugyō nōryoku kaihatsu sokushin hō (職業能力開発促進法) Vocational Ability Development Promotion Law
shokugyō nōryoku kaihatsu sokushin sentā (職業能力開発促進センター) Vocational Training Center
shokugyō shidō (職業指導) career guidance
shotō chūtō kyōiku kyoku (初等中等教育局) Elementary and Secondary Education Bureau

shūshoku hyōgaki (就職氷河期) hiring Ice Age
sōgōteki na chi (総合的な知) comprehensive knowledge
sōgōteki na gakushū (総合的な学習) integrated studies
sōgōteki na shikōryoku (創造的な思考力) imaginative thinking
suberidai shakai (すべり台社会) slide society
taido (態度) attitude
taiikukan (体育館) gymnasiums
terakoya (寺子屋) temple schools
tōgi (討議)
tōgōtekina gakushū keiken (統合的な学習経験) integrated learning experiences
tokutei hieiri katsudō hōjin (特定非営利活動法人, NPO) specified non-profit cooperation
toshokan (図書館) libraries
toshokan hō (図書館法) Library Law
toyama kenmin shōgai gakushū karreji (富山県民生涯学習カレッジ) Toyama citizens' lifelong learning college
tsunagari (つながり) network
tsūshin kyōiku (通信教育) correspondence courses
wakamono jiritsu chōsen puran (若者自立挑戦プラン) Young People's Independence and Challenge Plan
yaritori no fukkatsu (やりとりの復活) revival of communication
yoka (余暇) leisure
yōkyū kadai (要求課題) desired topics
yutori (ゆとり) low pressure
zaidan (財団) foundation
21 seiki gata shimin (21世紀型市民) citizens for the twenty-first century
"21 seiki nihon no kōsō" kondankai (「２１世紀日本の構想」懇談会) Prime Minister's Commission on Japan's Goals in the Twenty-first Century

References

Abe, Aya. 2007. "Nihon ni okeru shakaiteki haijo no jittai to sono yōin" (The Circumstances and causes of social exclusion in Japan). *Shakai hoshō kenkyū* 43(1): 27–40.
Adam, Barbara, Ulrich Beck and Joost Van Loon, eds. 2000. *The Risk Society and Beyond: Critical Issues for Social Theory*. London; Thousand Oaks, CA: Sage Publications.
Adams, John. 2002. *Risk*. London; New York: Routledge.
Ad Hoc Council on Education (*rinji kyōiku shingikai*). 1988. *Kyōiku kaikaku ni kansuru tōshin: Rinji kyōiku shingikai daiichiji—daiyoji (saishū)* (Report on Education Reform: Ad Hoc Council on Education: the First Report through the Fourth (Final) Report). Tokyo: Ministry of Finance Printing Bureau.
Agency for Cultural Affairs. 2002. *Bunka borantia tsūshin dai 2 gō* (*Journal of Culture Volunteers 2*). Tokyo: Agency for Cultural Affairs.
Amano, Ikuo. 1989. *Kawaru shakai kawaru kyōiku—seijukuka nihon no gakushū zō* (Changing Society, Changing Education—Learning Style of a Matured Japanese Society). Tokyo: Yūshindōkōbunsha.
Annette, John. 2009. "'Active Learning for Active Citizenship': Democratic Citizenship and Lifelong Learning." *Education, Citizenship and Social Justice* 4(2): 149–160.
Appadurai, Arju, ed. 2001. *Globalization*. Durham, NC: Duke University Press.
Arai, Ikuo. 1982. *Gakushū shakai ron* (Theory on Learning Society). Tokyo: Daiichi hōki.
Arnoldi, Jakob. 2009. *Risk: An Introduction*. Cambridge: Polity.
Arthur, James. 2005. "Introduction." In *Citizenship and Higher Education: The Role of Universities in Communities and Society*, ed. Arthur James, and Karen E. Bohlin, 1–5. Milton Park, UK: RoutledgeFalmer.
———. 2010. "Universities Help Develop Tomorrow's Good Citizens." Economic and Social Research Council. Available at http://www.esrc.ac.uk/

news-and-events/press-releases/2923/universities-help-develop-tomorrows-good-citizens.aspx. Accessed July 15, 2011.
Arthur, James, and Karen E. Bohlin, eds. 2005. Citizenship and Higher Education: The Role of Universities in Communities and Society. Milton Park, UK: RoutledgeFalmer.
Asahi Shimbun. 2007. *Rosuto jenerēshon—samayoeru 2000 mannin* (Lost Generation—The Wandering 20 Million People). Tokyo: Asahi shimbunsha.
———. 2009 (January 30). "Kanmin kyōdō e shikō" (Trial of Public-Private Cooperation).
———. 2009 (November 4). "Shasetsu: 15.7 pāsento no shōgeki—hinkonritsu ga utsusu nihon no kiki" (Editorial: Impact of 15.7 Percent—Japan in Crisis as Represented by the Poverty Rate).
———. 2010 (September 9). "Keizai taisaku yowami ari" (Weak Points in Economic Policies).
———. 2011 (June 14). "Seikatsu hogo 200 mannin wo toppa, 3 gatsu, yaku hanseikiburi, sarani zōka mo" (The Number of People Who Received the Livelihood Protection Exceeds 2 Million in March for the First Time in Half a Century, Expecting Further Increase).
Avenell, Simon A. 2010a. Making Japanese Citizens: Civil Society and the Mythology of the Shimin in Postwar Japan. Berkeley: University of California Press.
———. 2010b. "Facilitating Spontaneity: The State and Independent Volunteering in Contemporary Japan." *Social Science Japan Journal* 13(1): 69–93.
Azuma, Kentaro, Junpei Ichinozawa, Shuhei Kimura, and Taku Iida, eds. 2014. *Risuku no jinruigaku* (*Anthropology of Risk*). Kyoto: Sekai shisōsha.
Baker, Tom, and Jonathan Simon, eds. 2002. *Embracing Risk: The Changing Culture of Insurance and Responsibility*. Chicago, IL: University of Chicago Press.
Barata, Pedro. 2000. *Social Exclusion in Europe: Survey of Literature*. Toronto: LaidlawFoundation.
Barry, Monica. 1998. "Social Exclusion and Social Work: An Introduction." In *Social Exclusion and Social Work: Issues of Theory, Policy and Practice*, ed. Monica. Barry and Christine Hallett, 1–12. London: Russell House Printing.
Bauman, Zygmunt. 2000. *Liquid Modernity*. Cambridge: Polity.
Baumeister, Roy F., and Mark R. Leary. 1996. "The Need to Belong: Desire for Interpersonal Attachment as a Fundamental Human Motivation." *Psychological Bulletin* 117(3): 497–529.
Beck, Ulrich. 1992. *Risk Society: Towards a New Modernity*. London: Sage Publications.
———. 1994. "The Reinvention of Politics." In *Reflexive Modernization: Politics, Tradition and Aesthetics in the Modern Social Order*, ed. Ulrich Beck, Anthony Giddens, and Scott Lash, 1–23. Cambridge: Polity.

References

———. 1995. *Ecological Enlightenment: Essays on the Politics of the Risk Society*. AtlanticHighlands, NJ: Humanities Press.
———. 1997. *The Reinvention of Politics: Rethinking Modernity in the Global Social Order*. Cambridge: Polity.
———. 1998. "Politics of Risk Society." In *The Politics of Risk Society*, ed. Jane Franklin, 9–22. Cambridge: Polity.
———. 1999a. *Globalisation*. Cambridge: Polity.
———. 1999b. *World Risk Society*. Cambridge: Polity.
———. 2000a. "Risk Society Revisited: Theory, Politics, and Research Programmes." In *The Risk Society and Beyond: Critical Issues for Social Theory*, ed. Barbara Adam, Ulrich Beck, and Joost Van Loon, 211–229. London: Sage Publications.
———. 2000b. *The Brave New World of Work*. Cambridge: Polity.
———. 2002. "The Terrorist Threat: World Risk Society Revisited." *Theory, Culture and Society* 19(4): 39–55.
———. 2005. *Power in the Global Age: A New Global Political Economy*. Cambridge: Polity.
———. 2006. *Cosmopolitan Vision*. Cambridge: Polity.
———. 2008. "World at Risk: The New Task of Critical Theory." *Development and Society* 37(1): 1–21.
———. 2009a. "Critical Theory of World Risk Society: A Cosmopolitan Vision." *Constellations* 16(1): 3–22.
———. 2009b. Keynote Speech: Reflexive Modernity in Non-European Contexts. The German Association for Social Science Research on Japan. Berlin, November 20, 2009.
Beck, Ulrich, and Elisabeth Beck-Gernsheim. 1995. *The Normal Chaos of Love*. Cambridge: Polity.
———. 2002. Individualization: *Institutionalized Individualism and Its Social and Political Consequences*. Thousand Oaks, CA: Sage Publications.
Beck, Ulrich, Wolfgang Bonss, and Christoph Lau. 2003. "The Theory of Reflexive Modernization: Problematic, Hypotheses and Research Programme." *Theory, Culture and Society* 20(2): 1–33.
Beck, Ulrich, Anthony Giddens, and Scott Lash. 1994. *Reflexive Modernization: Politics, Tradition and Aesthetics in the Modern Social Order*. Cambridge: Polity.
Beck, Ulrich, and Edger Grande. 2007. *Cosmopolitan Europe*. Cambridge: Polity.
Beck, Ulrich, and Christoph Lau. 2005. "Second Modernity as a Research Agenda: Theoretical and Empirical Exploration in the 'Meta-change' of Modern Society." *British Journal of Sociology* 56(4): 525–557.
Beck, Ulrich, and Natan Znaider. 2006. "Unpacking Cosmopolitanism for the Social Sciences: A Research Agenda." *British Journal of Sociology* 57(1): 1–23.
Beck-Gernsheim, Elisabeth. 2002. *Reinventing the Family*. Oxford: Blackwell.

Becker, Gary S., 1964. *Human Capital: A Theoretical and Empirical Analysis, with SpecialReference to Education*. New York: Columbia University Press.
Bestor, Theodore C. 2002. "Networks, Neighborhoods, and Markets: Field Research in Tokyo." In *Urban Life: Readings in the Anthropology of the City*, ed. George Gmelch and Walter P. Zenner, 146–161. Long Grove, IL: Waveland Press.
Bhalla, A. S., and Frédéric Lapeyre. 2004. *Poverty and Exclusion in a Global World*. New York: Palgrave Macmillan.
Bjork, Christopher. 2009. "Local Implementation of Japan's Integrated Studies Reform: A Preliminary Analysis of Efforts to Decentralize the Curriculum." *Comparative Education* 45(1): 23–44.
Boholm, Åsa. 2003. "The Cultural Nature of Risk: Can There Be an Anthropology of Uncertainty?" *Ethnos: Journal of Anthropology* 68(2): 1–21.
Boltanski, Luc, and Eve Chiapello. 2007. *The New Spirit of Capitalism*. London: Verso.
Bora, Alfons. 2007. "Risk, Risk Society, Risk Behavior, and Social Problems." In *Blackwell Encyclopedia of Sociology* Vol. III, ed. George Ritzer, 3926–3932. Oxford: Blackwell.
Borg, Camel, and Peter Mayo. 2005. "The EU Memorandum on Lifelong Learning: Old Wine in New Bottles?" *Globalisation, Societies and Education* 3(2): 203–225.
Bowles, Samuel, and Herbert Gintis. 2002. "Social Capital and Community Governance." *The Economic Journal* 112: 419–36.
Bradley, William. 2012. "Risk, Media and Japanese Young People." In *Education and the Risk Society: Theories, Discourse and Risk Identities in Education Contexts*, ed. Steven Bialostok, Robert L. Whitman, and William S. Bradley, 265–278. Rotterdam, the Netherlands: Sense Publisher.
Brinton, Mary C. 2008. *Ushinawareta ba wo sagashite, rosuto jenerēshon no shakaigaku (Lost in Transition, Sociology of Youth, Education, and Work in Post-industrial Japan)*. Tokyo: NTT Shuppan.
Bunka Borantia National Forum. 2007. *Bunka borantia, asu kara no dezain (Culture Volunteers, a Design for the Future)*. Tokyo: Um Promotion.
Burchell, Graham. 1996. "Liberal Government and Techniques of the Self." In *Foucault and Political Reason: Liberalism, Neo-liberalism and Rationalities of Government*, ed. Andrew Barry, Thomas Osborne, and Nikolas Rose, 19–33. London: UCL Press.
Burgess, Chris, Ian Gibson, Jay Klaphake, and Mark Selzer. 2010. "The 'Global 30' Project and Japanese Higher Education Reform: An Example of a 'Closing in' or an 'Opening Up'? *Globalisation, Societies and Education* 8(4): 461–475.
Bynner, John. 1998. *Use of Longitudinal Data in the Study of Social Exclusion*. Paris: OECD Centre for Educational Research and Innovation.
Cabinet Office (*naikaku fu*). 2007. *Abe naikaku sōri daijin shisei hōshin enzetu (Policy Speech Made by Prime Minister Abe)*, January 26, 2007. Available

at http://www.kantei.go.jp/jp/abespeech/2007/01/26sisei.html. Accessed March 25, 2010.
———. 2008a. *Shōgai gakushū ni kansuru yoron chōsa* (*Public Opinion Survey on Lifelong Learning*). Tokyo: Cabinet Office.
———. 2008b. *Kokumin seikatsu hakusho, shōhisha shiminshakai e no tenbō* (*White Paper on National Life: Toward the Creation of a Consumer-Based Civil Society*), Tokyo: Cabinet Office.
———. 2009. *Kokumin seikatsu senkōdo chōsa* (*Study on Citizens' Lifestyle Preferences*). Tokyo: Cabinet Office.
———. 2010a. *Shin seichō senryaku: "Genki na nihon" fukkatsu no shinario* (*New Growth Strategy: Toward the Revival of an Active Japan*). Tokyo: Cabinet Office.
———. 2010b. *Atarashii kōkyō shien jigyō ni tsuite* (*On Business Support for the New Public Commons*). Tokyo: Cabinet Office. Released on October 8, 2010.
———. 2011a. *Hōjin ga teikan ni kisai shiteiru bunya no kazu* (*The Number of Activity Areas NPO States in Their Article of Association*). Available at https://www.npohomepage.go.jp/data/bunnya.html. Accessed June 23, 2011.
———. 2011b. *NPO no ninshōsū nado* (*The Number of Recognized NPOs*). Available at https://www.npo-homepage.go.jp/data/pref.html. Accessed September 2, 2011.
———. 2011c. *Shakaiteki hōsetsu seisaku wo susumerutame no kihonteki na kangaekata* (*Basic Stance for Promoting Social Inclusion Policies*). Tokyo: Cabinet Office. Released on May 31, 2011.
Calhoun, Craig. 2010. "Beck, Asia and Second Modernity." *British Journal of Sociology* 61(3): 597–619.
Cave, Peter. 2009. *Primary School in Japan: Self, Individuality and Learning in Elementary Education*. London: Routledge.
Central Council for Education (*chuō kyōiku shingikai*). 1966. *Kōki chūtō kyōiku no kakujū seibi ni tsuite* (*On Expansion and Development of Post-secondary Education*). Tokyo: Central Council for Education. Available at http://www.mext.go.jp/b_menu/shingi/12/chuuou/toushin/661001.htm. Accessed May 6, 2011.
———. 1981. *Shōgai kyōiku ni tsuite* (*On Lifelong Education*). Tokyo: Central Council for Education. Available at http://www.mext.go.jp/b_menu/shingi/12/chuuou/toushin/810602.htm. Accessed May 6, 2011.
———. 1990. *Shōgai gakushū no kiban seibi ni tsuite* (*Development of a Lifelong Learning Infrastructure*). Tokyo: Central Council for Education. Available at http://www.mext.go.jp/b_menu/shingi/12/chuuou/toushin/900101.htm. Accessed May 6, 2011.
———. 1991. *Atarashii jidai ni taiō suru kyōiku shoseido no kaikaku ni tsuite* (*Reform of Educational Systems to Deal with a New Era*). Tokyo: Central Council for Education. Available at http://www.mext.go.jp/b_menu/shingi/12/chuuou/toushin/910401.htm. Accessed August 6, 2011.

———. 1996. *21 seiki wo tenbō shita wagakuni no kyōiku no arikata ni tsuite, dai ichiji tōshin* (*On Japanese Education's Prospectus towards the 21st Century, Preliminary Report*). Tokyo: Central Council for Education. Available at http://www.mext.go.jp/b_menu/shingi/12/chuuou/toushin/960701e.htm. Accessed August 6, 2011.

———. 1999. *Shotō chūtō kyōiku to kōtō kyōiku tono setsuzoku no kaizen ni tsuite* (*Improvements in the Articulation between Elementary/Secondary Schools and Higher Education Institutions*). Tokyo: Central Council for Education. Available at http://www.mext.go.jp/b_menu/shingi/12/chuuou/toushin/991202.htm. Accessed August 6, 2011.

———. 2003. *Atarashii jidai ni fusawashii kyōiku kihonhō to kyōiku shinkō kihon keikaku no arikata ni tsuite* (*On the Fundamental Law of Education and a Basic Plan for Education Promotion in the New Era*). Tokyo: Central Council for Education. Available at http://www.mext.go.jp/b_menu/shingi/chukyo/chukyo0/toushin/030301.htm. Accessed August 6, 2011.

———. 2005. *Wagakuni no kōtō kyōiku no shōraizō* (*Future Plans for Japanese HigherEducation*). Tokyo: Central Council for Education. Available at http://www.mext.go.jp/b_menu/shingi/chukyo/chukyo0/toushin/05013101.htm. Accessed August 6, 2011.

———. 2007. *Atarashii jidai wo kirihiraku shōgai gakushū no shinkō hōsaku ni tsuite* (*On Lifelong Learning Policy Measures to Explore the New Era*). Tokyo: Central Council for Education. Available at http://www.mext.go.jp/b_menu/shingi/chukyo/chukyo0/toushin/07020806.htm. Accessed August 6, 2011.

———. 2008a. *Atarashii jidai wo kirihiraku shōgai gakushū no shinkō hōsaku nit tsuite, chi no junkangata shakai no kōchiku wo mezashite* (*On Lifelong Learning Policy Measures to Explore the New Era, Aiming to Construct a Knowledge-circulating Society*). Tokyo: Central Council for Education. Available at http://www.mext.go.jp/b_menu/shingi/chukyo/chukyo0/toushin/1216131_1424.html. Accessed August 6, 2011.

———. 2008b. *Gakushi katei kyōiku no kōchiku ni mukete* (*Development of Undergraduate Education*). Tokyo: Central Council for Education. Available at http://www.mext.go.jp/b_menu/shingi/chukyo/chukyo0/toushin/1217067.htm. Accessed August 6, 2011.

———. 2011. *Kongo no gakkō ni okeru kyaria kyōiku shokugyō kyōiku no arikata ni tsuite* (*The Future of Career and Vocational Education in Japanese schools*). Tokyo: Central Council for Education. Available at http://www.mext.go.jp/b_menu/shingi/chukyo/chukyo0/toushin/1301877.htm. Accessed August 6, 2011.

Chan, Jennifer. 2008. *Another Japan Is Possible: New Social Movements and Global Citizenship Education*. Stanford: Stanford University Press.

Chan-Tiberghien, Jennifer. 2004. *Gender and Human Rights Politics in Japan: Global Norms and Domestic Networks*. Stanford: Stanford University Press.

Chan, Raymond K. H., Mutsuko Takahashi, and Lillian Lih-Rong Wang, ed. 2010. *Risk and Public Policy in East Asia*. Surrey, UK: Ashgate.

Cheetham, Juliet, and Roger Fuller. 1998. "Social Exclusion and Social Work: Policy, Practice and Research." In *Social Exclusion and Social Work: Issues of Theory, Policy and Practice*, ed. Monica Barry and Christine Hallett, 118–132. London: Russell House.

Chiavacci, David. 2008. "From Class Struggle to General Middle-class Society to Divided Society: Societal Models of Inequality in Postwar Japan." *Social Science Japan Journal* 11(1): 5–27.

Christensen, Tom. 2011. "Japanese University Reform—Hybridity in Governance and Management." *Higher Education Policy* 24 (1): 127–142.

Citizenship Foundation. 2011. *What Is Citizenship Education?* Available at http://www.citizenshipfoundation.org.uk/main/page.php?286. Accessed July 15, 2011.

Cohen, Maurie J., ed. 2000. *Risk in the Modern Age*. London: Macmillan.

Council of the European Union. 2000. Presidency Conclusions. Lisbon European Council, March 23–24, 2000. Available at http://www.bologna-berlin2003.de/pdf/PRESIDENCY_CONCLUSIONS_Lissabon.pdf. Accessed May 6, 2011.

Council on National Life (*kokumin seikatsu shingikai*). 2005. *Komyuniti saikō to shimin katsudō no tenkai (On the Development of Community Rebuilding and Citizens' Activities)*. Tokyo: Council on National Life.

Cox, W. Michael, and Jabyeong Koo. 2006. "Miracle to Malaise: What's Next for Japan?" *Economic Letter Insights from the Federal Reserve Bank of Dallas* 1(1): 1–8.

Cruikshank, Barbara. 1999. *The Will to Empower: Democratic Citizens and Other Subjects*. Ithaca, NY: Cornell University Press.

Daly, Mary. 2006. *Social Exclusion as a Concept and Policy Template in the European Union*. Center for European Studies Working Paper Series 135. Cambridge, MA: Harvard University Center for European Studies.

Dean, Mitchell. 1999a. *Governmentality: Power and Rule in Modern Society*. London: Sage Publications.

———. 1999b. "Risk, Calculable and Incalculable." In *Risk and Sociocultural Theory: New Directions and Perspectives*, ed. Deborah Lupton, 131–159. Cambridge: CambridgeUniversity Press.

Dean, Mitchell, and Paul Henman. 2004. "Governing Society Today: Editors' Introduction." *Alternatives: Global, Local, Political* 29(5): 483–94.

Defourny, Jacques, and Marthe Nyssens. 2008. "Social Enterprise in Europe: Recent Trends and Developments." *Social Enterprise Journal* 4(3): 202–228.

Delanty, Gerard. 2003. "Citizenship as a Learning Process: Disciplinary Citizenship versus Cultural Citizenship." *International Journal of Lifelong Education* 22(6): 597–605.

Delors, Jacques. 1996. *Learning: The Treasure Within—Report to UNESCO of the International Commission on Education for the Twenty-first Century*. Paris: UNESCO.

Denscombe, Martyn. 2001. "Uncertain Identities and Health-risking Behaviour." *British Journal of Sociology* 52(1): 157–177.

Dingwall, Robert. 1999. "'Risk Society': The Cult of Theory and the Millennium?" *Social Policy and Administration* 33(4): 474–491.
Dolowitz, David, and David Marsh. 2000. "Learning from Abroad: The Role of Policy Transfer in Contemporary Policy-Making." *Governance: An International Journal of Policy, Administration, and Institution* 13(1): 5–24.
Doogan, Kevin. 2009. *New Capitalism?: The Transformation of Work*. Cambridge: Polity.
Douglas, Mary. 1966. *Purity and Danger: An Analysis of Concepts of Pollution and Taboo*. London: Routledge and Kegan Paul.
———. 1985. *Risk Acceptability according to the Social Sciences*. London: Routledge.
———. 1990. "Risk as a Forensic Resource." *DAEDALUS* 119(4): 1–16.
———. 1992. *Risk and Blame: Essays on Cultural Theory*. London: Routledge.
Douglas, Mary, and Aaron Wildavsky. 1982. *Risk and Culture: An Essay on the Selection of Technological and Environmental Dangers*. Berkeley: University of California Press.
Dudley, Janice, Judith Robinson, and Anthea Taylor. 1999. "Educating for an Inclusive Democracy: Critical Citizenship Literacy." *Discourse: Studies in the Cultural Politics of Education* 20(3): 427–441.
Economic Planning Agency (*keizai kikaku chō*). 1967. *Kokumin seikatsu hakusho* (*White Paper on National Life*). Tokyo: Ministry of Finance Printing Bureau.
Edwards, Richard. 2008. "Actively Seeking Subjects?" In *Foucault and Lifelong Learning: Governing the Subject*, ed. Andreas Fejes and Katherine Nicoll, 21–33. London; New York: Routledge.
Ekberg, Merryn. 2007. "The Parameters of the Risk Society: A Review and Exploration." *Current Sociology* 55(3): 343–366.
Elliott, Anthony. 2002. "Beck's Sociology of Risk: A Critical Assessment." *Sociology* 32(11): 2423–2434.
Employment and Human Resources Development Organization of Japan (*koyō nōryoku kaihatsu kikō*). 2010. *Machikado no kikō* (*Voices from Users*). Available at http://www.ehdo.go.jp/machikado/machikado.html. Accessed November 11, 2010.
Ericson, Richard V., and Aaron Doyle. 2003. *Risk and Morality*. Toronto: University of Toronto Press.
———. 2004a. "Catastrophe Risk, Insurance and Terrorism." *Economy and Society* 33(2): 135–173.
———. 2004b. *Uncertain Business: Risk, Insurance and the Limits of Knowledge*. Toronto: University of Toronto Press.
Ericson, Richard V., Aaron Doyle, and Dean Barry. 2003. *Insurance as Governance*. Toronto: University of Toronto Press.
Eriksen, Thomas Hylland. 2005. *Engaging Anthropology: The Case for a Public Presence*. Oxford: Berg.
European Commission. 1992. *Towards a Europe of Solidarity: Intensifying the Fight against Social Exclusion, Fostering Integration*. COM (92) 542, final.

———. 2000. *A Memorandum on Lifelong Learning*. Brussels: European Commission.

———. 2001. *Making a European Area of Lifelong Learning a Reality*. Brussels: European Commission.

———. 2004. *Facing the Challenges: The Lisbon Strategy for Growth and Employment*, Report from the High Level Group chaired by Wim Kok, November 2004. Brussels: European Commission.

———. 2005. *Working Together for Growth and Jobs: A New Start for the Lisbon Strategy*. Brussels: European Commission.

———. 2010. *Europe 2020*. Available at http://ec.europa.eu/europe2020/index_en.htm. Accessed June 15, 2011.

European Commission Employment and Social Affairs Program. 2008. European Employment Strategy, Mutual Learning. Available at http://ec.europa.eu/employment_social/employment_strategy/peer_en.htm. Accessed May 27, 2008.

European Council. 2000. *Presidency Conclusions, Lisbon European Conclusion, 23 and 24 March 2000*. Available at http://www.consilium.europa.eu/uedocs/cms_data/docs/pressdata/en/ec/00100-r1.en0.htm. Accessed March 27, 2008.

European Investment Bank. 2008. *Innovation 2010 Initiative*. Available at http://www.eib.org/projects/topics/innovation. Accessed May 26, 2008.

European Union. 2008. *Lifelong Learning as a Key Factor in a Knowledge-based Economy*. Available at http://www.eu2008.si/en/News_and_Documents/Press_Releases/March/0311MVZTlll.html. Accessed May 27, 2008.

Evans, Martin. 1998. "Behind the Rhetoric: The Institutional Basis of Social Exclusion and Poverty." *IDS Bulletin* 29 (1): 42–49.

Ewald, François. 1991. "Insurance and Risk." In *The Foucault Effect: Studies in Governmentality*, ed. Graham Burchell, Colin Gordon, and Peter Miller, 197–210. Chicago, IL: University of Chicago Press

———. 1993. "Two Infinities of Risk." In *The Politics of Everyday Fear*, ed. Brian Massumi, 221–228. Minneapolis, MN: University of Minnesota Press.

Faure, Edger, Felipe Herrera, Abdul-Razzak Kaddoura, Henri Lopes, Arthur V. Petrovsky, Majid Rahnema, and Frederick Champion Ward. 1972. *Learning to Be: The World of Education Today and Tomorrow*. Paris: UNESCO.

Ferguson, James, and Akhil Gupta. 2002. "Spatializing States: Toward an Ethnography of Neoliberal Governmentality." *American Ethnologist* 29(4): 981–1002.

Ferreira, Celio, Åsa Boholm, and Ragnar Löfstedt. 2001. "From Vision to Catastrophe: A Risk Vent in Search of Images." In *Risk, Media and Stigma: Understanding Public Challenges to Modern Science and Technology*, ed. James Flynn, Paul Slovic, and Howard Kunreuther, 283–300. London: Earthscan.

Field, John. 2006. *Lifelong Learning and the New Educational Order*. Stoke on Trent, UK: Trentham Books.

Fien, John, Rupert Maclean, Man-Gon Park. 2009. *Work, Learning and Sustainable Development: Opportunities and Challenges*. New York: Springer.

Financial Times. 2011 (June 23). "Millionaires Shrug Off Downturn."
Foucault, Michel. 1991. "Governmentality." In *The Foucault Effect: Studies in Governmentality,* ed. Graham Burchell, Colin Gordon, and Peter Miller, 87–104. Chicago, IL: University of Chicago Press.
Fujita, Teruyuki. 2011. "The Current State and Future Tasks of Japan's Career Education Promotion Policies—Embarking on the Road Less Traveled." *Japan Labor Review* 8(1): 26–47.
Fukuhara, Hiroyuki. 2007. *Shakaiteki haijo/hōsetsu to shakai seisaku (Social Exclusion/Inclusion and Social Policies).* Kyoto: Hōritsu Bunkasha.
Furlong, Andy, and Fred Cartmel. 2007. *Young People and Social Change: New Perspectives.* Maidenhead, UK: Open University Press.
Fuwa, Kazuhiko. 2001. "Lifelong Education in Japan, a Highly School-Centred Society: Educational Opportunities and Practical Educational Activities for Adults." *International Journal of Lifelong Education* 20(1/2): 127–136.
———. 2009. "Is the Expansion of Higher Education in Japan for Young Students Only or for All?: A Critical Analysis from a Lifelong Learning Perspective." *International Journal of Lifelong Education* 28(4): 459–471.
Garland, David. 2003. "The Rise of Risk." In *Risk and Morality,* ed. Richard. V. Ericson and Aaron Doyle, 48–86. Toronto: University of Toronto Press.
Genda, Yuji. 2001. *Shigoto no naka no aimai na fuan: Yureru wakamono no genzai.* Tokyo: Chuōkōron shinsha. An English translation of this book, *A Nagging Sense of Job Insecurity: The New Reality Facing Japanese Youth*, is available from the I House Press in Tokyo in 2006.
Giddens, Anthony. 1990. *The Consequences of Modernity.* Cambridge: Polity.
———. 1991. *Modernity and Self Identity: Self and Society in the Late-modern Age.* Cambridge: Polity.
———. 1994. "Living in a Post-traditional Society." In *Reflexive Modernization: Politics, Tradition and Aesthetics in the Modern Social Order,* ed. Ulrich Beck, Anthony Giddens,and Scott Lash, 56–109. Cambridge: Polity.
———. 1998a. *The Third Way: The Renewal of Social Democracy.* Cambridge: Polity.
———. 1998b. "Risk Society: The Context of British Politics." In *The Politics of Risk Society,* ed. Jane Franklin, 23–34. Cambridge: Polity.
———. 1999. "Risk and Responsibility." *Modern Law Review* 62(1): 1–10.
Goodman, Roger. 2001. "The State of Higher Education in East Asia: Higher Education in East Asia and the State." *Ritsumeikan Journal of Asia Pacific Studies* 8: 1–29.
———, ed. 2002. *Family and Social Policy in Japan: Anthropological Approaches.* Cambridge: Cambridge University Press.
———. 2010. "The Rapid Redrawing of Boundaries in Japanese Higher Education." *Japan Forum* 22(1): 65–87.
Gouthro, Patricia A. 2007. "Active and Inclusive Citizenship for Women: Democratic Considerations for Fostering Lifelong Education." *International Journal of Lifelong Education* 26(2): 143–154.

Greenhouse, Carol J., ed. 2010. *Ethnographies of Neoliberalism*. Philadelphia, PA: University of Pennsylvania Press.
Greenwood, Davydd J., and Morten Levin. 1998. *Introduction to Action Research: Social Research for Social Change*. Thousand Oaks, CA: Sage Publications.
———. 2007. *Introduction to Action Research: Social Research for Social Change*. Second edition. Thousand Oaks, CA: Sage Publications.
Griffin, Colin. 2009. "Policy and Lifelong Learning." In *The Routledge International Handbook of Lifelong Learning*, ed. Peter Jarvis, 261–270. Abingdon, UK: Routledge.
Group of Eight. 1999. *The Cologne Charter: Aims and Ambitions for Lifelong Learning*. Cologne, Germany: Group of Eight.
Habermas, Jürgen. 1996. *Between Facts and Norms: Contributions to a Discourse Theory of Law and Democracy*. Cambridge, MA: MIT Press.
Hacking, Ian. 1999. *The Social Construction of What?* Cambridge, MA: Harvard University Press.
———. 2003. "Risk and Dirt." In *Risk and Morality*, ed. Richard V. Ericson and Aaron Doyle, 22–47. Toronto: University of Toronto Press.
Haddad, Mary. A. 2010. "A State-in-society Approach to the Nonprofit Sector: Welfare Services in Japan." *Voluntas* 22(1): 26–47.
Han, Soonghee. 2007. "Asian Lifelong Learning in the Context of a Global Knowledge Economy: A Task Re-Visited." *Asia Pacific Education Review* 8(3): 478–486.
Harvey, David. 2005. *A Brief History of Neoliberalism*. Oxford: Oxford University Press.
Hashimoto, Kenji. 2009a. *"Kakusa" no sengoshi—kaikyū shakai nihon no rirekisho* (*Postwar History of Socioeconomic Divide—Class Society, Japanese Curriculum Vitae*). Tokyo: Kawade shobō.
———. 2009b. *Hinkon rensa—kakudai suru kakusa to andā kurasu no shutsugen* (*Poverty Chain—Expanding Socioeconomic Divide and the Emergence of an Underclass*). Tokyo: Daiwa shobō.
Hatano, Kanji. 1972. *Shōgai kyōiku ron* (*Lifelong Education Theory*). Tokyo: Shōgakkan.
———. 1995. "Shōgai gakushū no hassei to hatten" (*The Emergence and Development of Lifelong Learning*). *Shakai Kyōiku* 572: 4–5.
Hidaka, Tomoko. 2010. *Salaryman Masculinity: Continuity and Change in Hegemonic Masculinity in Japan*. Leiden, the Netherlands: Brill.
Hilgers, Mathieu. 2002. "The Three Anthropological Approaches to Neoliberalism." *International Social Science Journal* 61(2): 351–364.
Hiroi, Yoshinori. 2008. "'Komyuniti no chūshin' to komyuniti seisaku" (The Center of Community and Community Development Policy). *Chiba daigaku kōkyō kenkyū* 5(3): 48–72.
———. 2009. *Komyuniti wo toinaosu—tsunagari, toshi, nihon shakai no mirai* (*Revising Communities—Networks, Cities, and the Future of Japanese Society*). Tokyo: Chikuma shōbō.

Hirosaki Municipal Board of Education (*hirosaki shi kyōiku iinkai*). 2010. *Heisei 22 nendo hirosaki no shakai kyōiku* (*Social Education in the City of Hirosaki in 2010*). Hirosaki: Hirosaki Municipal Board of Education.

Hokkaido Shimbun. 2009 (March 14). "Juyō takamaru kōkyō shokugyō kunren" (Increase in the Demands for Public Vocational Training).

Honda, Yuki. 2005. *Tagenka suru "nōryoku: to nihon shakai—haipā meritokurashī ka no nakade* (*Diversified "Abilities" and Japanese Society—amid Hyper-meritocracy*). Tokyo: NTT Shuppan.

———. 2009. *Kyōiku no shokugyōteki igi: wakamono, gakkō, shakai wo tsunagu* (*The Vocational Meaning of Education: Connecting Youth, School, and Society*). Tokyo: Chikuma Shinsho.

Hood, Christopher P. 2001. *Japanese Education Reform: Nakasone's Legacy*. London: Routledge.

Hood, Christopher, Henry Rothstein, and Robert Baldwin. 2001. *The Government of Risk: Understanding Risk Regulation Regimes*. Oxford: Oxford University Press.

Hook, Glenn D., ed. 2010. "Special Issue: Risk and Security in Japan." *Japan Forum* 22 (1&2): 139–237.

Hook, Glenn D., and Hiroko Takeda. 2007. "'Self-responsibility' and the Nature of the Postwar Japanese State: Risk through the Looking Glass." *Journal of Japanese Studies* 33(1): 93–123.

Humbert, Marc, and Yoshimichi Sato, eds. 2012. *Social Exclusion: Perspectives from France and Japan*. Melbourne, Australia: Trans Pacific Press.

Hutchins, Robert M. 1968. *The Learning Society*. New York: Frederick A. Praeger.

Ichikawa, Shogo. 1995. *Rinkyōshin igo no kyōiku seisaku* (*Education Policies after the Ad Hoc Council on Education National*). Tokyo: Kyōiku kaihatsu kenkyūsho.

———. 2009. *Kyōiku kihonhō kaiseiron shi—kaisei de kyōiku wa dōnaru* (*History of the Revision of the Fundamental Law of Education—What Will Happen to Japanese Education after the Revision*). Tokyo: Kyōiku kaihatsu kenkyūjo.

Imamura, Haruhiko, Shino Sonoda, and Ikuyo Kaneko. 2010. *Komyuniti no chikara—"enryogachi" na sōsharu kyapitaru no hakken* (*Power of Community—Discovery of "Hesitant" Social Capital*). Tokyo: Keiogijku daigaku shuppankai.

Inui, Akio. 2003. "Restructuring Youth: Recent Problems of Japanese Youth and Its Contextual Origin." *Journal of Youth Studies* 6(2): 219–233.

Ishida, Hiroshi, and David Slater. 2009. *Social Class in Contemporary Japan*. London; New York: Routledge.

Ishiguro, Kuniko. 2008. "Japanese Employment in Transformation: The Growing Number of Non-regular Workers." *Electronic Journal of Contemporary Japanese Studies*. Available at http://www.japanesestudies.org.uk/articles/2008/Ishiguro.html. Accessed July 30, 2011.

Ito, Midori, and Munenori Suzuki. 2013. "Acceptance of Beck's Theory in Japan: From Environmetnal Risks to Individualization." In *Routledge Companion to Contemporary Japanese Social Theory: From Individualization to Global-*

ization in Japan Today, ed. Anthony Elliott, Masataka Katagiri, and Atsushi Sawai, 114–131. London; New York: Routledge.
Iwata, Masami. 2008. *Shakaiteki haijo, sanka no ketsujo, futashikana kizoku (Social Exclusion, Lack of Participation, and Uncertain Belongingness)*. Tokyo: Yūhikaku.
———. 2010. "Shakaiteki haijo, wākingu puā wo chūshin ni" (Social Exclusion from the Perspective of the Working Poor). *Nihon rōdō kenkyū zasshi* 597: 10–13.
Iwata, Masami, and Akihiko Nishizawa, eds. 2008. *Poverty and Social Welfare in Japan*. Melbourne, Australia: Trans Pacific Press.
Japan Association of Corporate Executives (*keizai dōyukai*). 2008. *21seiki no atarashii hatarakikata: "wāku ando raifu integurēshon" wo mezashite (A New Working Style in the Twenty-first Century: Towards the Integration of Work and Life)*. Tokyo: Japan Association of Corporate Executives.
Japan Business Federation (*nippon keidanren*). 2010. *Sangyōkai no motomeru jinzaizō to daigaku kyōiku e no kitai ni kansuru ankēto (Survey on the Human Resources That Industries Want to Hire and Expectations Regarding University Education)*. Tokyo: Japan Business Federation.
Japan Federation of Economic Organizations (*keidanren*). 1996. *Sōzōteki na jinzai no ikusei ni mukete (Toward Nurturing Creative People)*. Tokyo: Japan Federation of Economic Organizations.
Japan Federation of Employers' Associations (*nikkeiren*). 1995. *Shin jidai no nihon teki keiei (Japanese Management in a New Era)*. Tokyo: Japan Federation of Employers' Associations.
Japan Library Association (*nihon toshokan kyōkai*). 2010. *Nihon no toshokan (Libraries in Japan)*. Tokyo: Japan Library Association.
Jarvis, Peter. 1983. *Adult Education and Lifelong Learning: Theory and Practice*. Milton Park, UK: Routledge Falmer.
———. 2007. *Globalization, Lifelong Learning and the Learning Society: Sociological Perspectives*. London; New York: Routledge.
———, ed. 2009a. *The Routledge International Handbook of Lifelong Learning*. Abingdon, UK: Routledge.
———. 2009b. "The European Union and Lifelong Learning Policy." In *The Routledge International Handbook of Lifelong Learning*, ed. Peter Jarvis, 271–280. Abingdon, UK: Routledge.
Jones, Hywel Ceri. 2005. "Lifelong Learning in the European Union: Whither the Lisbon Strategy?" *European Journal of Education* 40(3): 247–60.
Kagawa, Masahiro, and Kosaku Miyasaka. 1994. *Shōgai gakushū no sōzō (The Creation of Lifelong Learning)*. Kyoto: Minerva shobō.
Kagawa, Masahiro, Makoto Suzuki, and Hidekazu Sasaki, eds. 2007. *Yoku wakaru shōgai gakushū (An Introductory Guide to Lifelong Learning)*. Kyoto: Minerva shobō.
Kainose, Shigeru. 2010. *Shō chū ikkan komyuniti sukūru no tsukurikata—mitakashi kyōikuchō no chōsen (How to Make Elementary School and Junior High School Linked Community Schools—A Challenge for the Head of the Mitaka Municipal Department of Education)*. Tokyo: Popura sha.

Kaneko, Ikuyo. 2002. *Komyuniti sorūshon* (*Community Solution*). Tokyo: Iwanami shoten.
Kaneko, Ikuyo, Hiroshi Suzuki, and Kyoko Shibuya. 2000. *Komyuniti skūru kōsō: gakkō wo henkaku suru tameni* (*The Community School Idea: A Plan about Reforming the School*). Tokyo: Iwanami shoten.
Kaneko, Isamu. 2007. *Kakusa fuan jidai no komyuniti shakaigaku—sōsharu kyapitaru kara no shohōsen* (*Community Sociology in the Era of Uncertainties Generated from Socioeconomic Divide—Prescription from Social Capital Theory*). Kyoto: Minerva shobō.
Kawachi, Paul. 2008. "Education Reform in Japan for Lifelong Learning." *International Journal of Lifelong Education* 27(5): 509–516.
Kawanobe, Satoshi. 1994. "Lifelong Learning in Japan." *International Review of Education* 40(6): 485–493.
Kelly, Peter. 2001. "Youth at Risk: Processes of Individualization and Responsibilisation in the Risk Society." *Discourse: Studies in the Cultural Politics of Education* 22(1): 23–33.
Kemshall, Hazel. 2002. *Risk, Social Policy and Welfare*. Buckingham, UK: Open University Press.
Kerlin, Janelle A. 2010. "A Comparative Analysis of the Global Emergence of Social Enterprise." *Voluntas* 21: 162–179.
Kingston, Jeff. 2010. *Contemporary Japan: History, Politics, and Social Change since the 1980s*. Hoboken, NJ: Wiley, John and Sons.
Kinoshita, Tatsufumi. 2005. "Myūziamu borantia ni kansuru jittai chōsa" (Survey on Volunteers at Museums). *Musée* 68: 12.
Kirzner, Israel M. 1973. *Competition and Entrepreneurship*. Chicago, IL: University of Chicago Press.
Kisby, Ben. 2009. "Social Capital and Citizenship Lessons in England: Analyzing the Presuppositions of Citizenship Education." *Education Citizenship and Social Justice* 4(41): 41–62.
Kloprogge, Jo. 1998. *Social Exclusion in the Netherlands: Discussions and Initiatives*. Paris:OECD Centre for Educational Research and Innovation.
Kobayashi, Miki. 2008. *Rupo: "Seishain" no wakamonotachi: Shūshoku hyōgaki sedai wo ou* (*Report:"Regular Worker" Youth: Chasing after the Hiring Ice Age Generation*). Tokyo: Iwanami shoten.
Komazaki, Hiroki. 2007. *"Shakai wo kaeru" wo shigoto ni suru* (*Working towards "Changing Society"*). Tokyo: Eichi Shuppan.
Komikawa, Koichiro. 2007. *Kenri to shiteno kyaria kyōiku* (*The Right to Career Education*).Tokyo: Akashi shoten.
Konno, Haruki. 2012. *Burakku kigyō, nihon wo kuitsubusu yōkai* (*Black Companies, Phantoms Destroying Japan*). Tokyo: Bunshun shinsho.
Kuno, Osamu. 1960. "Shimin shugi no seiritsu—hitotsu no taiwa" (Development of Citizen-ism: A dialogue). *Shisō no kagaku* 19: 9–16.
Kusumi, Takashi, Masuo Koyasu, and Yasushi Michita, eds. 2011. *Hihanteki shikōryoku wo hagukumu* (*Developing Critical Thinking in Higher Education*). Tokyo: Yuhikaku.

Kymlicka, Will. 1996. *Multicultural Citizenship: A Liberal Theory of Minority Rights*. Oxford: Oxford University Press.

Lash, Scott. 1994. "Reflexivity and Its Doubles: Structure, Aesthetics, Community." In *Reflexive Modernization: Politics, Tradition and Aesthetics in the Modern Social Order*, ed. Ulrich Beck, Anthony Giddens, and Scott Lash, 111–73. Cambridge: Polity.

LeBlanc, Robin. M. 1999. *Bicycle Citizens: The Political World of the Japanese Housewife*. Berkeley: University of California Press.

Lengrand, Paul. 1970. *An Introduction to Lifelong Education*. Paris: UNESCO.

Lister, Ruth. 2007. "Inclusive Citizenship: Realizing the Potential." *Citizenship Studies* 11(1): 49–61.

LLC (Lifelong Learning Council, Shogai gakushū shingikai). 1992. *Kongo no shakai no dōkō ni taiōshita shōgai gakushū no shinkō hōsaku ni tsuite* (*On Promotion of Lifelong Learning Responding to Ongoing Changes in Society*). Tokyo: LLC. Available at http://www.mext.go.jp/b_menu/hakusho/nc/t19920803001/t19920803001.html. Accessed May 6, 2011.

———. 1996. *Chiiki ni okeru shōgai gakushū kikai no jūjitsu hōsaku ni tsuite* (*On Measures to Expand Lifelong Learning Opportunities in Local Communities*). Tokyo: LLC. Available at http://www.mext.go.jp/b_menu/shingi/12/shougai/toushin/960402.htm. Accessed May 6, 2011.

———. 1997. *Shōgai gakushū no seika wo ikasutame no hōsaku ni tsuite* (*On Measures to Make the Best Use of Results of Lifelong Learning*). Tokyo: LLC. Available at http://www.mext.go.jp/b_menu/shingi/12/shougai/toushin/970301.htm. Accessed May 6, 2011.

———. 1998. *Shakai no henka ni taiō shita kongo no shakai kyōiku gyōsei no arikata ni tsuite* (*On Social Education Administration Responding to Social Changes in the Future*). Tokyo: LLC. Available at http://www.mext.go.jp/b_menu/shingi/12/shougai/toushin/980901.htm. Accessed May 6, 2011.

———. 1999a. *Gakūshū no seika wo habahiroku ikasu* (*On Encouraging the Use of Learning Results through Lifelong Learning Activities*). Tokyo: LLC. Available at http://www.mext.go.jp/b_menu/shingi/12/shougai/toushin/990601.htm. Accessed May 6, 2011.

———. 1999b. *Seikatsu taiken, shizen taiken ga nihon no kodomo no kokoro wo hagukumu* (*On Nurturing Japanese Children through Real Experiences in Actual Daily Life and Nature*). Tokyo: LLC. Available at http://www.mext.go.jp/b_menu/shingi/12/shougai/toushin/990602.htm. Accessed May 6, 2011.

Luhman, Niklas. 1993. *Risk: A Sociological Theory*. New York: A. de Gruyter.

Lupton, Deborah. 1999a. *Risk (Key Ideas)*. London: Routledge.

———. 1999b. "Introduction: Risk and Sociocultural Theory." In *Risk and Sociocultural Theory: New Directions and Perspectives*, ed. Deborah Lupton, 1–11. Cambridge: Cambridge University Press.

Lyng, Stephen. 1990. "Edgework: A Social Psychological Analysis of Voluntary Risk Taking." *American Journal of Sociology* 95(4): 851–886.

———. ed. 2004. *Edgework: The Sociology of Risk-taking*. New York; London: Routledge.

———. 2008. "Edgework, Risk, and Uncertainty." In *Social Theories of Risk and Uncertainty: An Introduction*. Jens O. Zinn, ed. Malden, MA: Blackwell.

Mainichi Shimbun. 2014 (July 16). "Kodomo no hinkon 16.3 pāsento, kako saiaku" (Children's Poverty Rate Hits 16.3 percent, the Worst on Record).

Makino, Atsushi. 2005. *"Watashi" no saikōchiku to shakai, shōgai kyōiku—gurōbaru ka, shōshi kōreika soshite daigaku (Reconstructing Myself and Social and Lifelong Education—Globalization, Aging Society and Universities)*. Okayama: Daigaku kyōiku shuppankai.

———. 2013. "Changing Grassroots Communities and Lifelong Leanring in Japan." *Comparative Education* 49(1): 42–56.

Marcus, George E. 1995. "Ethnography in/of the World System: The Emergence of Multi-Sited Ethnography." *Annual Review of Anthropology* 24: 95–117.

Marshall, T. H. [1950] 1992. *Citizenship and Social Class*. London: Pluto Press.

Martin, Ian. 2003. "Adult Education, Lifelong Learning and Citizenship: Some Ifs and Buts." *International Journal of Lifelong Education* 22(6): 566–579.

Martin, Sherry. 2011. *Popular Democracy in Japan: How Gender and Community Are Changing Modern Electoral Politics*. Ithaca, NY: Cornell University Press.

Matsuura, Masahiro. 2010. "How the New Government Utilizes Emerging Internet Media in Japan." *Asian Politics and Policy* 2(4): 671–674.

Matten, Dirk. 2004. "The Impact of the Risk Society Thesis on Environmental Politics and Management in a Globalizing Economy—Principles, Proficiency, Perspectives." *Journal of Risk Research* 7(4): 377–398.

McCann, Eugene, and Kevin Ward. 2013. "A Multi-Disciplinary Approach to Policy Transfer Research: Geographies, Assemblages, Mobilities, and Mutations." *Policy Studies* 34(1): 2–18.

Mebrahtu, Teame, Michael Crossley, and David Johnson, eds. 2000. *Globalization, Educational Transformation and Societies in Transition*. Oxford: Symposium Books.

Medel-Añonuevo, Carolyn, Toshio Ohsako, and Werner Mauch. 2001. *Revisting Lifelong Learning for the 21st Century*. Hamburg: UNESCO Institute for Education.

Melucci, Alberto. 1996. *The Playing Self: Person and Meaning in the Planetary Society*. Cambridge: Cambridge University Press.

METI (Ministry of Economy, Trade and Industry, Keizai sangyō shō). 2005. *Heisei 17 nendo tokutei sābisu sangyō jittai chōsa (Survey on Specific Service Industry in 2005)*. Tokyo: METI.

———. 2008. *Sōsharu bijinesu kenkyūkai hōkokusho (Report on Social Enterprises)*. Tokyo: METI.

MEXT (Ministry of Education, Culture, Sports, Science and Technology, Monbu kagaku shō). 2001. *Shōgai gakushū fesutibaru kaisai yōkō (Outline for the National Festival forLifelong Learning)*. Tokyo: MEXT.

———. 2003. *Gakkō kihon chōsa hōkokusho* (*Basic Survey Report on Schools*). Tokyo: MEXT.

———. 2008a. *Shakai kyōiku chōsa hōkoku* (*Report on Social Education*). Tokyo: MEXT.

———. 2008b. *Kyōiku shinkō keikaku* (*Basic Plan for the Promotion of Education*). Tokyo: MEXT.

———. 2008c. *Ima no gakkō kyōiku ni okeru kyaria kyōiku shokugyō kyōiku no arikata ni tsuite* (*Career and Vocational Education in Current School Education*). Tokyo: MEXT.

———. 2009a. *Heisei 21 nendo monbu kagaku hakusho* (*White Paper on Policies of Education, Culture, Sports, Science and Technology in 2009*). Tokyo: MEXT.

———. 2009b. *Shin gakushū shidō yōryō* (*New Teaching Guidelines*). Tokyo: MEXT.

———. 2010a. *Heisei 22 nendo shōgai gakushū, shakai kyōiku shinkō shisaku ni kansuru kiso shiryō* (*Basic Materials for Policymaking on Lifelong Learning and Social Education in 2010*). Tokyo: MEXT.

———. 2010b. *Monbukagakushō e no teiansho* (*Proposal to MEXT*). Tokyo: MEXT.

———. 2010c. *Komyuniti sukūru, chiiki komyuniti to ittai to natta gakkō zukuri* (*The Community School: Integrating Schools and the Local Community*). Tokyo: MEXT.

———. 2010d. *Ikiru chikara* (*Zest for Living*). Tokyo: MEXT.

———. 2010e. *"Atarashii kōkyō" gata gakkō no sōzō jigyō* (*On the "New Public Commons"Type of School*). Tokyo: MEXT.

———. 2010f. *"Atarashii kōkyō" gata gakkō no sōzō ni tsuite* (*On the Creation of the "New Public Commons" Type of School*). Tokyo: MEXT.

———. 2010g. *Mondai kōdō chōsa* (*Survey on Deviant Behaviors*). Tokyo: MEXT.

———. 2011a. *Monbukagakushō shokan ippan kaikei, saishutsu yosan kakumoku meisaisho* (*Details of MEXT Budget*). Tokyo: MEXT.

———. 2011b. *Shakai kyōiku chōsa hōkoku chūkan hōkoku* (*Interim Report on Social Education*). Tokyo: MEXT.

———. 2011c. "Atarashii kōkyō, jukugi" (*New Public Commons and Due Deliberation*). *Gekkan Shōgai Gakushū* 4(1): 2–5. Tokyo: MEXT.

———. 2011d. *Manabipia Tokyo 2011, zenkoku shōgai gakushū nettowāku fōramu* (*Manabipia Tokyo 2011, National Forum of Lifelong Learning*). Tokyo: MEXT.

———. 2014. *Community school no shitei jōkyō* (*Current Circumstances of Community Schools*) Tokyo: MEXT. Available at http://www.mext.go.jp/a_menu/shotou/community/shitei/detail/1348142.htmAccessed August 6, 2014.

MHLW (Ministry of Health, Labor and Welfare, Kōsei rōdō shō). 2009. *Heisei 21 nendo 8 gatu yūkō kyūjin bairitsu* (The National Ratio of Job Offers to Job Seekers in August 2009). Tokyo: MHLW.

———. 2010a. *Shotoku saihaibun chōsa* (*Survey on Income Redistribution*). Tokyo: MHLW.

———. 2010b. *Hiseiki rōdōsha no yatoidome nado no jōkyō* (*On the Situation of Layoffs among Non-regular Workers*). Tokyo: MHLW. Released on August 27, 2010.

———. 2010c. *Shinsotsusha taiken koyō jigyō no kakujū ni tsuite* (*On the Trial of Employment for New Graduates*). Tokyo: MHLW. Released on May 21, 2010.

———. 2010d. *Chingin kōzō kihon tōkei chōsa* (*A Basic Statistical Survey on the Wage Structure*). Tokyo: MHLW. Released on January 13, 2010.

———. 2010e. *Rōdō keizai no bunseki* (*Analysis of Labor Economy*). Tokyo: MHLW.

———. 2011. *Shūgyōkeitai no tayōka ni kansuru sōgō chōsa* (*Comprehensive Survey on the Diversity of Working Styles*). Tokyo: MHLW. Released on August 29, 2011.

MHLW (Ministry of Health, Labor and Welfare, Kōsei rōdō shō) and MEXT (Ministry of Education, Culture, Sports, Science and Technology, Monbu kagaku shō). 2011. *Daigakusei naiteiritsu chōsa* (*Survey on the Number of College-graduating Students who Secured Jobs before Graduating*). Tokyo: MHLW and MEXT.

MIAC (Ministry of Internal Affairs and Communications, Sōmu shō). 2010. *Heisei 21 nendo rōdōryoku chōsa nenpō* (*Annual Survey on Labor Forces in 2009*). Tokyo: MIAC.

Mierendorff, Johanna. 1998. *Childhood Social Exclusion: Children's Situation and Social Exclusion in Germany*. Paris: OECD Centre for Educational Research and Innovation.

Milana, Marcella, and John Holford, eds. 2014. *Adult Education Policy and the European Union: Theoretical and Methodological Perspectives*. Rotterdam, the Netherlands: Sense Publishers.

Miller, Riel. 1997. "Economic Flexibility and Social Cohesion." *OECD Observer* 207: 24–27.

Miller, Toby. 2007. *Cultural Citizenship: Cosmopolitanism, Consumerism, and Television in a Neoliberal Age*. Philadelphia, PA: Temple University Press.

Mills, C. Wright. 1958. *The Sociological Imagination*. New York: Oxford University Press.

Mimura, Takao. 2010. "Wagakuni no kyaria kyōiku no genjō to korekara" (Current Situations and the Future of Japan's Career Education). *Business Labor Trend*, March2010, 7–10.

Mincer, Jacob. 1962. "On-the-job Training: Costs, Returns and Some Implications. *Journal of Political Economy*" 70 (suppl.): 50–79.

Miura, Seiichiro, Tomoko Matsushita, Masayuki Nakamura, and Fujimi Suezaki, eds. 1991. *Lifelong Learning in Japan: An Introduction*. Tokyo: National Federation of Social Education, Japan.

Miyamoto, Michiko. 2002. *Wakamono ga "shakaiteki jyakusha" ni tenraku suru* (*The Youth Becomes "Socially Vulnerable"*). Tokyo: Yōsensha.

Miyazaki, Hirokazu. 2010. "The Temporality of Hope." In *Ethnographies of Neoliberalism*, ed. Carol J. Greenhouse, 238–250. Philadelphia: University of Pennsylvania Press.
Miyazaki, Saeko. 2007. *Kyaria kyōiku: riron to jissen, hyōka* (*Career Education: Theory, Practice, and Evaluation*). Tokyo: Koyō mondai kenkyūkai.
Mok, Ka Ho. 2007. "Globalization, New Education Governance and State Capacity in East Asia." *Globalisation, Societies and Education* 5(1): 1–21.
Moutsios, Stavros. 2009. "International Organizations and Transnational Education Policy." *Compare* 39(4): 467–478.
Mulder, Regina H., and Peter F. E. Sloane, eds. 2004. *New Approaches to Vocational Education in Europe*. Oxford: Symposium Books.
Murphy, Mark, and Ted Fleming. 2006. "The Application of the idea of Habermas to Adult Learning." In *Lifelong Learning: Concepts and Contexts*, ed. Peter Sutherland and Jim Crowther, 48–57. New York: Routledge.
Mutual Learning Program. 2008. *Mutual Learning Program of the European Employment Strategy*. Available at http://www.mutual-learning-employment.net. Accessed May 27, 2008.
Mythen, Gabe. 2007. "Reappraising the Risk Society Thesis: Telescopic Sight or MyopicVision?" *Current Sociology* 55(6): 793–813.
Nakamura, Kengo. 2006. *Shakai riron kara mita haijo: Furansu ni okeru giron wo chūshin ni* (Exclusion from the Perspective of Social Theory: An Introduction to the Discussion in France). CREI Discussion Paper Series No. 2. Osaka City University Centre for Research and Economic Inequality.
Nakano, Lynne. Y. 2005. *Community Volunteers in Japan: Everyday Stories of Social Change*. London; New York: Routledge.
National Commission on Educational Reform (*kyōiku kaikaku kokumin kaigi*). 2000. *Kyōiku wo kaeru 17 no teian*. Tokyo: National Commission on Educational Reform. The official English Translation *17 Proposals for Changing Education* is available at http://www.kantei.go.jp/foreign/education/report/report.html.
National Curriculum. 2011. Citizenship Key Stage 3. Available at http://curriculum.qcda.gov.uk/key-stages-3-and 4/subjects/key-stage-3/citizenship/index.aspx. Accessed July 15, 2011.
National Institute for Education Policy Research (*kokuritsu kyōiku seisaku kenkyūjo*). 2002. *Jidō seito no shōkugyōkan kinrōkan wo hagukumu kyōiku no suishin ni tsuite* (*The Promotion of Education Which Nurtures the Work Ethics of Children and Students*). Tokyo: National Institute for Education Policy Research.
———. 2009. *Heisei 21 nendo zenkoku gakuryoku gakushū jōkyō chōsa kekka* (*Results on the National Academic Achievement Test*). Tokyo: National Institute for Education Policy Research.
———. 2010. *Heisei 21 nendo shokuba taiken, intānshippu jisshi jōkyō nado chōsa kekka* (*Results of a Survey Regarding the State of Work Experience and*

Internship Implementation during Fiscal 2009). Tokyo: National Institute for Education Policy Research.

———. 2011a. *Kyaria hattatsu ni kakawaru shonōryoku no ikusei ni kansuru chōsa kenkyū hōkokusho* (*Report on the Abilities Related to Career Development*). Tokyo: National Institute for Education Policy Research.

———. 2011b. *Kyaria kyōiku no saranaru jūjitsu no tameni* (*The Further Enhancement of Career Education*). Tokyo: National Institute for Education Policy Research.

National Police Agency (*keisatsu chō*). 2011. *Heisei 22 nenchū ni okeru jisatsu no gaiyō shiryō* (*Outline Material on Suicides in 2010*). Tokyo: National Policy Agency Community Safety Bureau Community Safety Planning Division.

New Public Commons Roundtable (*atarashii kōkyō entaku kaigi*). 2010a. "*Atarashii kōkyō" sengen* (Declaration of "New Public Commons"). Tokyo: Cabinet Office. Available at http://www5.cao.go.jp/npc/pdf/declaration-nihongo.pdf. Accessed June 29, 2011. The official English translation *Declaration of "New Public Commons"* is also available at http://www5.cao.go.jp/npc/pdf/declaration-english.pdf.

———. 2010b. "*Atarashii kōkyō" entaku kaigi ni okeru teian to seidoka nado ni muketa seifu no taiō*. Available at http://www5.cao.go.jp/npc/pdf/goverment-actions-nihongo.pdf. Accessed June 29, 2011. The official English translation *Proposals by the "New Public Commons" Roundtable and Government Actions toward Their Institutionalization* is available at http://www5.cao.go.jp/npc/pdf/goverment-actions-english.pdf.

NHK (Japan Broadcasting Corporation). 2010. Muen Shakai: 32,000 "Muenshi" no Shōgeki. (The No-relationship Society: The Shock of 32,000 Solitary Deaths). Aired on Januarny 31, 2010.

Obinger, Julia. 2009. "Working on the Margins: Japan's Precariat and Working Poor." *Electronic Journal of Contemporary Japanese Studies*. Available at http://www.japanesestudies.org.uk/discussionpapers/2009/Obinger.html. Accessed March 16, 2011.

OECD. 1996. *Lifelong Learning for All: Meeting of the Education Committee at Ministerial Level*, January 16 and 17, 1996. Paris: OECD.

———. 2005. Promoting Adult Learning. Paris: OECD.

———. 2006. *Economic Survey of Japan*. Paris: OECD.

———, ed. 2010. *Shakaiteki kigyō no shuryūka, "atarashii kōkyo" no ninaite to shite*. Tokyo: Akashi Shoten. This is a Japanese translation of *The Changing Boundaries of Social Enterprises* originally published by the OECD in 2009.

Ogawa, Akihiro. 2009a. *The Failure of Civil Society?: The Third Sector and the State in Contemporary Japan*. Albany: State University of New York Press.

———. 2009b. "Japan's New Lifelong Learning Policy: Exploring Lessons from the European Knowledge Economy." *International Journal of Lifelong Education* 28(5): 601–614.

———. 2013. "Risk Management by a Neoliberal State: Construction of New Knowledge through Lifelong Learning in Japan." *Discourse: Studies in the Cultural Politics of Education* 34(1): 132–144.
Ogawa, Seiko. 2005. "Lifelong Learning and Demographics: A Japanese Perspective. *International Journal of Lifelong Education* 24(4): 351–368.
Ohsako, Tohio, and Yukiko Sawano. 2006. "The Situation in Japan." In *Promoting Lifelong Learning for Older Workers: An International Overview*, ed. Tarja Tikkanen and Barry Nyham, 90–106. Luxembourg: Office for Official Publications of the European Communities.
Okamoto, Kaoru. 1994. *Lifelong Learning Movement in Japan: Strategy, Practices and Challenges*. Tokyo: Sun Printing.
———. 2001. "Lifelong Learning and the Leisure-Oriented Society: The Developments and Challenges in the Far East." In *International Handbook of Lifelong Learning* Part One, ed. Daivd Aspin, Judith Chapman, Michael Hatton, and Yukiko Sawano, 317–328. Dordrechet, the Netherlands: Kluwer Academic Publishers.
———. 2004. *Nyūmon, shogai gakushū seisaku, shintei ban* (*Introduction, Lifelong Learning Policies, Revised Edition*). Tokyo: Zen nihon shakai kyōiku rengōkai.
———. 2006. *Education of the Rising Sun 21—An Introduction to Education in Japan*. Tokyo: National Federation of Social Education in Japan.
Okano, Kaori, and Motonori Tsuchiya. 1999. *Education in Contemporary Japan: Inequality and Diversity*. Cambridge: Cambridge University Press.
Okuma-Nyström, Michiyo Kiwako. 2007. "Risk Society and School Education in Japan." *Stockholm Journal of East Asian Studies* 17: 133–148.
Okumoto, Kaori. 2008. "Lifelong learning in England and Japan: Three translations." *Compare* 38(2): 173–188.
Okuno, Nobuhiro, and Takuya Kurita. 2010. *Atarashii kōkyō wo ninau hitobito* (*People Who Are in Charge of Creating the New Public Commons*). Tokyo: Iwanami shoten.
Olsson, Ulf, and Kenneth Petersson. 2008. "The Operation of Knowledge and Construction of the Lifelong Learning Subject." In *Foucault and Lifelong Learning: Governing the Subject*, ed. Andreas Fejes and Katherine Nicoll, 61–73. London; New York: Routledge.
O'Mahony, Patrik. 2010. "Habermas and Communicative Power." *Journal of Power* 3(1): 53–73.
O'Malley, Pat. 1998. *Crime and Risk Society*. Aldershot, UK: Ashgate.
———. 2000. "Uncertain Subjects: Risks, Liberalrism and Contract." *Economy and Society* 29(4): 460–484.
———. 2003. Moral Uncertainties. In *Risk and Morality*, ed. Richard V. Ericson and Aaron Doyle, 231–257. Toronto: University of Toronto Press.
———. 2004. *Risk, Uncertainty and Government*. London: Glasshouse Press.
———. 2006. "Criminology and Risk." In *Beyond the Risk Society*, ed. Gabe Mythen and Sandra Walklate, 43–59. Maidenhead, UK: Open University Press.

Ong, Aihwa. 1999. *Flexible Citizenship: The Cultural Logics of Transnationality.* Durham, NC: Duke University Press.
———. 2006. *Neoliberalism as Expection: Mutations in Citizenship and Sovereignty.* Durham, NC: Duke University Press.
Ong, Aihwa, and Stephen Collier. 2005. *Global Assemblages: Technology, Politics, and Ethics as Anthropological Problems.* Malden, MA: Blackwell.
Open University of Japan (*hōsō daigaku*). 2011. *Sotsugyōsei no gaiyō* (*Information on Graduates*). Available at http://www.ouj.ac.jp/hp/gaiyo/gaiyo09.html#sotugyou. Accessed June 2, 2011.
Osaka University School of International Public Policy. 2003. *NPO hōjin zaimu dēta bēsu* (*Database Indicating the Financial Situation of NPOs*). Available at http://npodb.osipp.osaka-u.ac.jp. Accessed March 9, 2010.
Osawa, Machiko, Myoung Jung Kim, and Jeff Kingston. 2013. "Precarious Work in Japan." *American Behavioral Scientist* 57(3): 309–334.
Ouane, Adama. 2009. "UNESCO's Drive for Lifelong Leanring." In *The Routledge International Handbook of Lifelong Learning*, ed. Peter Jarvis, 302–311. Abingdon, UK: Routledge.
Pawley, Laurence. 2008. "Cultural Citizenship." *Sociology Compass* 2(2): 594–608.
Peacock, James L. 2001. *The Anthropological Lens: Harsh Lights, Soft Focus.* Cambridge: Cambridge University Press. 2nd edition.
Pekkanen, Robert. 2006. *Japan's Dual Civil Society: Members without Advocates.* Stanford, CA: Stanford University Press.
Percy-Smith, Janie, ed., 2000. *Policy Responses to Social Exclusion: Towards Inclusion?* Buckingham, UK and Philadelphia, PA: Open University Press.
Peters, Michael A. 2001. "Education, Enterprise Culture and the Entrepreneurial Self: A Foucau ldian Perspective." *Journal of Educational Enquiry* 2(2): 58–71.
Peters, Michael A., and A. C. (Tina) Besley. 2006. *Building Knowledge Culture: Education and Development in the Age of Knowledge.* Lanham, MD: Rowan and Littlefield Publishers.
Pharr, Susan J. 2003. "Conclusion: Targeting by an Activist State: Japan as a Civil Society model." In *The State of Civil Society in Japan*, ed. Frank J. Schwartz and Susan J. Pharr, 316–336. Cambridge: Cambridge University Press.
Pidgeon, Nick, Roger E. Kasperson, and Paul Slovic, eds. 2003. *The Social Amplification of Risk.* Cambridge: Cambridge University Press.
Poole, Gregory. S. 2003. "Higher Education Reform in Japan: Amano Ikuo on 'the University in Crisis.'" *International Education Journal* 4 (3): 149–176.
Prime Minister's Commission on Japan's Goals in the 21st Century ("21 seiki nihon no kōsō" kondankai). 2000. *Nihon no furontia wa nihon no naka ni aru: jichi to kyōchi de kizuku shinseiki.* Tokyo: Prime Minister's Commission on Japan's Goals in the 21st Century. The official English translation *The Frontier Within: Individual Empowerment and Better Governance in the New Millennium* is available at www.kantei.go.jp/jp/21century/report/pdfs/index.html. Accessed March 15, 2011.

Prime Minister Hatoyama's Cabinet E-mail Magazine No. 17. 2010. *Atarashii kōkyō (New Public Commons)*. Available at http://www.mmz.kantei.go.jp/jp/m-magazine/backnumber/2010/0204/index.html. Accessed February 5, 2011.

Prime Minister Kan's Blog. 2011. *Jisatsu wo herasu, shakai no chikara de, seiji no chikara de (Decreasing the Number of Suicides through the Strength of Society and the Strength of the Government)*. Tokyo: Cabinet Office. Available at http://kanfullblog.kantei.go.jp/2011/03/20110302-2.html. Accessed March 2 2011.

Putnam, Robert D. 2000. *Bowling Alone: The Collapse and Revival of American Community*. New York: Simon and Schuster.

Qualifications and Curriculum Authority. 1998. *Education for Citizenship and the Teaching of Democracy in Schools—Final Report of the Advisory Group on Citizenship*. London: Qualifications and Curriculum Authority.

Rausch, Anthony. 2004. "Lifelong Learning in Rural Japan: Relevance, Focus and Sustainability for the Hobbyist, the Resident, the Careerist and the Activist as Lifelong Learner." *Japan Forum* 16(3): 473–493.

Reich, Robert B. 1991. *The Work of Nations: Preparing Ourselves for 21st-century Capitalism*. New York: Vintage Books.

Renn, Ortwin. 2008. *Risk Governance: Coping with Uncertainty in a Complex World*. London: Earthscan.

Rohlen, Thomas P. 1983. *Japan's High Schools*. Berkeley, CA: University of California Press.

Rosaldo, Renato. 1997. "Cultural Citizenship, Inequality, and Multiculturalism." In *Latino Cultural Citizenship: Claiming Identity, Space, and Rights*, ed. William. V. Flores and Rina Benmayor, 27–38. Boston: Beacon Press.

Rose, Nikolas. 1996. "The Death of the Social? Refiguring the Territory of Government." *Economy and Society* 25(3):327–356.

———. 1998. *Inventing Ourselves: Psychology, Power, and Personhood*. Cambridge: Cambridge University Press.

———. 1999. *Powers of Freedom: Reframing Political Thought*. Cambridge: Cambridge University Press.

———. 2000. "Government and Control." *British Journal of Criminology*. 40(2): 321–329.

Rychen, Dominique Simone. 2003. "Key Competencies: Meeting Important Challenges in Life." In *Key Competencies for a Successful Life and a Well-functioning Society*, Dominique Simone Rychen, and Laura Hersh Salganik, 63–107. Cambridge, MA: Hogrefe and Huber.

Rychen, Dominique Simone, and Laura Hersh Salganik. 2003. *Key Competencies for a Successful Life and a Well-functioning Society* Cambridge, MA: Hogrefe and Huber. Tatsuta (2006) is a Japanese translation of this book.

Saitama Prefecture Education Department (*saitama ken kyōiku kyoku*). 2010. *Manabu kokoro (A Mind for Learning)*. Saitama: Saitama Prefecture Education Department.

Sasai, Hiromi. 1998. "An Analysis of Lifelong Learning Policy in Japan." In *International Perspectives on Lifelong Learning*, ed. John Holford, Peter Jarvis, and Colin Griffin, 180–185. London: Kogan Page.

Sasaki, Hidekazu. 2006. "Minkan sekutā ni yoru shakai kyōiku" (Social Education by the Private Sector). In *Shakai Kyōiku no Kiso (Basics of Social Education)*, ed. Makoto Suzuki and Koji Matsuoka, 65–76. Tokyo: Gakubunsha.

Sasaki, Minoru. 1992. *Shōgai gakushū jidai no gakkō kaihō, daigaku kaihō (Opening up Schools and Universities in the Era of Lifelong Learning)*. Tokyo: Zen nihon shakai kyōiku rengōkai.

Sato, Haruo. 2008. *Chiiki renkei de gakkō wo mondai zero ni suru—jissen gata komyuniti sukūru no hiketsu (Linking Schools to Local Communities Reduces Social Problems—the Secret of Practice-Oriented Community Schools)*. Tokyo: Gakuji shuppan.

———. 2009. "Shakai kyōiku hō seitei kara genzai madeno shakai kyōiku gyōsei no kiseki" (Trajectory of Social Education Administration from the Enactment of Social Education Law to the Present). Shakai Kyōiku 760: 8–14.

———. 2010. *Komyuniti sukūru no kenkyū (A Study on the Community School)*. Tokyo: Kazama shobō.

Sato, Hiroki, and Shizuko Koizumi. 2007. *Fuantei koyō to iu kyozō: pāto, furīta, haken no jitsuzō (The False Image of Insecure Employment: The Reality of Part-timers, Freeters, and Temporary Workers)*. Tokyo: Keisō shobō.

Sato, Katsuko. 1998. *Shōgai gakushū to shakai sanka; otona ga manabu koto no imi (Lifelong Learning and Social Participation: Meaning of Adult Learning)*. Tokyo: Tokyo daigaku shuppankai.

———. 2004. *NPO no kyōiku ryoku—shōgai gakushū to shiminteki kōkyōsei (Educational Capacity of NPOs—Lifelong Learning and Public Citizenry)*. Tokyo: Tokyō daigaku shuppankai.

Sato, Sanzo. 2003. "Shakai kyōiku ni okeru kadai to tenbō—kodomo no shakai kyōiku to gakkō kyōiku no kankei" (Agendas and Prospects in Social Education—the Relationship between Social Education Centering on Children and Formal School Education). In *Henkaku jidai no kyōiku wo saguru: gakkō, katei, chiiki ni okeru kyōiku no kadai to tenbō (Exploring Education in the Transition Era: Agendas and Prospectus of Education in School, Family, and Community)*, ed. Hiroshi Ozawa, Sanzo Sato, and Masaaki Murayama, 127–145. Tokyo: Toshindo.

Sawano, Yukiko. 2007. "The Learning Society in Japan." In *New Society Models for a New Millennium: The Learning Society in Europe and Beyond*, ed. Michael Kuhn, 471–488. New York: Peter Lang.

Schoppa, Leonard. 1991. *Education Reform in Japan: A Case of Immobilist Politics*. London: Routledge.

Schuetze, Hans G., and Catherine Casey. 2006. "Models and Meanings of Lifelong Learning: Progress and Barriers on the Road to a Learning Society." Compare 36(3): 279–87.

Schuller, Tom. 2009. "The OECD and Lifelong Learning." In *The Routledge International Handbook of Lifelong Learning*, ed. Peter Jarvis, 292–301. Abingdon, UK: Routledge.

Schultz, Theodore W. 1961. "Investment in Human Capital." *The American Economic Review* 51: 1–17.

Schwartz, Frank J., and Susan J. Pharr, eds. 2003. *The State of Civil Society in Japan*. Cambridge: Cambridge University Press.

Science Council of Japan (*nihon gakujutsu kaigi*). 2009. *Keizai kiki ni tachimukau hōsetsuteki shakai seisaku no tameni* (*Social Inclusion Policies to Respond to the Ongoing Economic Crisis*). Tokyo: Science Council of Japan.

———. 2010. *Kaitō: Daigaku kyōiku no bunyabetsu shitsu hoshō ni tsuite* (*Response: Quality Assurance of University Education by Disciplines*). Tokyo: Science Council of Japan.

Sennett, Richard. 1998. *The Corrosion of Character: The Personal Consequences of Work in the New Capitalism*. New York: W. W. Norton.

Senuma, Yoshiaki. 2006. *Jūmin shudō no shōgai gakushu chiiki zukuri* (*Lifelong Learning and Community Development Led by Local Residents*). Kyoto: Sekai shisōsha.

Shibuya, Nozomu. 2010. *Midoru kurasu wo toinaosu, kakusa shakai no mōten* (*Revisiting Middle Class, Pitfalls of a Socioeconomic Divided Society*). Tokyo: NHK Shuppan.

Shimizutani, Satoshi. 2011. "Education Reform in Japan: A Course for Lifelong Learning." *Asia-Pacific Review* 18(2): 105–114.

Shinmura, Junichi. 2007. *Shōgai gakushū, machizukuri wa sonkaku, toshikaku* (*Lifelong Learning and Community Development as Local Pride*). Osaka: Seibunsha.

Shiraishi, Katsumi, Masafumi Tanaka, and Takahito Hirose, eds. 2001. *"Min" ga hirogeru gakushū sekai* (*Learning World Expanded by the Private Sector*). Tokyo: Gyōsei.

Shore, Cris, and Susan Wright, eds. 1997. *Anthropology of Policy: Critical Perspectives on Governance and Power*. London; New York: Routledge.

———. 2011. "Introduction. Conceptualising Policy: Technologies of Governance and the Politics of Visibility." In *Policy Worlds: Anthropology and the Analysis of Contemporary Power*, ed. Cris Shore, Susan Wright, and David Però, 1–25. Oxford: Berghahn.

Shore, Cris, Susan Wright, and David Però, eds. 2011. *Policy Worlds: Anthropology and the Analysis of Contemporary Power*. Oxford: Berghahn.

Simons, Maarten, and Jan Masschelein. 2008. "Our 'Will to Learn' and the Assemblage of a Learning Apparatus." In *Foucault and Lifelong Learning: Governing the Subject*, ed. Andreas Fejes and Katherine Nicoll, 48–60. London; New York: Routledge.

Smith, Martin J. 2009. "Risk." In *Power and the State*, 198–219. London: Palgrave Macmillan.

Social Education Council (*shakai kyōiku shingikai*). 1971. *Kyūgekina shakai kōzō no henka ni taisho suru shakai kyōiku no arikata ni tsuite* (*On the Arrangement of Social Education to Cope with Rapid Changes in the Social Structure*). Tokyo: Social Education Council.

Sorensen, Annemette. 1999. "Family Decline, Poverty, and Social Exclusion: The Mediating Effects of Family Policy." *Comparative Social Research* 18: 57–78.

Spring, Joel. 2009. *Globalization of Education: An Introduction*. London; New York: Routledge.

Starkey, Ken, and Alan McKinlay. 1998. "Afterword: Deconstructing Organization—Discipline and Desire." In *Foucault, Management and Organization Theory: From Panopticon to Technologies of Self*, ed. Alan McKinlay and Ken Starkey, 230–41. London: Sage Publications.

Stevens, Carolyn. S. 1997. *On the Margins of Japanese Society: Volunteer Work with the Urban Underclass*. London: Routledge.

Stevenson, Nick. 2003. *Cultural Citizenship: Cosmopolitan Questions*. Maidenhead, UK: Open University Press.

Stromquist, Nelly P. 2002. *Education in a Globalized World: The Connectivity of Economic Power, Technology, and Knowledge*. Lanham, MD: Rowman and Littlefield Publishers.

Somers, Margaret R. 1995. Narrating and Naturalizing Civil Society and Citizenship Theory: The Place of Political Culture and the Public Sphere. *Sociological Theory* 13(3): 229–74.

Suginami Board of Social Education (*suginami ku shakai kyōiku iin no kaigi*). 2009. *"Yaritori no fukkatsu" ga tsumugidasu atarashii kōkyō kūkan* (*Creating the "New Public Commons" through the Revival of Communication*). Tokyo: Suginami Board of Social Education.

Suginami Ward Government (*suginami ku*). 2011. *Seikatsu gaido, seikatsu hogo* (Guide for Livelihood and Livelihood Assistance). Available at http://www2.city.suginami.tokyo.jp/guide/guide.asp?n1=60&n2=100&n3=210. Accessed July 10, 2011.

Sutherland, Peter, and Jim Crowther. 2006. "Introduction: 'The Lifelong LearningImagination.'" In *Lifelong Learning: Concepts and Contexts*, ed. Peter Sutherland and Jim Crowther, 3–11. New York: Routledge.

Suzuki, Kan. 2010. *Reforming Japanese Education through Jukugi*. Available at http://jukugi.mext.go.jp/archive/412.pdf. Accessed February 21, 2011.

Suzuki, Makoto. 1994. "Sengo seijin gakushūron no tokuchō" (Characteristics of Adult Learning Theory in Postwar Japan). In *Seijin gakushūron to shōgai gakushū keikaku* (*Adult Learning Theory and Lifelong Learning Planning*), ed. Shiro Kurauchi and Toshiki Doi, 27–50. Tokyo: Akishobo.

Suzuki, Munenori, Midori Ito, Mitsunori Ishida, Norihiro Nihei, and Masao Maruyama. 2010. "Individualizing Japan: Searching for Its Origin in First Modernity." *British Journal of Sociology* 61(3): 513–553.

Suzuki, Toshimasa. 2004. *Shōgai gakushū no kyōikugaku: Gakushū nettowāku kara chiiki shōgai kyōiku keikaku e* (*Education of Lifelong Learning: From Learning Networks to Local lifelong Education Planning*). Tokyo: Hokuju shuppan.
Suárez-Orozco, Marcelo M., ed. 2007. *Learning in the Global Era: International Perspectives on Globalization and Education*. Berkeley, CA: University of California Press.
Tachibanaki, Toshiaki, ed. 2004. *Risuku shakai wo ikiru* (*Surviving Risk Society*). Tokyo: Iwanami shoten.
———. 2005. *Confronting Income Inequality in Japan*. Cambridge, MA: MIT Press.
Takayama, Keita. 2008. "The Politics of International League Tables: PISA in Japan's Achievement Crisis Debate." *Comparative Education* 44(4): 387–407.
Takenaka, Heizo, and Yasuyuki Nanbu, ed. 2010. *Korekarano "hatarakikata" wa dōnarunoka* (*In What Way Are We Going to Work?*). Tokyo: PHP.
Tanimoto, Kanji. 2006. *Sōsharu entāpuraizu—shakaiteki kigyō no taitō* (*Social Enterprises—the Emergence of Social Enterprises*). Tokyo: Chuō Keizaisha.
Tarohmaru, Hiroshi. 2009. *Jyakunen hiseiki koyō no shakaigaku: kaisō, jendā, gurōbaruka* (The Sociology of Irregular Youth Employment: Class, Gender, and Globalization). Osaka: Osaka Daigaku shuppankai.
Tatsuta, Yoshihiro, ed. 2006. *Kī konpetenshī: kokusai hyōjun no gakuryoku wo mezashite* (*Key Competencies: Aiming to Achieve International Academic Standards*). Tokyo: Akashi shobō. This is a Japanese translation of Rychen and Salganik (2003).
Taylor, Matthew. 2012. "Not with a Bang but a Whimper: Muen Shakai and Its Implications." *Anthropoetics: Journal of Generative Anthropology* 18(1). Available at http://www.anthropoetics.ucla.edu/ap1801/1801taylor.htm. Accessed March 14, 2013.
Taylor-Gooby, Peter, ed. 1999a. *Risk, Trust and Welfare*. London: Macmillan.
———. 1999b. "Risk and the Welfare State." *British Journal of Sociology* 50(2): 177–194.
———. 2004. *New Risks, New Welfare: The Transformation of European Welfare State*. Oxford: Oxford University Press.
———. 2008. *Reframing Social Citizenship*. Oxford: Oxford University Press.
Taylor-Gooby, Peter, and Jens O. Zinn. 2001. *Risk in Social Science*. Oxford: Oxford University Press.
———. 2006. "Current Directions in Risk Research: New Developments in Psychology and Sociology." *Risk Analysis* 26(2): 397–411.
Te Riele, Kitty. 2006. "Youth 'at Risk': Further Marginalizing the Marginalized?" *Journal of Education Policy* 21(2): 129–45.
Thang, Leng L. 2001. *Generations in Touch: Linking the Old and the Young in a Tokyo Neighborhood*. Ithaca, NY: Cornell University Press.

Thompson, Hunter S. 1971. *Fear and Loathing in Las Vegas: A Savage Journey to the Heart of the American Dream*. New York: Random House

Thompson, John, and Bob Doherty. 2006. "The Diverse World of Social Enterprise: A Collection of Social Enterprise Stories." *International Journal of Social Economics* 33(5/6): 361–375.

Tilly, Charles. 1984. *Big Structures, Large Processes, Huge Comparisons*. New York: Russell Sage Foundation.

Tokyo Metropolitan Government. 2008. *Tokyoto ni okeru chiiki kyōiku wo shinkō surutameno kyōiku gyōsei no arikata ni tsuite* (*On the Development of Community-focused Education in Tokyo*). Tokyo: Tokyo Metropolitan Government.

Tsukamoto, Ichiro, and Hideo Yamagishi. 2008. *Sōsharu entāpuraizu—shakai kōken wo bijinesu ni suru* (*Social Enterprises—Making Social Contribution a Business*). Tokyo: Maruzen.

Tuijnman, Albert, and Ann-Kristin Boström. 2002. "Changing Notions of Lifelong Education and Lifelong Learning." *International Review of Education* 48(1/2): 93–110.

Tulloch, John, and Deborah Lupton. 2003. *Risk and Everyday Life*. London: Sage Publications.

Uchida, Kenzo. 1987. *Rinkyōshin no kiseki—kyōiku kaikaku 100 nichi* (*Track of Ad Hoc Council on Education—100 days of Educational Reform*). Tokyo: Daiichihōki.

University Council (*daigaku shingikai*). 1991. *Daigaku kyōiku no kaizen ni tsuite* (*On Improvements to University Education*). Tokyo: University Council.

Watanabe, Hideo. 2005. "Changing Adult Learning in Japan: The Shift from Traditional Singing to Karaoke." *International Journal of Lifelong Education* 24(3): 257–267.

White, Merry I. 1987. *The Japanese Educational Challenge: A Commitment to Children*. New York: Free Press.

Williamson, Piers R. 2014. *Risk and Securitization in Japan 1945–60*. London: Routledge.

Wilson, John Dewar. 2001. "Lifelong Learning in Japan—A Lifelong for a 'Maturing' Society." *International Journal of Lifelong Education* 20(4): 297–313.

Wishart, Diane, Alison Taylor, and Lynette Shultz. 2006. "The Construction and Production of Youth 'at Risk.'" *Journal of Education Policy* 21(3): 291–304.

Work Foundation. 2007. *The Knowledge Economy in Europe: A Report Prepared for the 2007 EU Spring Council*. London: Work Foundation.

Yamamoto, Shigeri. 2001. *Otonatachi no gakkō, shōgai gakushū wo tanoshimu* (*Schools for the Adults, Enjoying Lifelong Learning*). Tokyo: Chūkō shinsho.

Yamamoto, Yoshihiro. 1996. *Shōgai gakushū no gendaiteki kadai* (*Contemporary Topics Studied in Lifelong Learning*). Tokyo: Zen nihon shakai kyōiku rengōkai.

Yergin, Daniel, and Joseph Stanislaw. 1998. *The Commanding Heights: The Battle betweenGovernment and the Market Place That Is Remaking the Modern World*. New York: Simon and Schuster.

Yomiuri Shimbun. 2009 (September 17). "Nīzu takamaru shokugyō kunren" (Increase in the Demand for Vocational Training).

———. 2010 (July 22). "Shūshoku ryūnensha kyūzō, shokugyō ishiki wo takame saichōsen shiyō" (The Number of Students Repeating the College Senior Year to Search for Jobs Is Increasing: Encourage Them to Take Chances by Enhancing Vocational Consciousness).

Yorimoto, Katsumi, and Takaharu Kohara, eds. 2011. *Atarashii kōkyō to jichi no genba (The New Public Commons and Local Autonomy)*. Tokyo: Commons.

Yuasa, Makoto. 2008. *Hanhinkon—"suberidai shakai" kara no dashuttsu (Anti-poverty—Escape from the "Slide Society")*. Tokyo: Iwanami shinsho.

Zinn, Jens O., 2006. "Recent Developments in Sociology of Risk and Uncertainty." *Historical Social Research* 31(2): 275–286.

———, ed. 2008. *Social Theories of Risk and Uncertainty: An Introduction*. Malden, MA: Blackwell.

Index

Abe, Shinzo, 57, 61
action research, 170, 172
Ad Hoc Council on Education, 29, 37, 38–40, 48, 177, 178
adult education, 7, 30, 35, 36, 41, 112
   adult and community-oriented education, 30
   See also community-oriented learning
   See also non-formal education
Agency for Cultural Affairs (*Bunka chō*), 75, 77, 188
agenda-setting, 63, 67
aging, 2, 11, 45, 46, 50, 132, 134, 139, 160, 186
Anpo, 76
Aomori Model, 138
Aomori Prefecture, 3, 23, 68, 114, 119, 126, 127, 135, 138, 141, 153
   Aomori (city of), 129
   Dazai, Osamu, 23
   Hirosaki (city of), 3, 23, 114, 131, 172
   Kuroishi (city of), 135
Appadurai, Arju, 22
Arai, Ikuo, 35
Arnoldi, Jakob, 17
Arthur, James, 164
Avenell, Simon, 81

Bauman, Zygmunt, 14, 56
Beck, Ulrich, 12–17, 19, 55, 115, 137, 185
   See also risk society
black companies (*burakku kigyō*), 163
bunka borantia (culture volunteers), 23, 26, 73, 74, 75, 77–83, 95, 96, 97, 172, 173, 188

Cabinet Office, 66, 71, 139, 150, 171, 189, 190
career, 20, 45, 56, 75, 77, 106, 121, 122, 128, 129, 142, 147, 148, 151, 152, 159, 162, 169, 170
career education, 27, 67, 116, 148, 149, 150–154, 158, 161–163, 166, 173, 179, 190
   basic and versatile competencies, 27, 148, 151–153, 162
   career counseling (*shinro shidō*), 150
   career guidance (*shokugyō shidō*), 106, 122, 162
   meaning of career, 151
Central Council for Education, 27, 29, 35, 36, 40, 41, 49, 53, 57, 59, 61–63, 84, 87, 107, 149, 151, 153, 164, 177–179, 187
Chambers of Commerce and Industry (*shōko kaigi sho*), 46

citizens (*shimin*), 3, 6, 7, 8, 17, 18, 26, 31, 33, 34, 42, 45, 46, 50, 53, 54, 55, 57, 58, 63, 66, 69, 73, 74, 76, 80, 81, 83, 86, 88, 94, 95, 97, 100, 112, 121, 125, 132, 133, 163, 164, 166, 172
   citizens for the twenty-first century (*21 seiki gata shimin*), 164
   neoliberal citizens, 166
citizens' public hall (*kōminkan*), 2, 3, 31, 32, 37, 45, 47, 57, 58, 67, 73–75, 79, 81, 83, 96, 111, 129, 172, 174, 175
   courses, 32
   number (of citizens' public hall), 31, 32
   users, 32
citizenry, 27, 149
citizenship, 1, 8, 22, 32, 45, 58, 73, 80, 163–165, 166, 187
   citizenship education (*shimin kyōiku*), 165
   cultural citizenship, 73
   self-governing citizenship, 80
civic knowledge (*shimin chi*), 26, 74, 78–80, 83, 96, 97, 181
   See also knowledge
civil servants, 78
civil society, 17, 19, 68, 86, 94, 96, 97, 119, 125, 128, 140, 143, 162–164, 170–172, 174
   See also third sector
collaboration, 63, 80, 83, 102, 112, 126, 128, 150, 182
   collaborative engagement, 78, 96
   collaborative relationship, 77, 83
   kyōdō, 83
collective learning, 2, 62, 80
Cologne Charter (1999), 6
communication, 11, 45, 88, 99, 100, 102, 107, 108, 109, 110, 112, 115, 132, 142, 153, 154, 157, 165, 169, 173, 188

communication skills, 142, 153, 154, 157, 173
Revival of Communication (*Yaritori no fukkatsu*), 99, 100, 102, 107, 110
communicative power, 86
community / communities
   see local communities
community development, 50, 67, 75, 79, 92, 128, 129, 131, 140, 181, 183, 186
community-oriented learning, 22, 171
   adult and community-oriented education, 30
   community-oriented social education, 38, 48, 92
   community-oriented lifelong learning, 51, 81, 170
   nonformal, community-oriented social education, 26
   See also non-formal education
   See also social education
community revitalization, 46, 94, 140, 170
community school, 26, 49, 67, 68, 88, 89–92, 99, 101–105, 107, 109–111, 113, 114, 115, 154, 173, 178, 187
   school council, 89–93, 104–107
   School Support Community Headquarters (*gakkō shien chiiki honbu*), 111
community solutions, 26, 102, 112, 169
comprehensive knowledge (*sōgōteki na chi*), 18, 19, 26, 52, 59, 60, 62–64, 68, 69, 79, 107, 168, 169
disciplinary knowledge, 4, 18, 26, 56, 59, 68, 69, 74, 95
Copenhagen, Denmark, 22
council, 3, 29, 34, 35, 37–40, 43, 44, 47, 48, 63, 66, 71, 81, 110, 146, 164, 177, 178, 187

Ad Hoc Council on Education, 29, 37–40, 48, 177, 178
Council on Comprehensive Measures to Prevent Suicide, 146
Council on National Life, 66
Council on the Promotion of New Public Commons, 71
Lifelong Learning Council, 3, 29, 43, 44, 47, 63, 81, 110, 178, 187
Social Education Council, 29, 34, 35, 177
University Council, 44, 164, 178, 187
Council on National Life, 66
credentialed society (*gakureki shakai*), 37, 38
Crick, Bernard, 164
cultural model, 1, 4, 6, 25, 52, 58
culture centers (*karuchā sentā*), 2, 38, 46, 47, 111, 175
  courses, 47
  fee, 47
  housewives, 2
  numbers (of culture centers), 47

Delors, Jacques, 5, 7
democracy, 78, 85
  deliberative democracy, 85
Democratic Party of Japan (DPJ), 23
deregulation, 19, 20, 59, 66
devolution, 64, 82, 83
Diet, 49, 61, 76, 84, 86
  divided Diet (*nejire kokkai*), 84
diploma-oriented society (*gakureki shakai*), 2, 51, 169
diversity, 78, 80, 129, 131
Douglas, Mary, 12, 13, 55
  cultural-symbolic approach, 12
  See also risk

economic development, 102, 109, 173

Economic Planning Agency, 46, 55
Education Ministry, 2, 3, 23, 26, 30, 33, 37, 40, 43, 45, 46, 50, 60, 67, 74, 83, 84, 86, 88, 89, 91, 94, 103, 107, 111, 112, 114, 150, 151, 155, 168, 185, 188
  Community Development Support Unit, 67
  Community Policy Unit, 67
  Elementary and Secondary Education Bureau, 111
  Higher Education Bureau, 155
  Lifelong Learning Bureau, 40
  Lifelong Learning Policy Bureau, 40, 67, 84, 111
  manabipia, 50, 168
  Social Education Bureau, 30, 40
  Social Education Division, 111
  See also councils
Education Order (*Gakusei*) (1872), 37
educational reform, 38, 39, 43, 60, 84, 103, 104, 188
employability, 8, 9, 140, 147, 148, 165
employment, 7, 10, 20, 26, 27, 38, 54, 66, 94, 116, 117, 120, 121–126, 132, 133–139, 142, 143, 145–148, 150, 151, 154, 156, 159–162, 163, 165, 169, 171, 189, 190
Employment and Human Resources Development Organization, 121–123, 189
  See also vocational training
empowerment, 80
entrepreneurship, 9, 82, 120, 125, 135, 137, 138, 140
  entrepreneurial self, 26, 74, 80, 82, 83, 96
ethnography, 17, 22, 114, 170
Eriksen, Thomas, 23
Europe, 7–11, 22, 24, 125, 158, 159, 167, 186

European Commission, 5, 8–11, 159
European Council, 8
   A Memorandum on Lifelong Learning (2000), 8
   Europe 2020 Strategy, 11
   Lisbon Strategy (2000), 8–11, 159
   Making a European Area of Lifelong Learning a Reality (2001), 9
European Union (EU), 7, 11, 159
   Amsterdam Treaty (1997), 7
   Luxemburg Summit (1997), 7
   White Paper on Growth, Competitiveness, and Jobs (1993), 7

family / families, 1, 14, 16, 20, 23, 34, 35, 39, 45, 60, 65, 76, 99, 100–102, 107, 111, 122, 127, 131, 136, 138, 139, 149, 153, 154, 159, 161, 167, 173, 186
   nuclear families, 99, 100
Faure Report—Learning to Be (1972), 4, 5, 36
   See also UNESCO
Field, John, 1, 4
flexibility, 6, 14, 54, 59, 155
   flexible workforce, 25, 147
   See also labor market
formal school education, 26, 27, 37, 40, 43, 48, 57, 102, 104, 110, 113, 169, 170, 173, 175
Foucault, Michel, 12, 14, 15, 17, 55, 56, 74, 185
France, 158
freeters, 146, 149
   See also labor market
Fundamental Law of Education, 1, 18, 53, 54, 57, 60, 61, 67, 110, 148, 150, 151, 165, 177, 178

gakusha yūgō (integration of school and society), 110
gakushiryoku (standards for bachelor's degrees), 155

Germany, 16, 55, 167
Giddens, Anthony, 13, 14, 16, 21, 55, 82, 120
globalization, 4, 6, 8, 22, 24, 25, 57, 69, 160, 161
governance, 12, 18, 26, 54, 64, 82–84, 95, 96, 115, 147, 169, 187
governmental risk, 17, 18, 19, 26, 52, 56, 64, 69, 74, 96, 115, 168, 171
   See also risk
governmentality, 12, 14, 15, 17, 18, 26, 52, 56, 68, 82, 169
   See also Foucault, Michel
Great East Japan Earthquake, 167
Greenhouse, Carol, 22, 95
Gross Domestic Product (GDP), 94
G8 (Group of Eight), 6
   Cologne Charter, 6
gymnasiums (*taiikukan*), 2, 3, 32–34, 37, 175, 185
   number (of gymnasiums), 34

Habermas, Jurgen, 85, 86
   communicative power, 86
   deliberative democracy, 85
Hatoyama, Yukio, 65, 71, 72, 119
Hello Work, 117, 124, 127, 188, 189
Hiroi, Yoshinori, 101, 115
Hirosaki, Aomori Prefecture, 3, 23, 114, 131, 138, 172, 190
Hirosaki University, 23, 138
hōkago kodomo puran (provision of after-school activities), 111, 113
home education, 34
Honda, Yuki, 131, 190
Hook, Glenn, 16, 56
Hutchins, Robert, 36
human capital, 5, 7, 9, 10, 11

ikiru chikara (zest for living), 20, 48, 49, 60, 107–109, 112, 162, 169, 178

individualization, 14, 16, 17, 19, 20, 116, 137, 159
  See also risk
inequality, 10, 55, 65
  Gini-coefficient, 10, 65
  See also *kakusa* (socioeconomic divide)
information disclosure, 72
information society, 8
Italy, 125, 167

Japan Association of Corporate Executives (*Keizai dōyukai*), 147
Japan Federation of Economic Organizations (*Keidanren*), 147
Japan Federation of Employers' Associations (*Nikkeiren*), 147
Japan Vocational Ability Development Association, 122, 126
  See also vocational training
Jarvis, Peter, 1, 4, 5, 7, 30
Jukugi (Due Deliberation), 26, 74, 83–91, 93–96, 173, 188
  five key steps, 85, 89
  online *jukugi*, 86
  real *jukugi*, 86, 88, 89, 91, 188
  virtual *jukugi*, 86
junior colleges, 41, 43, 190

Kakegawa (city of), Shizuoka Prefecture, 49
kakusa (socioeconomic divide), 19, 26, 55, 101, 160
  divided society, 55, 66
  divided and polarized Japanese population, 26, 55
  socioeconomically polarized, 19
  winner and losers, 160
Kan, Naoto, 71, 72, 84, 94, 123, 124, 146, 161
Kaneko, Ikuyo, 20, 102, 103
Kawai, Hayao, 75
  See also *bunka borantia* (culture volunteers)

  See also Prime Minister's Commission on Japan's Goals in the Twenty-first Century
Kawazoe, 114
  See also SLG
key competencies, 60, 162, 166
  acting autonomously, 60
  interacting in socially heterogeneous groups, 60
  using tools interactively, 60
  See also OECD
kizuna (bonding), 167, 168, 170–174
Koizumi, Junichiro, 55, 66, 187
Koizumi administration, 61
Knowledge, 2, 4, 6, 7, 8, 9, 11–15, 17–21, 23, 26, 27, 31, 33, 44, 48, 51, 52, 54, 56–60, 62–64, 68, 69, 73–75, 78–83, 94–97, 107, 109, 116, 117, 119–123, 126, 128–131, 134, 142, 143, 145, 148, 151, 154–158, 161–166, 168–170, 172, 178, 181
  civic knowledge (*shimin chi*), 26, 74, 78–80, 83, 96, 97, 181
  comprehensive knowledge (*sōgōteki na chi*), 18, 19, 26, 52, 59, 60, 62–64, 68, 69, 79, 107, 168, 169
  disciplinary knowledge, 4, 18, 56, 59, 68
  neoliberal knowledge, 68, 69
  state-sponsored knowledge, 54, 56
knowledge society, 9, 10
  knowledge-based society, 25, 57, 155
  knowledge-constructing subjects, 26, 73, 74, 80–83, 94–97
knowledge economy, 1, 7–11, 54, 169
  global knowledge economy, 1, 8

labor education (*rōdō kyōiku*), 163

labor market, 2, 7, 10, 14, 16, 20, 25, 27, 54, 65, 120, 124, 127, 131, 136, 137, 147, 148, 157, 160, 161, 162, 166
  adaptability, 8, 9, 10
  employability, 8, 9, 140, 147, 148, 165
  flexibility, 6, 14, 54, 59, 155
  freeters, 146, 149
  labor market dualism, 20, 160
  labor market liberalization, 65
  lifetime employment, 20, 66, 121, 161
  non-regular type of jobs, 54
  precarious (employment), 56, 66, 147, 160
Laidlaw Foundation, 158, 190
Lash, Scott, 66
Law for the Promotion of Youth Class (1953), 31, 177
learning society (*gakushū shakai*), 2, 6, 35, 36, 186
Lee, Young-Jun, 138
Lehman Brothers, 121, 123, 146
leisure (*yoka*), 21, 46
  leisure-oriented lifelong learning, 38, 51, 111, 169
  See also Ministry of International Trade and Industry
Lengrand, Paul, 35, 177
Lenor, René, 158
libraries (*toshokan*), 2, 3, 23, 37, 57, 67, 68, 73–75, 79, 81, 83, 111, 112, 169, 172, 174, 175
  Japan Library Association, 33
  Library Law (1950), 33, 177
  number (of libraries), 33
lifelong education (*shōgai kyōiku*), 7, 25, 29, 34, 37, 57, 177
lifelong learning centers (*shōgai gakushū sentā*), 2, 22, 23, 41, 50, 58, 80, 175
lifelong learning city (*shōgai gakushū toshi*), 49

Lifelong Learning Council, 29, 43, 44, 63, 81, 110, 178, 187
  prefectural lifelong learning councils, 3, 47
lifelong learning imagination, 4
lifelong learning infrastructure, 40, 178
Lifelong Learning Promotion Law (1990), 3, 41, 44–47, 49, 57, 178
lifelong learning society (*shōgai gakushū shakai*), 38, 39, 44, 57, 195
lifetime employment, 20, 66, 121, 161
Liberal Democratic Party (LDP), 23
liquid modernity, 14
  See also Bauman, Zygmunt
local communities (*chiiki*), 1, 2, 19, 21, 22, 25, 26, 29, 30, 37, 39, 42, 45, 48, 49, 58, 62–64, 66–69, 71, 73, 81, 83, 100–103, 106, 110–112, 114, 115, 126, 133, 139, 149, 154, 157, 162, 166, 168, 172–174, 187
  See also agenda setting
  See also problem solving
lost generation (*rosugene sedai*), 146, 147
Lyng, Stephen, 20, 21, 120
  edgework, 21
  voluntary risk taking, 20, 21
  See also risk

manabi (learning), 50, 77, 168
manabipia, 50, 168
Marshall, T. H., 73
meritocracy, 102, 131, 150, 169
  hyper-meritocracy, 131
  school-oriented meritocracy, 102, 131, 150, 169
middle-class society, 19, 55
  See also kakusa (socioeconomic divide)
Ministry of Economy, Trade and Industry, 46, 125, 134

Ministry of Health and Welfare / Ministry of Health, Labor and Welfare (since 2001), 46, 65, 117, 119, 122, 126, 150
Ministry of Internal Affairs, 66
Ministry of International Trade and Industry, 46
  Lifelong Learning Development Office, 46
Ministry of Labor, 46
Ministry of Transportation, 46
museums (*hakubutsukan*), 2, 3, 23, 33, 34, 37, 57, 67, 68, 73, 74, 75, 79, 81, 83, 111, 112, 135, 169, 172, 174, 175, 177
Museum Law (1951), 33, 34, 177

Nakasone, Yasuhiro, 37, 38
National Institute for Education Policy Research, 114, 150, 152, 154
National Police Agency, 46, 145
National University Corporation Law, 155
network / networking, 11, 23, 48, 50, 63, 64, 77–80, 83, 92, 100, 109, 111, 114, 129, 131, 139, 151, 172, 183
neoliberalism, 17, 18, 19, 22, 56, 78, 95, 96
  neoliberal economy, 27, 149, 160, 161
  neoliberal governance, 95
  neoliberal governmentality, 26, 56, 68, 82
  neoliberal ideology, 62, 160
  neoliberal Japan, 4, 27, 56, 69, 165
  neoliberal knowledge, 68, 69
  neoliberal model, 74
  neoliberal politics, 17, 21, 55, 74, 96, 165
  neoliberal state, 19, 21, 26, 52, 53, 69, 74, 82, 83, 95, 166
neighborhood associations, 105, 107, 112, 115, 130, 172

New Public Commons (*atarashii kōkyō*), 18, 19, 20, 23, 26, 54, 56, 58, 59, 61–64, 66, 68, 69, 71–75, 77, 78, 79, 80, 83, 94–97, 100, 112, 115, 118–121, 125, 126, 130, 139–143, 187, 189
  Council on the Promotion of New Public Commons, 71, 73
  New Public Commons Roundtable, 18, 73, 95, 96, 100, 119, 189
  sociopolitical imagery, 71, 100, 120
  See also societal restructuring
ningen ryoku (ability as a human being), 60
no-relationship society (*muen shakai*), 173
  See also solitary death
non-formal education, 31
  See also community-oriented learning
  See also social education
NPOs (Non-profit organizations), 2, 20, 48, 51, 63, 68, 71–73, 83, 95, 97, 112, 126, 128, 129, 134–136, 139, 140, 142, 143, 151, 157, 162, 170–172, 174, 175, 185, 188
  GoNPO (*gonpo*), 171
  tax incentive, 95
  See also civil society
  See also third sector

Obuchi, Keizo, 61, 65, 72, 103
  Prime Minister's Commission on Japan's Goals in the 21st Century, 61, 72, 75
OECD (Organization for Economic Co-operation and Development), 4, 5, 6, 7, 8, 25, 52, 55, 60, 65, 108, 149, 160, 186, 189
  key competencies, 60, 162, 166
  Lifelong Learning for All (1996), 5
  Promoting Adult Learning (2005), 5

OJT (on-the-job training), 122, 129, 131, 134, 136, 137, 139, 142
Okamoto, Kaoru, 37
Open University of Japan (*Hōsō daigaku*), 2, 43, 175, 186
   University of the Air Foundation, 44, 177, 186

Parent-Teacher Association (PTA), 77
Peacock, James, 171
poverty, 65, 66, 72, 158, 159, 160, 173
   poverty rate, 65, 72
power, 14, 15, 18, 19, 24, 45, 47, 56, 60, 61, 67, 72, 80, 82, 86, 94, 97, 138, 155, 162, 163, 167, 168
precarious (employment), 56, 66, 147, 160
Prime Minister's Commission on Japan's Goals in the Twenty-first Century, 72, 75
privatization, 19, 73
problem solving, 14, 19, 20, 26, 54, 58, 63, 64, 67, 84, 93, 152, 153, 162, 165, 169
   See also local communities (*chiiki*)
Program for International Student Assessment (PISA), 108
public management, 155
public sphere, 18, 21, 54, 58, 59, 61, 68, 72, 73, 119, 174
   See also New Public Commons

reform, 10, 25, 38, 39, 40, 43, 59, 60, 61, 66, 72, 84, 95, 103, 104, 155, 178, 187, 188
   administrative reform, 40, 59, 84
   educational reform, 38, 39, 43, 60, 84, 103, 104, 188
   structural reform (*kōzō kaikaku*), 66, 72
reflexivity, 13
   reflexive biography, 137

reflexive modernity, 13
reflexive modernization, 13, 16, 55
Reich, Robert, 59
recurrent education, 2, 7, 44, 149, 186
relationality, 64, 101
responsibility / responsibilities, 6, 10, 17, 18, 19, 26, 31, 39, 54–56, 58, 59, 61, 71, 73, 74, 76, 82, 85, 86, 96, 106, 111, 120, 125, 131, 147, 160, 164, 165, 183
   distribution of responsibility, 18, 26, 56
   self-responsibility, 56, 59, 82, 96, 120, 131
risk, 6, 9, 12–22, 25–27, 52–56, 64, 66–69, 74, 82, 83, 96, 100, 115, 116, 120, 121, 136–138, 140, 146, 148, 158, 159, 160–162, 167–169, 171, 173, 186
   at-risk for being socially excluded, 67, 68
   governmental risk, 17–19, 26, 52, 56, 64, 69, 74, 96, 115, 168, 171
   individualization, 14, 16, 17, 19, 20, 116, 137, 159
   reflexive modernization, 13, 16, 55
   risk governance, 12
   risk managing, 54, 56, 64
   risk society, 12–17, 55, 56, 66, 68, 137
   risk taking, 9, 19–21, 120, 137
   second modernity, 14, 55
   socioeconomic risk, 17, 19, 20, 27, 52, 115, 120, 121, 148, 162
   voluntary risk taking, 20, 21, *see also* Lyng, Stephen
risk society, 12–17, 55, 56, 66, 68, 137
Rose, Nikokas, 18, 74, 168, 169, 185

salarymen, 126

Science Council of Japan (*Nihon gakujutsu kaigi*), 154, 157, 161, 164, 165, 179, 190
  quality assurance, 154, 155, 163, 179
second modernity, 14, 55
  See also risk
self-regulation, 54, 71
Shinmura, Junichi, 50
SLG, 22, 23, 51, 142, 170–172
  See also Kawazoe
small- and medium-sized companies, 121, 122, 124
socialization, 100, 101, 115
social capital, 64, 100
social class, 73
  socially vulnerable class, 138
  See also *kakusa* (socioeconomic divide)
social cohesion, 1, 4, 6, 8, 10, 55, 159
social education (*shakai kyōiku*), 2, 3, 23, 25, 27, 29–35, 38, 40, 42, 43, 46–49, 51, 57, 58, 73, 92, 99–102, 107, 110–114, 169, 172, 175, 177–179
  Arrangement of Social Education to Cope with Rapid Changes in the Social Structure (1971), 34
  board of social education, 33, 99, 100, 101, 107
  Social Education Council, 29, 34, 35, 177
  Social Education Law (1949), 3, 31–33, 49, 57, 112, 177–179
  social education officers (*shakai kyōiku shuji*), 32, 33, 57, 112
  social education section (*shakai kyōiku ka*), 47
  See also non-formal education
social enterprises, 6, 117, 121, 125, 126, 128, 133–140, 157, 189
  entrepreneurship, 9, 82, 120, 125, 133, 137, 138, 140

social exclusion (*shakaiteki haijo*), 55, 148, 158, 159–163
social inclusion (*shakaiteki hōsetsu*), 6, 8, 27, 115, 149, 158, 159, 161, 162, 165, 174
social integration, 56, 158
societal restructuring, 26, 71, 73, 97
socioeconomic risk, 17, 19, 20, 27, 52, 115, 120, 121, 148, 162
  See also risk
solidarity, 18, 19, 26, 32, 54, 55, 58, 64, 66, 69, 74, 100, 158, 167, 171, 186
solitary death (*muen shi*), 173
  See also no-relationship society (*muen shakai*)
specialized training college, 123
stimulus package, 123, 125, 126
Stockholm, Sweden, 22, 24, 167
suicide, 16, 145, 146, 173
  Council on Comprehensive Measures to Prevent Suicide, 146
  Suicide Prevention and Awareness Month, 146
Suzuki, Kan, 84, 103

teaching guideline (*gakushū shidō yōryō*), 107, 108, 110
third sector, 17, 22, 48, 72, 73, 117, 186
third sector method, 51
  See also civil society
Tokai, Kisaburo, 57
Tokyo, Japan, 22, 23, 37, 51, 63, 64, 76, 80, 88, 100, 104, 105, 113–115, 122, 123, 130, 137–139, 142, 153, 156, 162, 170, 186–190
Suginami, 22, 23, 99–101, 104, 106, 107, 110, 111, 115, 187
Sumida, 22
Tokyo Metropolitan Government, 63

Toyama Prefecture, 24, 51
trainability, 150
trust, 13, 64, 171, 183, 186

uncertainty, 4, 12–14, 66, 167
unemployment, 7, 120, 145, 159, 160, 165, 189
   rate of unemployment, 66
   youth unemployment, 136, 137, 151, 16
UNESCO (United Nations Educational, Scientific and Cultural Organization), 4, 5, 7, 25, 35, 36, 52, 177
   Delors, Jacques, 5, 7
   Faure Report—Learning to Be (1972), 4, 5, 36
   Learning: The Treasure Within (1996), 5
   Lengrand, Paul, 35, 177
   Third International Committee for the Facilitation of Adult Education (1965), 35
United Kingdom / UK, 16, 17, 103, 187
United States, 16, 66, 102, 105, 125, 145
university / universities, 1, 2, 11, 23, 24, 33, 37, 41, 43, 44, 50, 64, 87, 103, 112, 124, 137, 138, 145, 146, 148, 150, 154–157, 161, 162, 164–166, 169, 175, 177–179, 186–190
   basic attainments (*kihonteki na soyō*), 157, 161
   gakushiryoku (standards for bachelor's degree), 155
   general education (*kyōyō kyōiku*), 155
   specialized education (*senmon kyōiku*), 155, 157
   university education, 44, 137, 148, 154–157, 164, 165, 178, 179
university corporations, 155

University Council, 164, 178, 187
university extension, 2, 175

vocation (*shokugyō*), 1, 2, 7, 20, 21, 23, 24, 27, 35, 40, 46, 68, 116–123, 126, 127, 133, 136, 138–143, 148, 149, 151, 152, 154, 162–164, 166, 173, 175, 177, 178, 189
vocational education, 7, 148, 202
vocational training, 1, 2, 20, 21, 23, 24, 27, 46, 116–123, 126, 127, 133, 136, 138–143, 149, 151, 173, 175, 177, 189
   Employment and Human Resources Development Organization, 121–123, 189
   polytech center, 122, 189
   polytechnic college, 121, 122, 189
   polytechnic junior college, 121
   See also recurrent education
Vocation Training Law, 121, 177, 189

welfare state / statehood, 17, 55, 68, 74, 96, 159
   Keynesian welfare state, 68, 74
women's education centers, 2, 34, 58, 175
   National Women's Education Center, 34
   number (of women's education centers), 34
work ethics, 149, 151
work experience program, 67, 150
Work Foundation, 10
working poor, 66, 147, 161
   See also *kakusa* (socioeconomic divide)

Young People's Independence and Challenge Plan (*Wakamonor jiritsu chōsen puran*), 150, 165
Youth, 11, 27, 30–32, 34, 45, 50, 64, 66–68, 78, 99, 105, 106, 136,

137, 145, 146, 148–151, 153, 158, 161, 163, 166, 177, 190
youth development, 154, 190
Youth Friendship Centers, 34
Youth Outdoor Learning Centers, 34

youth unemployment, 136, 137, 151, 161
Yuasa, Makoto, 138
yutori (low-pressure), 108
sōgōteki na gakushū (integrated studies program), 108

www.ingramcontent.com/pod-product-compliance
Ingram Content Group UK Ltd.
Pitfield, Milton Keynes, MK11 3LW, UK
UKHW041917140426
5217IPUK00013B/198